Five Centuries *of* Lutheranism

FIVE CENTURIES
of
LUTHERANISM

Aaron Moldenhauer, Editor
for *LOGIA: A Journal of Lutheran Theology*

Assistant Editors
Jerry Gernander
Wade Johnston
Jason D. Lane
Paul Lehninger
Martin R. Noland
Carl D. Roth
Robert W. Paul

Luther Academy

ISBN: 978-1-935035-28-2 —hard cover
978-1-935035-29-9 —paperback
978-1-935035-30-5 —Kindle

Printed in the United States of America
Lulu.com

CONTENTS

Introduction

In the middle of the sixteenth century Matthias Illyricus Flacius organized the first church history written by Protestants. The *Magdeburg Centuries* devoted one volume to each century of church history through the thirteenth century. Its use of the term *century* to refer to one hundred years was an innovation, as was its approach to organizing the history of the church by century.

Building on that model, this volume surveys the history of the Lutheran church by century. Its publication marks the occasion of Lutheranism being five centuries old. While there is no clear-cut date for the emergence of Lutheranism from the Luther controversy, we are placing the birthdate of the Lutheran church in 1521. After the Diet of Worms in 1521, there was little hope of reconciliation between the excommunicated Martin Luther (now an outlaw in the Holy Roman Empire) and the church of Rome. As Electoral Saxony stood by Luther and protected him in the Wartburg, the churches of Electoral Saxony struck a course independent of Rome. By the end of the year, the churches in Wittenberg saw the first efforts at liturgical reform based on Luther's theology. These events make 1521 a good choice for the birth of Lutheranism. No longer was the Luther affair a struggle between a single Augustinian friar and Rome, but now a new church was emerging under the theological leadership of Martin Luther.

In the five centuries stretching from 1521 through 2020, the Lutheran church has spread from Electoral Saxony to the far reaches of the globe. This spread did not proceed along a single trajectory. It came about through missionary movements and migrations, through reforms and theological controversies. It has been marked by divisions and mergers. Its congregations and members have generated institutions of education and human care, and organized into synods and other church bodies. Along the way it has left a historical record located in theological texts, devotion and prayer books, church records, and other archives. There is a vast body of historical material that allows for study of the Lutheran church in the centuries of its existence.

Yet relatively few volumes attend to the history of the Lutheran church, and even fewer attempt a broad survey of Lutheranism in a single volume. This volume provides a brief survey of the history of Lutheranism, seeking to give equal weight to the various eras of the Lutheran church's life while keeping the length short enough to be useful in various settings. Drawing inspiration from the *Magdeburg Centuries*, we have organized this survey by century, devoting one article to each of the first five centuries of Lutheranism. Such a broad view of Lutheran history requires a survey of key figures and events rather than a detailed study of every significant moment in Lutheranism. The articles in this volume offer that kind of high-level survey by noting the key figures and developments in each century of Lutheranism.

The chapters of this book were originally published in *Logia* 29:4 (Reformation 2020). We offer the same essays here in booklet form as a resource for all interested in the history of Lutheranism. Researchers looking for a historical survey can use the book to locate their own work in the broader sweep of Lutheran history. They can turn to the bibliographies to find sources for more detailed historical work. Professors teaching church history can use the book as a textbook, as well as pastors looking to teach a Bible class or other course on the history of the Lutheran church.

One challenge in producing a survey of Lutheran church history is the lack of an institutional center in Lutheranism. The Roman Catholic Church relies on the papacy and its hierarchy to define who is and is not Roman Catholic. Anglicans look to the Book of Common Prayer as a central organizing element. Lutherans have no comparable structure or hymnal. Different Lutheran churches employ different polities and liturgical traditions. This lack is itself part of the history of Lutheranism, as various Lutheran churches developed different polities and liturgical traditions. That diversity arises from a Lutheran understanding of the church taking concrete form in different parts of the world.

What Lutheranism does have at its center is an interpretation of scripture centered on justification by faith in Christ. That soteriological and Christological center is confessed and fleshed out in the *Book of Concord*. Where Rome has the papacy and Anglicans have *The Book of Common Prayer*, Lutherans have a confession. This volume, accordingly, tends to focus on confessional Lutherans while also attending to other Lutheran movements. And, given our journal's location in North America, American Lutheranism receives more attention in the latter centuries. This focus is not intended to imply that other Lutheran churches are less important. Rather, this survey of Lutheranism in an invitation to develop more in-depth histories of Lutheran churches around the globe.

Such historical work is important because telling the history of a church is not just a record of what happened. For those in the Lutheran church, the history of Lutheranism is an essential part of defining who we are. Doctrines confessed, divisions recognized, fellowships formed, and mission efforts launched have contributed to shape Lutheranism as we know it today. Knowing this history helps Lutherans know who they are and how they came to be where they are today. The *Magdeburg Centuries* were themselves not a mere record of what happened, but an effort to show that the Lutheran church stood in a tradition stretching back to the apostles. Lutherans reading this volume can use this to deepen their understanding of Lutheran identity by attending to how the Lutheran church arrived at its present location.

We are grateful to the experts in Lutheran history who have contributed to this volume. They need no introduction, and collectively have contributed an impressive number of books and articles detailing different parts of the history of Lutheranism. They have each contributed a bibliography to assist other historians in their work. It is our hope that this volume will inspire new articles or books illuminating different periods of Lutheran church history. Such work will continue to shape and define Lutheranism in the coming centuries.

Aaron Moldenhauer
Assistant Professor of Theology
Concordia University Wisconsin
Senior Editor, *Logia*

The Lutheran Church in the Sixteenth Century

ROBERT KOLB

THROUGHOUT MUCH OF THE SIXTEENTH CENTURY, every deviation from the medieval Western church's teachings, rituals, and regulation earned the negative characterization of being Lutheran. In France, its frequent use almost always pointed to either a broad range of Erasmian humanist reformers or, later in the century, followers of John Calvin. Followers of Luther, and more reluctantly Luther himself, accepted the designation in the 1520s and 1530s. The Formula of Concord, and with it the Book of Concord, provided an anchor for the term *Lutheran* that corresponds roughly to the usage that has prevailed. Although in varying cultural situations some Lutherans resemble the church envisioned in the Book of Concord only remotely.[1]

LUTHER'S REDEFINITION OF BEING CHRISTIAN

The roots and antecedents of the Lutheran church, as it came to exist through the Concordian settlement, go back to the 1510s and 1520s to the reform movement that began with Wittenberg professor Martin Luther's call for reform of the church's teaching.[2] Luther captained a team that was centered in Wittenberg. Without his colleagues in the theological faculty, along with other university professors, the artist Lucas Cranach (1472–1553),[3] a dozen or more local printers,[4] and the electors and councilors at the castle across

1. Irene Dingel, "Confessional Transformations from the Wittenberg Reformation to Lutheranism," *Lutheran Quarterly* 33 (2019): 1–25.
2. Of the countless biographies of Luther to appear in recent years, I recommend Scott H. Hendrix, *Martin Luther, Visionary Reformer* (New Haven, CT: Yale University Press, 2016), Hermann J. Selderhuis, *Martin Luther, a Spiritual Biography* (Wheaton, IL: Crossway, 2017), Heiko Augustinus Oberman, *Luther: Man between God and the Devil*, trans. Eileen Walliser-Schwarzbart (German, 1982; New Haven, CT: Yale University Press, 1989), and Martin Brecht, *Martin Luther*, trans. James L. Schaaf, 3 vols. (German, 1981–1987; Philadelphia, PA: Fortress, 1985–1993).
3. Steven Ozment, *The Serpent and the Lamb: Cranach, Luther and the Making of the Reformation* (New Haven, CT: Yale University Press, 2011).
4. Andrew Pettegree, *Brand Luther: 1517, Printing, and the Making of the Reformation* (New York: Penguin, 2015).

town from the university, no Reformation would have been possible. But the impulses for the formation and activities of this team sprang initially and in continuing critical ways from Luther himself.

Reform movements had arisen throughout the Middle Ages in the Western church, and many had disappeared. Their concentration on moral practices and organizational issues had made very little impact on the fundamental understanding of being a Christian in the minds of the populace. When missionaries brought the faith to the German lands and tribal leaders imposed that faith on their people in the eighth and ninth centuries, the church had inadequate personnel to catechize the new Christians. They learned something of the Biblical teaching, but the fundamental structure of their religious thinking, their concept of the relationship between God and themselves, retained many characteristics of the traditional religions of the Germanic tribes. Most conceived of the relationship with God, even if initiated by grace, as ultimately dependent on the human approach to God through the performance of good works, most importantly the sacred rituals and religious regulations prescribed by the priestly hierarchy of the church.

Luther came to realize that Scripture presents a totally different framework for understanding the reality of the Christian way of living. He recognized that God as the Almighty Creator has human life in his own hands. He initiates and maintains his relationship with his people, and he does so through his Word. His Word expresses his expectations of his human creatures. Luther called that *law.* God speaks his re-creating word of forgiveness, life, and salvation with the promise that applies the benefits of Christ's death and resurrection to believers, and this, Luther called, *gospel.* Luther argued trust is the foundational response that God creates in his chosen people. That trust in God's absolving promise not only restores righteousness in God's sight to the passive recipient of the promise, but it also generates active righteousness in the godly life of the believer.[5]

Five factors contributed to Luther's reaching this new definition of being Christian. First, his own personality, with its highs and lows, enabled him to appreciate God's strict expectation of obedience and the passion of his wrath against sin as well as the sweet delight of his embrace of sinners through Christ.

Second, his study of theology under Ockhamist instructors, followers of the fourteenth-century English-born philosopher and theologian William of Ockham (ca. 1285–1347) and Ockham's later disciple, Tübingen professor Gabriel Biel (ca. 1413–95), affected him negatively with the expectation that a person must do his best (*facere quod in se est,* that is to do what is in him) to earn the grace that enables performance of truly God-pleasing works that gain heaven. But Ockham's accentuation of the almighty power of God generated Luther's perceptions of the Creator's lordship over all, his responsibility for all that happens in his creation. Ockham's focus on material things

5. Robert Kolb, *Martin Luther and the Enduring Word of God: The Wittenberg School and its Scripture-Centered Proclamation* (Grand Rapids, MI: Baker Academic, 2016), 8–10, 35–74.

generated Luther's appreciation of the created order that led him to perceive how God works his saving will through selected elements of that created order: his own incarnation, his use of human language and of the material elements of the sacraments, and human servants who speak his Word.

Third, Luther's entry into the Augustinian Order of Hermits placed him, through the ordination his superiors imposed upon him, in situations in which he exercised pastoral care. Augustinian brothers in the priesthood aided local parish priests with preaching and hearing confessions. That not only led to Luther's compulsion to question indulgence practices and teaching in his Ninety-five Theses of 1517; it also created an understanding of theology as the delivery of God's Word in such a way that sinners repent and receive the comfort and consolation of forgiveness and life in Christ. This concern for peace of conscience and trust that secures life permeated his thinking.

Fourth, as against his will Luther took up the task of teaching at the university, he looked to the latest methods for Biblical study. He immediately seized upon the helps for Hebrew reading supplied by the pioneer biblical humanist Johannes Reuchlin (1455–1522), the commentaries of the French biblical humanist Jacques Lefèvre d'Etaples (ca. 1450–1536), and especially the Biblical *Paraphrases* and the first printed edition of the New Testament in Greek of the Dutch biblical humanist Desiderius Erasmus (ca. 1466–1536). This shaped his reading of Scripture and his ability to get back to better definitions of key biblical terms, such as *faith*, *repentance*, and *promise*, as he submerged himself in the texts of the Psalms (1513–15), Romans (1515–16), Galatians (1516–17), Hebrews (1518), and again Psalms (1518–21), the fifth factor in his theological development.

The theological framework that Luther developed in the 1510s as his theology matured (no identification of a "magic moment of conversion" in this development can be identified despite the best efforts of dozens of twentieth-century scholars) rested on his theology of the cross or *theologia crucis*. Its initial form focused on God as God hidden and God revealed, distinguishing what God has told believers of himself and his will for humankind and what must remain off-limits for human speculation. It also focused on the nature of being human, not, as Aristotle defined humanity, as fundamentally an *animal rationalis*, a reasoning being, but rather as a trusting creature, who responds to the Word of the Lord with fear, love, and trust. This *theologia crucis* embraced Luther's understanding of God's atoning work in the death and resurrection of Christ—for the destruction and burial of the sinner and the resurrection of the believer restored to righteousness (Rom 4:25, 6:3–11). It also provided an explanation for human suffering and the church's persecution since God's people combat Satan and all evil weapons similar to those of their Savior. In addition, Christians bear the crosses of others in loving service to those around them.

Luther's perception of human life centered on God's justifying work in Christ. As he argued in *On Christian Freedom* (1520), this provided liberation from all oppressors, new birth or re-creation, reconciliation with the heavenly Father, and forgiveness of sins which brought about the restoration of righteousness, a passively bestowed gift, that through the faith that trusts God's pronouncement of righteousness then actively pursues living the righteous life that God designed for human creatures.

LUTHER'S TEAM

This new definition of what it means to be Christian might have simply been no more than one more theologian's idea had it not been for Luther's pastoral concern for people hoodwinked by Johann Tetzel's campaign to sell indulgences in 1517. Indulgence doctrine and practice was not well-defined in 1517, and Luther's Ninety-five Theses, as a call for academic discussion of one of many ecclesiastical problems, should not have caused a fuss. But his theses also implicitly and perhaps explicitly challenged papal power. Those people, whose concept of being Christian rested on ritual performance under the direction of the priestly hierarchy which proceeded from the Vicar of Christ in Rome, reacted as all people react when the very foundations of their system of interpreting reality are under attack.[6] At the same time, Luther's appeal struck a responsive chord with thousands of Germans and other Western Christians.

Had not several printers taken a risk and printed the Ninety-five Theses, and had not their modest sales convinced Luther that he could use the printing press to great advantage for his call for reform, nothing might have come of the furor over the Theses—except perhaps his execution on the heretic's pyre. But devotees among his students were already preaching the ideas that they had acquired in his lectures, and in the course of 1518 and 1519 the flood of his publications began to flow, attracting a wide, devoted readership as well as fierce opposition born of fear of the collapse of the old system.

Luther's redefinition of being Christian focused on God's approach through his Word, so the study of that Word became vital. This made schooling for all, girls and boys, a vital part of the Wittenberg program for change. The university, as the nursery for the preachers of the Word as well as the cultivation of all of God's good gifts, became central for church life among the adherents of the Wittenberg professors. Wittenberg's contributions to astronomy, botany, the development of history as a discipline, neo-Latin poetry, rhetoric and logic, among other disciplines, made a significant impact on Western learning. Two Wittenberg mathematicians and astronomers, Erasmus Reinhold (1511–53) and Georg Joachim Rheticus (1514–74) played essential roles in the publication of Nicolaus Copernicus's *De revolutionibus* and its early usage.[7]

6. David V. N. Bagchi, *Luther's Earliest Opponents: Catholic Controversialists* (Minneapolis, MN: Fortress, 1991).
7. Dennis Danielson, *The First Copernican: Georg Joachim Rheticus and the Rise of the Copernican Revolution* (New York: Walker, 2006), Robert S. Westman, *The Copernican Question: Prognostication, Skepticism, and Celestial Order* (Los Angeles: University of California Press, 2011).

Nonetheless, the Wittenberg theological faculty led the changes to the Western church. Luther's refocus of Christian thinking away from ritual performance of ecclesiastical prescriptions under the hierarchy's supervision did not mean the diminution of the liturgy and other pious practices or of the pastoral office. They were, however, subject to the Word. Thus, knowing Holy Scripture and how to interpret it became the center of theological instruction. Comment on the *Sententiae* of Peter Lombard no longer constituted the heart of university theological study. Lectures on the books of the Bible took command of the curriculum; it presumed knowledge of Greek and Hebrew provided in the faculty of arts. Melanchthon's arrival in 1518 heralded the transformation of the curriculum that quickly discarded Lombard, canon law, and other medieval elements and concentrated on Scripture's text and its interpretation. These changes were made official in 1533.[8] Other universities that joined Wittenberg reform followed suit.

This process found its heartbeat in the Wittenberg team. Philip Melanchthon's reputation as a leading expert on Greek among the Biblical humanists, brought him to the university that, when he arrived in August 1518, was where the action was in German academe at the time. He quickly absorbed Luther's theological insights while sharpening them through his command of Greek and Hebrew. His Biblical commentaries served students and pastors, shaping preaching the Biblical text throughout German lands and beyond. His pioneering work in rhetoric led him to compose a handbook for reading Romans, and thus all of Scripture, in 1521, based on the organizational principle of the commonplace or topic. This *Loci communes* replaced the *Sententiae* of Peter Lombard as the key textbook for the dogmatic organization of Biblical teaching although it was designed first of all as a tool for the pedagogical, homiletical delivery of the Biblical message. His skills at negotiating earned him the unofficial post of chief ambassador for the princely and municipal governments introducing and establishing the Wittenberg reform program across the German Empire.

Luther and Melanchthon found able colleagues in Johannes Bugenhagen and Justus Jonas, and later in the 1520s in their former student Caspar Cruciger. Bugenhagen not only authored Biblical commentaries that aided preachers in their ministry; he traveled repeatedly to north German towns and principalities and even to the kingdom of Denmark to reconstruct church life and to set down regulations for teaching and practice in church ordinances (*Kirchenordnung*). Justus Jonas and Caspar Cruciger supported them in teaching Scripture; Jonas translated both Latin and German works by Luther and Melanchthon into the other language and thus aided the propagation of the Wittenberg message.

8. Timothy J. Wengert, "Philip Melanchthon and Wittenberg's Reform of the Theological Curriculum," in *Church and School in Early Modern Protestantism: Studies in Honor of Richard A. Muller on the Maturation of a Theological Tradition*, ed. Jordan J. Ballor et al. (Leiden: Brill, 2013), 17–33.

The communication of that message rested upon preaching above all but also on the distribution and reading of printed treatises and tracts. Printers in Wittenberg and many other towns contributed a key element in the spread of Luther's thought. Printers had often studied at the university. They took part in the lively theological exchanges that were daily events in Wittenberg. Lucas Cranach, the official court painter of Electors Frederick the Wise, John, and John Frederick, painted Luther's message into the altarpieces produced by his workshop. His woodcuts aided understanding of some of the theologians' literary work, for instance, Luther's Small Catechism. Cranach and Luther became fast friends and learned from each other. Cranach provided border illustrations for Luther's published works; along with the addition of "Wittenberg" as place of publication and the name of the author, two new characteristics of a printed title page, these illustrated frames created what Andrew Pettegree labels "Brand Luther." Sales of his works soared, overshadowing all competing authors in the 1520s and 1530s. By using the latest techniques in public discourse, the Wittenberg team, especially its captain, managed to change minds across the populations of many places in Germany and beyond to a degree and in a brief period as had never before been experienced.

Luther's gift for music impelled him to make good use of song as a means of conveying his ideas. His own hymns sparked parallel efforts in a number of poets and composers who accepted his ideas.[9] Johann Walther (1496–1570), a Saxon court musician, and he became good friends. Walther, and others like him, slowly brought congregational singing alongside the traditional use of choirs, particularly of schoolboys, into the worship of the church.

Political leaders also exercised vital roles in establishing and spreading Wittenberg reform of teaching and practice. Most people in the German Empire, the Nordic kingdoms, and the kingdoms of Poland and Hungary were peasants, living in small villages, but the towns cultivated lively intellectual life along with trade and manufacture. The merchants and patricians and also the artisans of the towns often led efforts at reform and brought preachers to the churches they controlled who had studied in Wittenberg or who desired Luther-style reform. Lazarus Spengler (1479–1534), the city administrator of Nuremberg, is but one example of a civic leader, who not only accepted and promoted Luther's way of thinking but also wrote pamphlets of his own spreading the Wittenberg message,[10] as did the Nuremberg shoemaker Hans Sachs (1494–1576), a Meistersänger, whose poetry carried the ideas of the one Sachs called "the Wittenberg nightingale."

Critical for the possibility of setting down the roots of Luther's plan for the church and society was the support of territorial princes. Several were attracted to Luther's movement and not (or not only) because of the potential it gave them for expanding their own powers and lands. Throughout the fif-

9. Robin Leaver, *Luther's Liturgical Music: Principles and Implications* (Grand Rapids. MI: Eerdmans, 2007).
10. Harold J. Grimm, *Lazarus Spengler: A Lay Leader of the Reformation* (Columbus, OH: Ohio State University Press, 2015).

teenth century European rulers had increasingly interfered with church governance, often in the interests of reform (although this practice dates from the early Middle Ages). Not only Luther's supporters but also opponents such as Duke Georg of Saxony, actively promoted reform measures that remained faithful to Rome and to medieval teaching and practice, often in face of official ecclesiastical defiance.[11] The churches of the Reformation were no more under secular control than the Roman church in Spain or France in the later sixteenth and seventeenth centuries.

Without the support of the Saxon electors Luther's reform program would have had quite a different course. Elector Frederick the Wise (1463–1525) avoided meeting Luther personally and dealt with him through his right-hand aide, Georg Spalatin (1484–1545), who later became a parish pastor, cultivating reform in Altenburg. Frederick defended Luther and used his influence as one of the seven electors of the German Empire to stave off imperial and papal attempts to execute his prize theologian, the star at the university he had founded in 1502. His brother, John (1468–1532), committed himself firmly to Luther's faith early on. His brief rule from 1525 to 1532, witnessed the Saxon government's organization of the visitation of the congregations throughout his territories during 1527 and 1528. The *Visitation Articles* of 1528, authored by Melanchthon with Luther's aid, provided one model for ordinances governing church life in the Wittenberg circle.[12] John led the effort to gain imperial tolerance in 1530 at the Diet of Augsburg and risked his governance and his life in confessing his faith before the hostile Emperor Charles v (1500–58).[13] John's son, John Frederick (1503–54), was as enthusiastic a supporter of Wittenberg reform as his father though he was not bound quite as tightly in friendship to Luther.

Philip of Hesse (1504–67) stood by John and John Frederick in supporting Wittenberg reform, concentrating on political rather than theological interests.[14] His attempt to build a larger military alliance included his organization of the colloquy at Marburg in 1529, at which Philip hoped to resolve differences that were preventing an alliance between those committed to Luther's reform and the Swiss gathered around Ulrich Zwingli and Johannes Oecolampadius. Their critique of Luther's understanding of the presence of Christ's body and blood had caused a serious division among those striving for reform in the 1520s.[15] Zwingli and Oecolampadius believed that the sacramental ele-

11. Christoph Volkmar, *Catholic Reform in the Age of Luther: Duke George of Saxony and the Church, 1488–1525*, trans. Brian McNeil and Bill Ray (Leiden/Boston: Brill, 2017), esp. 80–416.
12. *"Der Unterricht der Visitatoren" und die Durchsetzung der Reformation in Kursachsen*, ed. Joachim Bauer and Stefan Michel (Leipzig: Evangelische Verlagsanstalt, 2017).
13. James Tracy, *Emperor Charles v, Impresario of War, Campaign Strategy, International Finance, and Domestic Politics* (Cambridge: Cambridge University Press, 2002).
14. John Helmke, *Philip of Hesse, Unlikely Hero of the Reformation* (St. Louis, MO: Concordia, 2018).
15. Amy Nelson Burnett, *Debating the Sacraments: Print and Authority in the Early Reformation* (New York: Oxford University Press, 2019).

ments only point to a heavenly reality. Their thinking rested on the Realist philosophy of medieval thinkers, such as Thomas Aquinas, and this perception of reality, unlike Ockham's, had no place for God to be working through earthly elements. Thus, they rejected Luther's concept of Christ's presence and the power of the promise in the sacraments to effect forgiveness, life, and salvation. The Marburg Colloquy produced theses that revealed widespread agreement between the two groups on a series of key doctrines, but not on the presence of Christ in the Lord's Supper.[16] Philip was sidelined from an active role in Reformation leadership by his bigamy in 1542 and ceased to play a significant part in developments in his last twenty years.

Examples of sincere commitment to the teachings of the Reformation among the princes abound. Count Georg of Brandenburg-Ansbach (1484–1543) told Emperor Charles that he would rather lose his head than his faith, to which Charles replied in his broken German, "head not off, head not off." Georg's brother, Albrecht (1490–1568), was serving as the Grand Master of the Order of the Teutonic Knights and master of their lands in Prussia when he converted himself and his territory to Luther's reform. The interest of such princes in reform created the structure in which Luther's thought could take institutional form.

DEFINING THE FAITH AS TAUGHT IN WITTENBERG

John of Saxony, Philip of Hesse, Georg of Brandenburg-Ansbach, and four other princes together with the cities of Nuremberg and Reutlingen made public confession of their commitment to Luther's teaching and the practices that grew out of it in the Augsburg Confession in 1530. These governments commissioned Melanchthon to compose a statement of their faith and a justification of their reforming measures. He called their statement a *confession*, the first time that a statement of faith bore this designation. It was a genre, a new way of understanding the church as defined by its teaching rather than its ritual. At the time no one realized the significance of a confession as a secondary authority. It was the mission statement of the Evangelical governments, aimed specifically at Emperor Charles. When his call for negotiations between the Roman party and the Wittenberg party ten years later set in place the opportunity to present the theology of Luther and his colleagues clearly, the princes asked for a strengthening of the text. Melanchthon obliged in 1540, expanding particularly the articles relating to justification by faith (AC IV–VI, XX). His alteration of Article X on the Lord's Supper in this *Confessio Augustana variata* was in line with the agreement that he had composed between Luther and his disciples and Martin Bucer of Strassburg, representative of a group that had worked to bridge the gap between Zwingli's Swiss supporter and Luther. The language on the Lord's Supper used formulations that Luther and those who held to his under-

16. Hermann Sasse, *This Is My Body: Luther's Contention for the Real Presence in the Sacrament of the Altar* (Minneapolis, MN: Augsburg, 1959).

standing of the presence of Christ's body and blood and the saving power of the sacrament's promise could accept. But this terminology was also given a different spin by Elector Frederick III of the Palatinate in 1561 in order to win legal standing for his own spiritualizing view of Christ's presence in the Supper. Therefore, those faithful to Luther's view insisted on abandoning the revised, updated version of the Confession that they had been using up to that time.[17]

In 1531 Melanchthon issued a defense of the Augsburg Confession, refuting the critique of it issued by a Roman Catholic commission appointed and guided by Emperor Charles. Luther urged Melanchthon to stop tinkering and publish it, so it appeared in April 1531. Luther immediately had suggestions for improvement, and so a second, *octavo*, edition appeared in September 1531. That version served as the basis for almost all of the German translations by Jonas and was incorporated into the Book of Concord of 1580.[18]

These two documents by Melanchthon slowly gained recognition as secondary authorities, prime interpreters of Biblical teaching, within the Wittenberg circle. Initially, the Confession commanded respect because it had some political standing, even if Emperor Charles had rejected it. In 1537 another document entered the running for status as a secondary authority for followers of Luther. Luther himself authored the Smalcald Articles, he claimed in its printed version, to help the Evangelical governments prepare for the council called by Pope Paul III in 1536. Some scholars argue that the document was designed to serve as a doctrinal last will and testament to give later generations a clear summary of Luther's teaching. It is true that Elector John Frederick had asked Luther to produce such a document. In 1528 he had appended a confession of his faith for that purpose to his *On the Lord's Supper, a Confession*; it followed a creedal outline. The Smalcald Articles appear in the form of bullet points for the Evangelical governments to use in orienting their theologians for activities in dialogue with Roman Catholic representatives at the council. Like the Augsburg Confession, these Articles must be read in the larger context of what the Wittenberg theologians were writing at the time since their brevity precludes their being clear and complete statements of Luther's thinking.

ORGANIZING REFORM ACCORDING TO THE WORD

The organization of the churches in territories and towns accepting Luther's reform program slowly took shape. Alongside the formal statements of the faith, publications played a key role in preparing the ground for institutional change. Luther's understanding of Scripture and thus of human life spread

17. Timothy J. Wengert, "Justifying the Variata: Observations on Melanchthon's 1540 edition of the Augsburg Confession," in *From Wittenberg to the Word, Essays on the Reformation and its Legacy*, ed. Charles P. Arand, Erik H. Hermann, Daniel L. Mattson (Göttingen: Vandenhoeck & Ruprecht, 2018), 207–225.

18. Christian Peters, *Apologia Confessionis Augustanae: Untersuchungen zur Textgeschichte einer lutherischen Bekenntnisschrift (1530–1584)* (Stuttgart: Calwer, 1997).

through several genres of writing, beginning with his postils, sermon books for the appointed lessons of the church year, in 1522.[19] His translation of the New Testament followed in 1522. Parts of the Old Testament appeared periodically until the team that Luther assembled for the translation task completed its work in 1534.[20] Luther and his colleagues also prepared liturgies and hymns centered on God's free grace, the work of Christ, and trust in him that modified but did not discard the medieval tradition of the worship service. Luther began in 1519 recasting medieval forms of devotional literature, such as meditations on Christ's passion and an art-of-dying book. He continued to prepare prayer books and other devotional literature. Most important were his postils, his biblical commentaries, published versions of his lectures, and his catechisms. His concern for the proper understanding of the Biblical message joined his pastoral desire to cultivate repentance and trust in the restoration of righteousness through Christ's work in children as well as adults. Therefore, his Small Catechism became a key text for conveying his way of thinking, in its law gospel Christian life framework. He transformed the order of the medieval catechism to do so, placing the Ten Commandments, the law, before the gospel of the Creed, and then following with the Lord's Prayer, which commits those who pray to participation in God's provision of life and salvation in his world. Luther followed medieval models and expanded their treatment of the baptismal base of Christian living as a daily drowning of the sinful identity and the resurrection of God's righteous children, who practices the righteousness that God has pronounced upon them. The Lord's Supper supports this life and affirms its setting in the Christian community. Luther then provided instruction for practicing the righteous life in the vertical relationship with God—through his texts for daily morning, evening, and mealtime prayer— and for the horizontal relationships with God's creatures in his *Table of Christian Callings*.[21]

The common people noticed the changes in the nature of the church and Christian living first of all in practices that were part of village life. Saints were no longer venerated; the Lord's Supper was offered in both kinds, without the canon of the mass. Pastors married, and confession and absolution took on a different accent as absolution was emphasized. Fasting rules fell away, and monastic life no longer was regarded as the ideal. Bishops no longer exercised power over local parishes. Territorial and municipal churches replaced bishops with superintendents, chosen under the direction of civil government (as had been the case for the most part in the Middle Ages); they were concerned above all with proper preaching and upright living by pastors and laity alike. Following Luther's admonition in 1526, the sermon de-

---

19. Benjamin T. G. Mayes, "Introduction to the Luther-Cruciger Church Postil (1540–1544)," in *LW* 75:xiii–xxxi.
20. Heinz Bluhm, *Martin Luther: Creative Translator* (St. Louis, MO: Concordia, 1965).
21. Albrecht Peters, *Commentary on Luther's Catechisms: Creed*, trans. Charles Schaum, Thomas H. Trapp, et al. (St. Louis, MO: Concordia, 2009–2013); Charles P. Arand, *That I May Be His Own: An Overview of Luther's Catechisms* (St. Louis, MO: Concordia, 2000).

livering God's Word to its hearers became the center of the liturgy.[22] Instead of initiating a long series of masses for the dead, believers heard sermons and sang hymns at funerals that were filled no longer with mourning and judgment but with resurrection hope.[23] Sermons were added to the wedding liturgy. The church exercised many functions in villages and towns, but instead of the ritual (that certainly continued to be present) the Word and its delivery stood at the center of the life of believers and church.

In the later 1530s and early 1540s a number of territories and towns introduced Wittenberg reforms. Most of these municipal governments joined the Smalcald League, formed in 1531 as a defensive alliance with the Augsburg Confession as its unifying commitment. The League undertook doctrinal discussions with England in 1536 though they produced no lasting results. In the late 1530s Emperor Charles felt increasing pressure to assert his authority over his German empire, also in its religious life, for which he believed God had made him responsible. His government pressed for a religious colloquy that brought Evangelicals and Roman Catholics together in conversations that took place in Hagenau, Worms, and Regensburg in 1540 and 1541. Melanchthon and Bucer with other Evangelical theologians met Johann Eck, the leading German Roman opponent of Luther and an author of the *Papal Confutation* in 1530, in exchanges focused on the doctrine of justification. They drafted a common position that in the end displeased Melanchthon and found rejection both in Rome and Wittenberg.

WITTENBERG GOES INTERNATIONAL

The medieval intellectual world knew no territorial boundaries. Students traveled from homeland to foreign schools, a movement facilitated by a common language of instruction, Latin. Some Wittenberg students from the kingdom of Hungary never learned German; Melanchthon conducted Bible study and prayer services for them in his home on Sunday mornings. Students from other lands, such as the Englishman, Robert Barnes, also heard Luther and Melanchthon and carried their theology back home. But chiefly in the Nordic lands and the kingdoms of Hungary and, to a lesser extent, Poland, the Wittenberg way of thinking took root in the East, suffering repeated persecution from Roman Catholic authorities.

The Slovaks, Magyars, and Siebenbürger from the kingdom of Hungary were not the first to find the infant university of Wittenberg an attractive place to study theology. Already in the 1510s students from the Nordic countries carried Luther's message back to Denmark, Norway, Sweden, Finland, and the lands along the eastern end of the Baltic Sea, where predominantly German populations slowly shared Luther's way of thinking with the native Estonians and Latvians.

---

22. WA 19:78, 26–27, *LW* 53:68.
23. Robert Kolb, "The Reformation of Dying and Burial: Preaching, Pastoral Care, and Ritual at Commital in Luther's Reform," *Concordia Theological Quarterly* 81 (2017): 77–93.

In Denmark the proximity to German centers of education and the fact that the duchies of Schleswig and Holstein had fallen to the Danish royal house contributed to the early access of Danish intellectuals to ideas from Wittenberg. A lively engagement with Erasmus's appeals for reform also paved the way for Luther's approach to reform centered on doctrine more than moral and institutional concerns. The preaching of Hans Tausen (1494–1561) after his return from Wittenberg made a particular impact since he became chaplain to King Frederick I (1471–1533), whom the Royal Council elected to the throne after his nephew Christian II (1481–1555) had weakened his hold on the throne by mismanagement and injustice, including the execution of eighty nobles in the Stockholm Bloodbath of 1520, in an effort to suppress rebellion in his Swedish domains. In the midst of continuing political tensions, Frederick's son and successor Christian III (1503–59), strongly committed to the Wittenberg theology, called Bugenhagen to Copenhagen to reorganize ecclesiastical life. During his stay in Copenhagen, 1537–39, Luther's colleague composed an ecclesiastical ordinance for the church in the Danish kingdom, recast university life, and advised the king on introducing reforms at the parish level.[24] Alongside Tausen, other Wittenberg students returned to Denmark to assume leading roles in spreading Luther's theology, including the brothers Peder (1503–60) and Niels Palladius (ca. 1510–60).

King Frederick II (1534–88) succeeded his father, whose piety and interest in theology exceeded his son's; nonetheless, Frederick strove to play a more active role in European religious politics, strongly opposing international Roman Catholic efforts to suppress and eliminate Wittenberg theology and practice, even with force. Under his rule the Danish translation of Holy Scripture was completed though not every parish obtained a copy immediately. Visitations made significant efforts at establishing the reformed practice mandated in the ordinance of 1537. In 1569 and 1580 Frederick mandated new standard altar books, prepared by bishops Peder Palladius and Poul Madsen. Frederick removed pastors for moral and liturgical wrongdoings, elevated educational standards for pastors, funded Latin schools throughout Denmark, and enforced salary specifications for local pastors. He demanded that pastors work to eliminate vagrancy, prostitution, drunkenness, and disrespect for authority in their parishes.

Frederick showed little interest in the theological struggles to define the Lutheran faith that occurred during his rule in German lands. His sister Anna (1532–85), wife of Elector August of Saxony, and like their father, Christian, a devoted follower of Luther, sent Frederick two copies of the Book of Concord, which he allegedly threw into the fire. Christian had expressed profound reservations over Georg Major's defense of the formula, "good works are necessary for salvation," but Frederick tended to favor Philippist positions, perhaps because his favorite theologian, Niels Hemmingsen (1513–

24. Eric Lund, "Nordic and Baltic Lutheranism," in Robert Kolb, ed., *Lutheran Ecclesiastical Culture, 1550–1675, 1550–1675*, ed. Robert Kolb (Leiden: Brill, 2008) , 411–454.

1600), shared the spiritualizing understanding of the Lord's Supper of the Crypto-Philippists. Pressure from Saxony finally led to Hemmingsen's dismissal, but he retained influence on the king and the church. His theological works spanned a range including Biblical commentaries, a handbook for teaching doctrine based on Melanchthon's *Loci communes*, a pastoral theology, a hermeneutics text, and doctrinal treatises, from his professorship. At the very end of the sixteenth century, under Christian IV (1577–1648), a dedicated Lutheran, the young theologian Hans Poulsen Resen (1561–1638) began bringing the church along his own path to the theology expressed in the Formula of Concord.

Norwegian and Icelandic resistance to rule from Copenhagen retarded the advance of this new way of thinking and worshipping. Leaders of the old faith, including the archbishop of Tronheim, Olaf Engelbrektsson (ca. 1480–1538), exploited this political discontent to slow the advance of the Reformation. But by the end of the sixteenth century Luther's catechism was reforming the way Norwegians and Icelanders understood life under the lordship of Christ, their Savior. Bishop Jørgen Erikssøn (1535–1604) studied in Wittenberg from 1568 to 1570. As bishop of Stavanger, he worked intensively to reform ecclesiastical life, rooting out ancient folk burial practices and forbidding the elevation of the chalice and ringing of bells at the consecration of the Lord's Supper. His published works, influenced by Johannes Brenz and Melanchthon, strove to instill the obedience that flows from faith in believers. In the 1540s Iceland's two bishops opposed each other as Gissur Einarsson (ca. 1512–46) introduced Luther's reform. In 1552 opposing Bishop Jón Arason (1484–1550) and two sons were executed for attacking Einarsson's diocese with military force. In 1584 Bishop Gudbrandur Thorlaksson (1541–1627) witnessed the publication of the Bible in Icelandic.

Luther's Ninety-five Theses and many of his publications into the early 1520s circulated in humanistic reform circles in the Kingdom of Hungary. Students from Upper Hungary (today Slovakia) and Siebenbürgen (Transylvania in Romania), the two areas in which Germans had settled centuries earlier, began coming to Wittenberg around 1530.[25] Following the deaths of seven bishops and additional other church officials on the battlefield at Mohács on 29 August 1526, the established church lacked leadership to combat divergent views effectively. The Slovakians and Germans of Upper Hungary remained under Habsburg control after King Louis II fell at Mohács; Siebenbürgen fell to a native Hungarian puppet of the victorious Turks, John Zápolya, and then his son. By the end of the sixteenth century, four legal religions were recognized in Siebenbürgen, the Orthodox, Roman Catholic, Reformed, and Lutheran. The Germans there organized politically and ecclesiastically in separate *universitates*, enjoying a large degree of self-governance.

---

25. David Paul Daniel, "Lutheranism in the Kingdom of Hungary," in *Lutheran Ecclesiastical Culture*, 455–507.

Committed nobles in many parts of Hungary provided protection, guidance, and leadership for the developing Wittenberg reforms; some members of the nobility also gradually shifted allegiance to the theology flowing into the region from Switzerland. Under the leadership of Wittenberg students Leonhard Stöckel (ca. 1510–60), rector of the school in Bardejov in the county Zips in Slovakia, and his pastoral colleague, Michael Radašin (ca. 1510–66), developed instructions for bringing the Wittenberg reform to several towns in Upper Hungary in 1540. They committed the church to the pure preaching of the gospel and proper administration of the sacraments, following the Augsburg Confession in adhering to Holy Scripture, the Confession, and Melanchthon's *Loci communes*. Luther's catechism was to be learned in Slovak. Stöckel and Radašin composed the *Confessio Pentapolitana* of 1549 for five towns in the Zips; it served as a model for the *Confessio Montana* (*Heptapolitana*) of 1559 and the *Confessio Scepusiana* of 1569 that affirmed Luther's and Melanchthon's teachings. Like Chemnitz and Chytraeus, Stöckel, who published the first commentary on Melanchthon's *Loci* in the year of the death of both student and mentor, 1560, believed that his two preceptors had shared the same views.

In 1547 under the leadership of John Honter, a humanist political leader in Brasov, whose reading of Luther was supplemented by works of Calvin and Bullinger, several pastors prepared a church ordinance for the Germans in Siebenbürgen. Likewise, the leading Hungarian voice for Luther's reform, Matthias Devai Biro, also demonstrated interest in Calvin's and Bullinger's thinking. In Upper Hungary the Wittenberg Crypto-Philippistic understanding of the Lord's Supper was condemned in four synods between 1595 and 1599. The Formula of Concord was a matter of contention among Slovaks and Siebenbürgers who adhered to the Augsburg Confession, but the Formula won acceptance slowly and not in all quarters.[26]

TOWARD A DEFINITION OF "LUTHERAN"

Movements that bring change always go through a stage of definition, often at the end of their first generation. It was less the death of Luther that set in motion this process of settling and setting boundaries than the fallout from the war that Emperor Charles launched against the political leaders of Wittenberg reform in the months after he died. He singled out John Frederick of Saxony and Philip of Hesse and managed to neutralize some of the members of the Smalcald League who had pledged unity in case of imperial attack. The Habsburg rulers even attracted Philip's son-in-law and John Frederick's cousin, Moritz of Saxony (1521–53), to their side. The imperial alliance defeated the forces of John Frederick and Philip; Charles commuted the death sentences pronounced upon the two rebellious princes, sending them to prison for five and four years respectively. Having established his rule by military force,

26. David P. Daniel, "The Acceptance of the Formula of Concord in Slovakia," *Archiv für Reformationsgeschichte* 70 (1979), 260–277.

the emperor called for a temporary religious settlement to govern German church life until the papal called council, which had begun its meeting in Trent in late 1545, could produce a lasting church-wide settlement.

At the imperial diet held in Augsburg from September 1547 to May 1548 an imperially appointed commission worked out a settlement dubbed the Augsburg Interim by its critics. The commission included two prominent reform-minded Roman Catholics, Julius Pflug (1499–1564) and Michael Helding (1506–61), a confessor of Charles' brother Ferdinand (1503–64), two Spanish theologians, and a renegade student of Luther, court theologian for the recently reformed electorate of Brandenburg, Johann Agricola (1494–1566). One of the brightest and best of Luther's early students, Agricola had stirred up controversy in the Wittenberg circle in 1527 and again from 1537 to 1540 with views labeled antinomian. He did not advocate a libertine way of life, but he confused law and gospel by turning the gospel into not only the justifying forgiveness of sins won by Christ but also commands for godly living. Luther's opposition restricted his activities in Wittenberg, and in 1540 Agricola fled the city to go to the court of Joachim II of Brandenburg (1505–71). His participation in the composition of the Augsburg Interim made him a despised traitor in the eyes of all of Luther's supporters.[27]

The Augsburg Interim essentially restored medieval teaching and practice though with reforms of superstitious practices and refinement of dogmatic language that Erasmian reformers such as Pflug and Helding had long advocated. The Augsburg Interim taught justification by faith, but for salvation, faith had to be completed or perfected by love, a doctrine of "double justification." It was founded on the continuing conviction that human righteousness ultimately is of only one kind, the active obedience to God's law. That righteousness in God's sight is a passively received gift lay beyond the imaginations of these reform-minded Catholics. Therefore, they maintained the perception that human righteousness is rooted in ritual practice; the Interim placed the doctrine of the mass at the center of Christian piety. This orientation indeed produced a view of much of church life cleansed of what both the Wittenberg theologians and these Roman reformers regarded as superstitious in medieval practice. Nonetheless, the fulfillment of God's commands along with the church's regulations, chiefly ritual, sealed the salvation of the faithful.[28]

After the Smalcald War Melanchthon made the difficult decision to remain in Wittenberg in order to fight for the preservation of the university,

---

27. On these developments and the subsequent controversies discussed below, see Charles P. Arand, Robert Kolb, and James A. Nestingen, *The Lutheran Confessions, History and Theology of the Book of Concord* (Minneapolis, MN: Fortress, 2012), 161–280. For editions of publications in these controversies, cf. *Controversia et Confessio: Theologische Kontroversen 1548–1577/80. Kritische Auswahledition*, ed. Irene Dingel, 9 vols. (Göttingen: Vandenhoeck & Ruprecht, 2008– [henceforth *C&C*]). See also the new critical edition of the Lutherans confessions, *Die Bekenntnisschriften der Evangelische—Lutherischen Kirche*, ed. Irene Dingel (Göttingen: Vandenhoeck & Ruprecht, 2014).
28. The text in *Sources and Contexts of the Book of Concord*, ed. Robert Kolb and James A. Nestingen (Minneapolis, MN: Fortress, 2001), 146–182.

no foregone conclusion since its new overlord, Moritz, could have closed it to support his family's traditional university in Leipzig. Moritz welcomed Melanchthon as an advisor as one measure to pacify the resistance of nobles and towns in both his traditional holdings and his newly annexed territory. Melanchthon was the first to criticize the Augsburg Interim, in a private memorandum that was leaked to the public rather quickly. A host of other followers of Luther sprang to his side, with critiques of varying depths.

This resistance compelled Moritz to seek an alternative solution. He called on his advisors, including members of the Wittenberg theological faculty, to formulate a religious policy for his lands that would appear to conform to the Augsburg Interim but would preserve Lutheran teaching. Melanchthon believed that it was better to compromise in adiaphora—neutral matters of practice neither forbidden nor commanded by Scripture—as he had formulated this principle in Article XV of the Augsburg Confession[29] than to invite invasion by Charles's forces since in the duchy of Württemberg and other places in southern Germany resistance to the Augsburg Interim had resulted in hundreds of pastors being driven from their pulpits. He aided in the composition of what opponents dubbed the Leipzig Interim.[30] Its formulation of the doctrine of justification omitted the word "alone" and had language that could suggest activity of the sinful will in coming to faith. It grouped baptism, absolution, and the Lord's Supper with confirmation (to be reintroduced in the hopes of aiding understanding of the faith), ordination, marriage, and extreme unction, implying a return to medieval views of the sacraments. It reintroduced other medieval customs, including mandatory fasting as a civil health-related regulation.

Some of Luther's and Melanchthon's brightest and best students from the previous decade felt betrayed by their beloved preceptor, from whom they had gained not only their theological method but much of their theological orientation.[31] Melanchthon and his colleagues in turn felt betrayed by the criticism of their attempt to save Lutheran pulpits for Lutheran preachers. Mutual recriminations and feelings of perfidious duplicity and infidelity governed the sorting out of the Wittenberg heritage for nearly a quarter century. The Saxon Diet rejected the Leipzig Proposal of Moritz's government; it never became law. Certain aspects of its prescribed practice were imposed on some, but by no means all, areas of Moritz's realm. Nonetheless, the perception of betrayal remained, on both sides, and shaped the debates over critical aspects of the definition of the faith.

29. Charles P. Arand, "The Apology as a Backdrop for the Interim of 1548," in *Politik und Bekenntnis: Die Reaktionen auf das Interim von 1548*, ed. Irene Dingel and Günther Wartenberg (Leipzig: Evangelische Verlagsanstalt, 2006), 211–227.

30. Text in *Sources and Contexts*, 184–196.

31. Robert Kolb, "Philipp's Foes but Followers Nonetheless: Late Humanism among the Gnesio-Lutherans," in *The Harvest of Humanism in Central Europe: Essays in Honor of Lewis W. Spitz*, ed. Manfred P. Fleischer (St. Louis, MO: Concordia, 1992), 159–177.

Scholars have identified two parties that developed out of the dispute over the Leipzig Proposal or Interim. Since the end of the eighteenth century they have been labeled Gnesio-Lutherans and Philippists. All wanted to be faithful to both their preceptors; all had been formed by the methods and theology of both. The Gnesio-Lutherans tended to be more radical, the Philippists more conservative, from a medieval perspective. In doctrine, Gnesio-Lutherans tended to emphasize God's saving action though they recognized that believers must respond with faith. Some, led by their foremost intellectual and spokesperson, Matthias Flacius (1520–75), held that original sin is the essence of the fallen sinner, using Luther's language to reinforce their view.[32] The "grandfather" figure of the Gnesio-Lutherans, Nikolaus von Amsdorf, repeated Luther's phrase, "good works are detrimental to salvation," though with little support even from fellow Gnesio-Lutherans. The Gnesio-Lutherans were more radical in their rejection of medieval practices and of any possible role for the Roman pontiff in governing the church; the Philippists were more prepared to compromise in matters of usage and polity so long as the doctrine of justification remained pure. Gnesio-Lutherans continually got into trouble by criticizing the doctrinal positions, the ecclesiastical policies, and unjust, oppressive treatment of their subjects by civil governments. Philippists tended toward compromise with those authorities. Nonetheless, the two parties were fluid in membership, and divisions among them crossed these simplified party lines.[33]

The disputes that issued from the Adiaphoristic Controversy have determined a good part of the Lutheran way of formulating theology since the Formula of Concord resolved these disputes to a large degree in 1577. The language of the Leipzig Proposal regarding "the necessity of good works for salvation" generated a dispute that ended in insistence that good works are necessary as a product of trust in Christ. This insistence stood against a minority of Gnesio-Lutherans which contended that *necessity* had to imply a compulsion not appropriate for the gospel-motivated new obedience. Related were differences in defining *law* and *gospel* as well as *repentance* (FC IV, V, VI). Melanchthon's efforts to preserve the view of human responsibility and of the nature of the creature created to think and will that he and Luther had shared resulted in argument over the precise formulation of the role of the human will in coming to faith and daily repentance, the synergistic controversy (FC II). This controversy generated disputes over the definition of original sin and election (FC I, XI).

Joachim Westphal (1510–74), Gnesio-Lutheran pastor in Hamburg, opened a new field for controversy in 1552 with his attack on John Calvin's accep-

32. Luka Ilic, *Theologian of Sin and Grace: The Process of Radicalization in the Theology of Matthias Flacius Illyricus* (Göttingen: Vandenhoeck & Ruprecht, 2014); Oliver K. Olson, *Matthias Flacius and the Survival of Luther's Reform* (Wiesbaden: Harrassowitz, 2002).

33. Robert Kolb, "Dynamics of Party Conflict in the Saxon Late Reformation, Gnesio-Lutherans vs. Philippists," in *Calvinismus in den Auseinandersetzungen des frühen konfessionellen Zeitalters* (Göttingen: Vandenhoeck & Ruprecht, 2013), 151–167.

tance of the *Consensus Tigurinus*, a document composed by Heinrich Bullinger which obligated the Swiss alliance to a doctrine of the Lord's Supper expressed in Zwinglian terms. The controversy between Westphal and Calvin generated a larger controversy,[34] in which in the late 1560s and early 1570s the electoral Saxon Philippists played a significant role. Some insisted that Luther and Melanchthon had maintained the same doctrine of Christ's presence in the Lord's Supper, while others, labeled Crypto-Calvinists by their opponents, but in reality developing their impression that Melanchthon had departed from Luther's belief in the true presence of Christ's body and blood in the elements, disagreed, agreeing with some Gnesio-Lutherans who criticized Melanchthon for turning to another concept of the presence of the person of Christ (not specifying the presence of his body and blood) shortly before his death.[35] A significant group of Gnesio-Lutherans held that their two instructors had maintained the same position, but unlike the Philippists who agreed, they expressed that common doctrine in Luther's terms. Two of this group, Martin Chemnitz (1522–86) and David Chytraeus (1530–1600), were responsible for drafting the articles on the Lord's Supper and the person of Christ in the Formula of Concord that established his view (FC VII, VIII, IX).[36]

Article X of the Formula of Concord did not address the Gnesio-Lutheran concern for the relative independence of the church from civil government because among its authors were those who did not hold the position represented by Martin Chemnitz, for example, that was always ready to call princes to repentance. This article affirmed the necessity of responsibility for clear communication through liturgical and other practices, the nonbinding nature of liturgical regulations, and the perception that the communication of the gospel takes place in the larger field of human transmission of a message. Article XII repeated the longstanding concern of the Wittenberg circle to distinguish its teaching from that of Anabaptists, spiritualists, and Anti-Trinitarians.

Both Philippists and Gnesio-Lutherans made common cause against the view of justification of sinners by faith advanced by Andreas Osiander (1498–1552). He had provided active leadership to the spread of Luther's reforms in southern Germany. As pastor in Nuremberg, he had composed a widely-used catechism and, with Johannes Brenz (1499–1570), pastor in Schwäbisch Hall, later counselor to the dukes of Württemberg, an influential church ordinance for Nuremberg and Brandenburg-Ansbach. Driven into exile by the enforcement of the Augsburg Interim in Nuremberg in 1549, he found refuge

34. Esther Chung-Kim, *Inventing Authority: The Use of the Church Fathers in Reformation Debates over the Eucharist* (Waco, TX: Baylor University Press, 2011).

35. *C&C* 8, *The Augsburg Interim*; Johannes Hund, *Das Wort ward Fleisch: Eine systematisch—theologische Untersuchung zur Debatte um die Wittenberger Christologie und Abendmahlslehre in den Jahren 1567 bis 1574* (Göttingen: Vandenhoeck & Ruprecht, 2006).

36. Irene Dingel, "The Creation of Theological Profiles: The Understanding of the Lord's Supper in Melanchthon and the Formula of Concord," in Irene Dingel et al., *Philip Melanchthon, Theologian in Classroom, Confession, and Controversy* (Göttingen: Vandenhoeck & Ruprecht, 2012), 263–281.

in Königsberg, at the court of Duke Albrecht of Prussia, who as Grand Master of the Teutonic Knights, had been brought to Luther's reform movement by Osiander's preaching. In Königsberg, Osiander fell into controversy on several issues with his colleagues. Most of these had studied in Wittenberg. It soon became apparent that Osiander's training at the University of Ingolstadt under Johannes Reuchlin had given him presuppositions shaped by the neo-platonic worldview of the Kabbalistic system that Reuchlin found fascinating. These presuppositions led him to dismiss Luther's understanding of God's justifying word and thus a forensic understanding of the re-creative word of absolution based on Christ's work. Almost all other followers of Luther and Melanchthon joined the latter in a steady chorus of critique that revealed the serious flaws in Osiander's understanding of God's word, faith as trust, the atonement, and the person of Christ.[37]

The Formula of Concord concluded a process that began soon after the outbreak of controversy around 1549 or 1550. Two approaches to finding concord emerged. One counted on princely leadership because of the fear that theologians would always find more differences than common ground. This program for concord found brief, general summaries sufficient grounds for unity and called for *amnistia*, forgetting or laying aside mutual recriminations, rejecting specific condemnations. Philippists tended to embrace this approach. Gnesio-Lutherans more often wished to place the search for concord in the hands of theologians, who could lay out in detail proper biblical teaching. They also insisted on specific condemnation of false teachings and false teachers.

Duke Christoph of Württemberg (1515–68) assumed leadership of the Evangelical princes of the empire in the early 1550s and thus led efforts to establish concord. His theologians stood apart from the north German parties. The Biblical commentaries and the Catechism if his leading theologian, Johannes Brenz (1499–1570) exercised wide influence in Lutheran circles into the seventeenth century. Brenz and his right-hand man, Jakob Andreae (1528–90), had contacts among both the Gnesio-Lutherans and the Philippists. In 1568 Christoph commissioned Andreae, while aiding Christoph's cousin, Duke Julius of Braunschweig-Wolfenbüttel (1528–89), to seek a new way to concord while in Braunschweig. Andreae's attempt ended in frustration because it embraced the former approach under princely direction, but in that process he switched his tactics to that of the Gnesio-Lutherans.[38] He sought critique of a rather explicit statement of the biblical answer to the disputes from Joachim Westphal, Martin Chemnitz, and David Chytraeus, three more or less committed Gnesio-Lutherans. Westphal died, but Chemnitz and Chytraeus revised Andreae's Swabian Concord into the Swabian-Saxon Concord, in the years between 1573 and 1575. Another attempt under princely su-

37. Timothy J. Wengert, *Defending Faith: Lutheran Responses to Andreas Osiander's Doctrine of Justification, 1551–1559* (Tübingen: Mohr/Siebeck, 2012).
38. Robert Kolb, *Andreae and the Formula of Concord: Six Sermons on the Way to Lutheran Unity* (St. Louis, MO: Concordia, 1977).

pervision, the Maulbronn Formula of 1576 became the basis for the work of a committee, finally reduced to six, Andreae, Chemnitz, Chytraeus, Nikolaus Selnecker (1530–92) (who had worked for the introduction of the Reformation in Braunschweig-Wolfenbüttel around 1570), Andreas Musculus (1514–81), and Christoph Körner (1518–94). In May 1576 they met in Torgau under the aegis of Elector August of Saxony (1532–85). Their *Torgau Book* was circulated to all Evangelical ministeria during the next twelve months. The committee took critiques into consideration in forging the *Bergen Book* at Bergen abbey near Magdeburg in May 1577. It formed the Solid Declaration of the Formula of Concord, which also contained Andreae's *Epitome of the Torgau Book*, prepared as a digest for the princes. Andreae also added a historical introduction to explain how the document had come about and was connected to earlier efforts to confess the faith in Wittenberg terms.

Efforts to bring all Evangelical ministerial into agreement through the Formula and the Book of Concord, 1577–80, failed, but some two-thirds of German Evangelical clergy subscribed to the Book by 1580, thus defining themselves as Lutheran. Objections kept some followers of Wittenberg reform from supporting the Concordia settlement—followers of Flacius's view of original sin from the Gnesio-Lutherans, for one, and the spiritualizing party among the Philippists for another.[39] Some territories did not subscribe but followed the theology of the Formula of Concord in a general way, such as Schleswig-Holstein (under the influence of its Danish overlord, King Frederick II) and Pomerania.

CHURCH LIFE IN THE SECOND HALF OF THE SIXTEENTH CENTURY

The governance of the church differed from one territory or town to the next, but in general the civil authorities assumed responsibility for managing property and finances for the churches in their domains. Across Europe, absolutistic tendencies among civil rulers placed the church under their subservience, the fate of Roman Catholics, Anglicans, Reformed, and Lutherans alike. That led inevitably to tensions between clergy and local authorities. The textbook picture of Lutheran submissiveness to secular rulers does not correspond to what happened often in parishes and on the level of the territorial church. The resistance theory formulated by the Gnesio-Lutheran *Magdeburg Confession* of 1550, in the midst of Moritz's efforts to reduce the Gnesio-Lutheran town which was resisting imperial imposition of the Interim, did not dominate Lutheran political thinking, but it did play a vital role in providing a basis for defiance of regulations imposed unjustly and counter to the interests of the church.[40]

39. Irene Dingel, *Concordia controversa: Die öffentlichen Diskussionen um das lutherische Konkordienwerk am Ende des 16. Jahrhunderts* (Gütersloh: Gütersloher Verlagshaus, 1996).
40. Robert von Friedeburg, *Luther's Legacy: The Thirty Years War and the Modern Notion of 'State' in the Empire, 1530s to 1790* (Cambridge: Cambridge University Press, 2016); idem, *Lutheran Ecclesiastical Culture*, 361–410.

Preaching remained the heart of the life of Lutheran congregations from Iceland to Siebenbürgen. Liturgical variations reflected Luther's own recommendation that liturgy follow the catholic tradition but incorporate local perspectives and practices. In Sweden the attempt of Roman Catholics to reverse the Reformation resulted in liturgy much closer to medieval usage than was found in the duchy of Württemberg, for instance, where a simplified form of divine service and less frequent celebration of the Lord's Supper defined the practice. The advance of congregational singing proceeded more slowly than often asserted; the custom of choirs from the schools persisted, and hymnals only gradually found their way into general usage as literacy increased.[41]

The exploration of God's creation alongside the study of Scripture continued to be important within the Wittenberg circle and its universities in the second half of the sixteenth century. The Danish Tycho Brahe (1546–1601), Tübingen professor Michael Mästlin (1550–1630), and his student Johannes Kepler (1571–1630) continued the Wittenberg tradition of cutting-edge research in astronomy. Historical contributions by the authors of the Magdeburg *Centuries*, a team initiated by Flacius, with the writers Johannes Wigand (1523–87) and Matthäus Judex (1528–64), by Cyriakus Spangenberg, and by Caspar Peucer's work on Johannes Carion's *Chronicle*[42] exemplify the ongoing commitment to historical study of the Wittenberg students. Wigand, a prominent theologian, also demonstrates that on a more amateur level, Luther's and Melanchthon's students carried on interests, in his case in botany, fostered by his Wittenberg professor, Valerius Cordus (1515–44). The reintroduction of metaphysics to the arts curriculum of the university in Helmstedt in the 1590s by Cornelius Martini (1568–1621) changed the academic course of study and discussion at all Lutheran universities profoundly.[43]

The final years of the sixteenth century witnessed increasing tensions with Reformed and Roman Catholic opponents. Jesuits arrived in German lands in the 1550s, launching a counter-reform movement that used the printing press far more effectively than earlier Roman Catholics had. Coordinated with imperial and Bavarian use of military force, the Jesuits made advances into lands committed to Wittenberg reform. Martin Chemnitz issued critiques of both Jesuit teaching and the canons and decrees of the Council of Trent (1565–73).[44]

Chemnitz's posthumously published commentary on Melanchthon's *Loci*[45] and *Postil* carried the theology of the Formula of Concord to pastors and people. Others also worked on fresh formulations of its theology, for

41. Joseph Herl, *Worship Wars in Early Lutheranism: Choir, Congregation, and Three Centuries of Conflict* (Oxford: Oxford University Press, 2004).
42. Mark A. Lotito, *The Reformation of Historical Thought* (Leiden: Brill, 2019).
43. Walter Sparn, *Wiederkehr der Metaphysik: Die ontologische Frage in der lutherischen Theologie des frühen 17. Jahrhunderts* (Stuttgart: Calwer, 1976).
44. *Examination of the Council of Trent*, 4. vols., trans. Fred Kramer (St. Louis, MO: Concordia, 1971–1986).
45. *Loci theologici: Martin Chemnitz*, trans. Jacob A. O. Preus (St. Louis: Concordia, 1989).

example, Leonhard Hütter (1563–1616), professor in Wittenberg,[46] and Matthias Hafenreffer (1561–1619), professor in Tübingen.[47] These works provided a bridge to the theological developments of the next century. The later controversy between two Wittenberg professors, Samuel Huber (1547–1624) and Aegidius Hunnius (1550–1603), over the doctrine of predestination demonstrated that the Formula had not solved all problems and still that Lutherans would find much to dispute.[48]

By the year 1600 the Lutheran church had defined its public teaching in the Book of Concord and had laid down ever deepening roots in the faith and public consciousness of people throughout a majority of German principalities, the Nordic kingdoms, the Baltic region, parts of the kingdoms of Poland and Hungary, and beyond.

ROBERT KOLB is professor of systematic theology emeritus at Concordia Seminary, St. Louis, Missouri.

46. *Compendium locorum theologicorum*, ed. Johann Anselm Steiger (Stuttgart-Bad Cannstatt: fromann-holzboog, 2006).
47. *Loci theologici, certa methode et ratione* . . . (Tübingen 1600).
48. Rune Söderlund, *Ex praevisa fide, Zum Verständnis der Prädestinationslehre in der lutherischen Orthodoxie* (Hamburg: Lutherisches Verlagshaus, 1983).

THE LUTHERAN CHURCH IN THE SIXTEENTH CENTURY
BIBLIOGRAPHY

PRIMARY SOURCES

Chemnitz, Martin. *Examination of the Council of Trent*. 4 Volumes. Translated by Fred Kramer. St. Louis, MO: Concordia, 1971-1986.

Chemnitz, Martin. *Loci theologici*. Translated by Jacob A. O. Preus. St. Louis: Concordia, 1989.

Dingel, Irene. *Controversia et Confessio: Theologische Kontroversen 1548-1577/80. Kritische Auswahledition*, 9 Volumes. Göttingen: Vandenhoeck & Ruprecht, 2008- .

Dingel, Irene. *Die Bekenntnisschriften der Evangelische-Lutherischen Kirche*. Göttingen: Vandenhoeck & Ruprecht, 2014.

Kolb, Robert and Timothy J. Wengert. *The Book of Concord*. Minneapolis, MN: Fortress, 2000.

Luther, Martin. *Luther's Works*. St. Louis, MO/Philadelphia, PA: Concordia/Fortress, 1958– .

SECONDARY LITERATURE

Arand, Charles P., Robert Kolb, and James A. Nestingen, *The Lutheran Confessions: History and Theology of the Book of Concord*. Minneapolis, MN: Fortress, 2012.

Brecht, Martin. *Martin Luther*. 3 Volumes. Translated by James L. Schaaf. Philadelphia: Fortress, 1985–1993.

Burnett, Amy Nelson. *Debating the Sacraments: Print and Authority in the Early Reformation*. New York: Oxford University Press, 2019.

Hendrix, Scott H. *Martin Luther: Visionary Reformer*. New Haven, CT: Yale University Press, 2016.

Herl, Joseph. *Worship Wars in Early Lutheranism: Choir, Congregation, and Three Centuries of Conflict*. Oxford: Oxford University Press, 2004.

Ilic, Luka. *Theologian of Sin and Grace: The Process of Radicalization in the Theology of Matthias Flacius Illyricus*. Göttingen: Vandenhoeck & Ruprecht, 2014.

Kolb, Robert. *Lutheran Ecclesiastical Culture: 1550-1675*. Leiden: Brill, 2008.

Kolb, Robert. *Martin Luther: Confessor of the Faith*. Oxford: Oxford University Press, 2009.

Kolb, Robert, Irene Dingel, and Lubomir Batka. *The Oxford Handbook of Martin Luther's Theology*. Oxford: Oxford University Press, 2014.

Leaver, Robin. *Luther's Liturgical Music: Principles and Implications*. Grand Rapids, MI: Eerdmans, 2007.

Lotito, Mark A. *The Reformation of Historical Thought*. Leiden: Brill, 2019.

Olson, Oliver K. *Matthias Flacius and the Survival of Luther's Reform*. Wiesbaden: Harrassowitz, 2002.

Peters, Albrecht. *Commentary on Luther's Catechisms: Creed*. Translated by Charles Schaum, Thomas H. Trapp, et al. St. Louis: Concordia, 2009-2013.

Pettegree, Andrew. *Brand Luther: 1517, Printing, and the Making of the Reformation*. New York: Penguin, 2015.

Sasse, Hermann. *This is My Body: Luther's Contention for the Real Presence in the Sacrament of the Altar*. Minneapolis, MN: Augsburg, 1959.

Wengert, Timothy J. *Law and Gospel: Philip Melanchthon's Debate with John Agricola of Eisleben over Poenitentia*. Grand Rapids: Baker, 1997.

Wengert, Timothy J. *Human Freedom, Christian Righteousness: Philip Melanchthon's Exegetical Dispute with Erasmus of Rotterdam*. New York: Oxford University Press, 1998.

Wengert, Timothy J. *Defending Faith: Lutheran Responses to Andreas Osiander's Doctrine of Justification, 1551–1559*. Tübingen: Mohr/Siebeck, 2012.

Lutheranism in the Seventeenth Century

TIMOTHY SCHMELING

SEVENTEENTH CENTURY LUTHERANISM (particularly Lutheran Orthodoxy) has often been described in monolithic and reductionist terms. Admittedly, Lutheranism had more theological continuity than other Western confessions (Roman Catholicism, Anglicanism, and Reformed). But while Orthodox Lutherans predominated in this period, there were also late Reformation Lutherans, Lutheran Irenicists, and early Lutheran Pietists. Just as there was never a homogeneous single Germany at this time, there could never be a homogeneous single German (or non-German) Lutheran Orthodoxy either, but rather distinct Orthodoxies, each with their own theological emphases, symbolic norms, liturgies, pieties, and cultural ethos.

Their world consisted of the states and imperial cities of the north, east, central, and southwest regions of the Holy Roman Empire of the German Nation. It comprised the Nordic kingdoms (including Estland and Livonia), East Prussia, as well as enclaves in the Dutch Republic, Habsburg lands, and Polish-Lithuanian Commonwealth (including Courland and Semigallia). Lutherans were likely present in South America in the sixteenth century, but permanent congregations were not established until the eighteenth. They became a fixture in North America in the seventeenth century. Lutherans had limited success evangelizing in Africa. By the century's end, the Danish-Halle mission was about to enter India.

TERRITORIAL CHURCHES, REFORMED, ROMAN CATHOLICS, AND CRISIS

When Heinz Schilling argued that the church orders' (*Kirchenordnungen*) mechanisms contributed to a modernizing process of social transformation, he reignited secular interest in the Confessional Era. Against Ernst Troeltsch, Schilling maintained that all four confessions were engaged in a macro-historical process called confessionalization. This occurred between 1560 and 1650 when the clergy collaborated with their prince to forge a confession (symbol) that shaped the identity of a territory, to form subjects through the social-disciplining measures of church and state, and to help build the early modern state via such collaboration. Textbooks have generally adopted confessionalization theory as a useful interpretative paradigm, but scholars have noted that it is too focused on modernizing, neglects theology, is state-driven, and overlooks resistance by the clergy, nobles, or lower classes. It mistakenly assumes that confession building only occurs in confessions (or at the confessional level) and homogenizes both confessional and inner-confessional (Swabian Lutheranism, Hessian-Darmstadt Lutheranism, etc.) distinctives as well.[1]

Imperial Lutherans ministered within the limits of their inherited territorial church system, but they did resist the state when theology necessitated it. Since the bishops rejected Martin Luther's (1483–1546) call to reform, he appealed to the princes as the most capable members of the priesthood of all believers to do so as "emergency bishops." Lutheranism's survival hinged on the princes. When their Augsburg Confession (1530) failed to become a reform platform for the church catholic, the princes had territorial churches on their hands. Visitations resulted in church orders that significantly regulated ecclesial life. Church orders spelled out the binding symbols, liturgical agenda, and ecclesial law of each church. Ecclesial and civil servants swore oaths to them.

As the sixteenth century progressed, the princes' prefaces to the church orders, despite clerical protests, increasingly claimed the prince was head of his church by divine right (*summus episcopus*). Many princes still recognized that clergy were to keep them accountable before God, but after 1648 princes started to view the clergy as a department of state that maintained moral order.[2] The Book of Concord (1580) replaced other binding symbols, but where the Formula of Concord (1577) was not accepted, other bodies of doctrine (*corpora doctrinae*) were sanctioned. Sometimes there were additional confessions that were only territorially binding (for example the *Saxon Visitation Articles* of 1592). The sixteenth century agendas, which laid out the Lutheran Divine Service, Offices, and Rites, generally provided a rich liturgical life, though the transition from choral to congregational worship occurred over the subsequent two centuries. Depending on when the reformation was introduced and the threats faced, some ultra-conservative agendas maintained more medieval ceremony (Electoral Brandenburg in 1540), and the chief service was shaped by the mass form; while other mediating or radical agendas maintained less, and the chief service was shaped by the Prone, a medieval service of the word (Ducal Württemberg in 1553). But the

1. Stefan Ehrenpreis and Ute Lotz-Heumann, *Reformation und konfessionelles Zeitalter* (Darmstadt: Wissenschaftliche Buchgesellschaft, 2002), 62–71.
2. Hans-Walter Krumwiede, *Zur Entstehung des landesherrlichen Kirchenregimentes in Kursachsen und Braunschweig-Wolfenbüttel* (Göttingen: Vandenhoeck & Ruprecht, 1967), 200–208; 261–65.

vast majority followed the Saxon pattern of central and north Germany.[3] The ecclesial law section made provisions for schools and universities to form clergy and civil servants for the territory and its church. It established a consistory comprised of the two other estates (clergy and lay lawyers) which assisted the prince in the church's oversight. The synod made ecclesial law and excommunicated. Superintendents or bishops cared for the parishes and reported the visitation findings to the consistory. Court preachers could exercise considerable influence.

The Peace of Augsburg (1555) established the principle of the ruler's religion defining the land's religion, *cuius regio, eius religio*. Episcopal and monastic estates conversely could not become Lutheran after 1552. The treaty only recognized two legal religions, Old Religion (Roman Catholicism) and the Augsburg Confession. German Reformed were not officially recognized. But since they believed that they were Lutheranism's logical conclusion, and because they lacked legal status in the empire, they asserted that they too were adherents of the Augsburg Confession (*Variata*) and insisted that turning Lutheran lands Reformed actually *completed* or *perfected* Luther's reforms. During the attempted Calvinization of Electoral Brandenburg, the Reformed audaciously claimed that they were Luther's true heirs and charged Lutherans with being "Formulists" or "New" and "Fake-Lutherans," if not closet papists.[4] Where this strategy was impossible, Reformed Irenicists, like David Pareus (1548–1622) in his *Irenicium* (1614), argued that because the two confessions were in fundamental doctrinal (teachings necessary for salvation) agreement, they ought to put aside their differences in mutual toleration, cultivate "pious syncretism," and focus on their real enemy: Roman Catholicism.[5]

The sometimes rancorous Lutheran polemics against the Reformed make more sense when one considers the following: Lutheran Electoral Palatinate became Reformed in 1559. There were two unsuccessful attempts to turn Electoral Saxony (1571–74 and 1586–91). Lutheran Anhalt and Hesse-Kassel became Reformed in 1596 and 1605 respectively. The Brandenburg Elector Johann Sigismund of the House of Hohenzollern (1572–1619) converted in 1613, but his Lutheran populace successfully resisted Calvinization. Still his successors' Hohenzollern church policy turned to Lutheran Irenicism and then to Lutheran Pietism to mollify the Orthodox Lutheranism of Brandenburg-

3. Herl, Joseph et al., eds., *Lutheran Service Book: Companion to the Hymns* (St. Louis, MO: Concordia Publishing House, 2020), 2:27–50; Luther Reed, *The Lutheran Liturgy: A Study of the Common Service of the Lutheran Church in America*, rev. ed. (Philadelphia, PA: Muhlenberg Press, 1960), 88–92.
4. Nischan, Bodo Nischan, "Reformation or Deformation? Lutheran and Reformed Views of Martin Luther in Brandenburg's 'Second Reformation,'" in *Lutherans and Calvinists in the Age of Confessionalism* (Aldershot: Ashgate Variorum, 1999), 1:203–13.
5. Howard Hotson, "Irenicism in the Confessional Age: The Holy Roman Empire, 1563–1648," in *Conciliation and Confession: The Struggle for Unity in the Age of Reform, 1415–1648*, ed. Howard P. Louthan and Randall C. Zachman (Notre Dame: University of Notre Dame Press, 2004), 239–45, 259.

Prussia. Between 1563 and 1619, thirty-three territories, residences, and cities of the empire became Reformed.[6]

The early modern Roman Catholic Counter-Reformation proved to be formidable too. After 1555 it recatholicized a number of prince-bishoprics and southeastern imperial territories as well as much of the Habsburg and Slavic lands. Heinrich Richard Schmidt outlines the strategy as follows: remove protestant officials; oaths to Tridentine decrees for officials, teachers, and graduates; expel protestant preachers and teachers; introduce only approved priests; confiscate protestant books and prohibit attendance at Protestant services; conduct visitations; and expel notorious Protestants.[7] The Jesuits were integral to the process. They wedded zeal for pope and mission with a Renaissance humanist and neo-Aristotelian priestly formation. The spearhead of German recatholicization was the Dutch Jesuit Peter Canisius (1521–97). Besides three German catechisms and popular preaching, he helped regain the intelligentsia and found many Jesuit colleges. The Italian Jesuit Robert Bellarmine (1542–1621) was the leading polemicist. His *Disputationes de controversiis* (1586–93) was the most comprehensive refutation of Protestantism. Its more historical than scholastic approach distinguished it among its peers. The greatest Roman thinker was the prolific Spanish Jesuit Francisco Suárez (1548–1617). His new reading of Thomas Aquinas (1225–74) was the apex of Salamanca University theology. Little interested in polemics, his philosophy became highly prized even by Orthodox Protestants.

The Counter-Reformation focused much on undermining Scripture's authority, clarity, and sufficiency. At the 1601 Regensburg Colloquy, the Ingolstadt Jesuit Adam Tanner (1572–1632) seeded doubts about Scriptures' ability to authenticate itself without the church's authoritative interpretation.[8] Lutherans thereafter started softening the distinction between antilegomena and homolegoumena. The Lutheran Irenicists actually agreed that the consensus of the fathers was needed to clarify Scripture. Many princes and intellectuals justified their conversion to Roman Catholicism with Lutheran Irenicism. By 1697 the leading Lutheran ruling house, the Electoral Saxon Albertine Wettins, notably August the Strong (1670–1733), converted to become Polish kings, causing problems for their church and the *Corpus evangelicorum* in the imperial diet.

The seventeenth century was a time of unprecedented crisis: Roman Catholics, Reformed, and the Muslim Turks (oft-considered the Oriental Antichrist) were gaining the upper hand, stoking the fires of eschatological

6. J. F. Gerhard Goeters, "Genesis, Formen und Hauptthemen des reformierten Bekenntnisses in Deutschland. Ein Übersicht," in *Die reformierte Konfessionalisierung in Deutschland—Das Problem der "Zweiten Reformation, Wissenschaftliches Symposion des Vereins für Reformationsgeschichte 1985*, ed. Heinz Schilling (Gütersloh: Gütersloher Verlagshaus Gerd Mohn, 1986), 46.
7. Heinrich Richard Schmidt, *Konfessionalisierung im 16. Jahrhundert* (Munich: R. Oldenbourg Verlag, 1992), 41.
8. Wilhelm Herbst, *Das Regensburger Religionsgespräch von 1601* (Gütersloh: C. Bertelsmann, 1928).

fervor. The cooling period called Little Ice Age climaxed, increasing want as planting got delayed and crops failed. New World precious metals caused hyperinflation. Apocalypticism and scapegoating yielded a rise in witch hunting. The Thirty Years' War (1618–48) devastated Europe on a level not known again until the twentieth century. Those not taken by war often succumbed to plague.[9] Through it all, clergy and professors did their best to care for souls and form godly pastors. Neither could be aloof for they served in the thick of things. The author of "Now Thank We All Our God" and Eilenburg archdeacon, Martin Rinckart (1586–1649), conducted up to fifty funerals a day, including his own wife's. Even the estate of the famous Jena theology professor Johann Gerhard (1582–1637) was plundered and burned multiple times by imperial troops and Swedish Lutherans, who both contemplated kidnapping him![10] It is no wonder that the finest Lutheran devotional literature and hymnody came from this time. Still the crisis provoked much soul searching: If the confessions could not agree on the interpretation of the same Scripture, was doctrinal agreement possible? If it was illusory, was the quest for it the real cause of the calamity? Even if it was possible, was it being sought at the expense of a more robust piety? Perhaps, this cross was actually sent to test the faithfulness of Orthodox Lutherans, especially if Luther was the first angel of Revelation 14:6–7.

LATE REFORMATION LUTHERANS

When Duke Moritz of Saxony (1521–53) sided with Emperor Charles V (1500–58) against Elector Johann Friedrich I of Saxony (1503–44) during the Schmalkaldic War (1546–47), the emperor expanded Moritz's Albertine Saxon lands by reducing Johann Friedrich I's Ernestine Saxon lands. He gave Moritz the University of Wittenberg, and bestowed upon him the title Saxon Elector, causing animosity between the two ever after. Philipp Melanchthon's (1497–1560) Leipzig Interim, then exposed theological tensions over the legitimate expression of Luther's legacy, initiating the Lutheran late Reformation. Two chief parties and others engaged in what it meant be Lutheran (that is, how the Augsburg Confession and its legacy should be interpreted). The Gnesio-Lutherans, who opposed the Leipzig Interim as a betrayal, became associated with Ernestine Saxon duchies and helped staff the Jena University, a new rival to Wittenberg. They were more radical interpreters of anthropology, soteriology, ecclesiology, and liturgical practice from a medieval perspective. They also resisted unsolicited government interference and deemed nothing adiaphora in the state of confession. The Philippists, who supported Melanchthon, were associated with Albertine Electoral Saxony and operated

---

9. Hartmut Lehmann, "Lutheranism in the Seventeenth Century," in *The Cambridge History of Christianity*, ed. R. Po-Chia Hsia (Cambridge: Cambridge University Press, 2007), 4:56–72.
10. Herl, *Lutheran*, 2:608–9; Erdmann Rudolph Fischer, *The Life of John Gerhard*, trans. Richard Dinda and Elmer Hohle (Malone, TX: Repristination Press, 2000), 136–37, 141–42.

the Wittenberg and Leipzig Universities. They were more conservative interpreters of aforementioned topics from a medieval perspective. They accepted more government control in the church and could accept imposed adiaphora, provided justification by grace was preserved. Both were shaped by Melanchthon's theology and method (that is Renaissance humanism and Neo-Aristotelianism) and Luther's teaching.[11]

Their mutual disagreement over adiaphora, good works, free will, original sin, coupled with Osianderian, antinomian, "Calvinizing" (Lord's Supper, Christology, and election), descent into hell, and sectarian errors were answered for most Lutherans by the Formula of Concord. When these parties proved unable to reach a resolution, Duke Christoph of Württemberg (1515–68) enlisted his theologian Jakob Andreae (1528–90) to engage in a Concord project while assisting his cousin Duke Julius of Braunschweig-Wolfenbüttel (1528–89) in his land's reform. After initial failure, Andreae worked with Braunschweig city Superintendent Martin Chemnitz (1522–86), representing Braunschweig-Wolfenbüttel; Rostock University professor David Chytraeus (1530–1600), representing Mecklenburg; Leipzig University professor Nikolaus Selnecker (1530–92), representing Electoral Saxony; and two other Electoral Brandenburg theologians to produce the Formula and the Book of Concord. Two thirds of Lutheranism accepted it as genuine resolution of these controversies and the proper explication of the Augustana. Despite the 1583 *Apology of the Book of Concord*, others still rejected the Formula as a politically-driven and flawed compromise.[12]

Gnesio-Lutherans and Philippists who repudiated it found calls in lands that refused subscription, but they were not always free of the Formula's influence. Duke Julius would not enforce it in Braunschweig-Wolfenbüttel because he was rebuked for letting his son receive Roman episcopal consecration to increase his lands and because Elector August I of Saxony (1526–86), who only recently expelled his Crypto-Calvinists or Philippists after finally realizing they were duping him, supplanted Julius's leadership in the Concord Project. Duke Julius then opened Helmstedt University to Gnesio-Lutherans that opposed the Formula, like Tilemann Heshusius (1527–88) and Daniel Hoffmann (1538–1611). His son, Duke Heinrich Julius (1564–1613), conversely, recruited leading Philippists to Helmstedt, like Johannes Caselius (1533–1613), a famous late humanist; and Cornelius Martini (1568–1621), the founder of Lutheran metaphysics. Nevertheless, Heinrich Julius was pressured to resolve a Christological controversy between Hoffmann and a former Swabian Wittenberg professor Polykarp Leyser I (1552–1610) by making his Gnesio-Lutheran and Philippist theologians subscribe

11. Robert Kolb, *Luther's Heirs Define His Legacy: Studies on Lutheran Confessionalization* (Ashgate: Variorum, 1996), ix–xii.

12. Irene Dingel, *Concordia controversa: Die öffentlichen Diskussionen um das lutherische Konkordienwerk am Ende des 16. Jahrhunderts* (Gütersloh: Gütersloher Verlagshaus, 1996).

to a *Revers/Abschied* (1591), sanctioning the Formula's position.[13] When the Philippist circle had the duke prohibit the Reformed philosophy of Peter Ramus (1515–72) in 1597, Hoffmann protested the general dominance of Neo-Aristotelianism and claimed Luther taught double truth, but the Orthodox Lutherans embraced Aristotle too and Hoffmann was removed in 1601. Until court preacher Basilius Sattler died (1549–1624), Gnesio-Lutheranism reined in the Philippists and the emerging Lutheran Irenicists in Braunschweig-Wolfenbüttel. Nevertheless, other Gnesio-Lutherans like Cyriacus Spangenberg (1528–1604), a committed Flacian, never found a permanent home.

LUTHERAN ORTHODOXY

Lutheran Orthodoxy was the prevailing movement of the century. It emerged with the 1580 Book of Concord, waned after 1675, and concluded in the 1740s. Confessionalization ensured that territorial universities advanced it, but many of its key elements cannot be reduced to professors and systematics (for example, dogmaticians) as often suggested. They called themselves "orthodox" to indicate their catholic and evangelical continuity with the consensus of the fathers and the Lutheran Confessions.[14] Since the Formula was not universally accepted, they felt tasked to achieve wider and deeper consensus about Scripture's theology via various theological genres and cultural forms of engagement. Theology had a pastoral and pious aim for them. It came to be understood as a God-given practical habit or ability, that is, a salvation-orientated way of being, gifted by God through the means of grace and exercised by a faith lived out or *pietas* in communal service under the cross until the blessed end. Since doctrine was an extension of Christ himself, they refuted teachings contrary to their Christocentric faith, especially as Roman Catholics and Reformed strived to convert Lutherans. To facilitate (pastoral and lay) formation, Lutheran consensus-building, and cross-confessional engagement, Orthodox Lutherans made use of the full spectrum of tools at their disposal, including various theological disciplines, Renaissance humanism, religious and secular thinkers of every age, and even Neo-Aristotelianism and natural science.

Württemberg Orthodoxy

Lutheran Orthodoxy took shape in Württemberg whose duke spearheaded the Concord Project and supported the South Slavic Bible Institute's mission to Slavs. The duchy's ecclesial life was forged by its reformer Johannes Brenz (1499–1570). The hallmark of his theology was a Swabian omnipresence-oriented Christology that made *genus maiestaticum* the glue

---

13. Inge Mager, *Die Konkordienformel im Fürstentum Braunschweig-Wolfenbüttel: Enstehungsbeitrag—Rezeption—Geltung* (Göttingen: Vandenhoeck & Ruprecht, 1993), 466–67, 476–501.
14. See *Dictionary of Luther and the Lutheran Traditions*, s.v. "Lutheran Orthodoxy"; *Encyclopedia of Martin Luther and the Reformation*, s.v. "Lutheran Orthodoxy"; *Religion Past & Present*, s.v. "Orthodoxy"; *Theologische Realenzyklopädie*, s.v. "Lutherische Orthodoxie."

of the person of Christ. The Tübingen University arts and philosophy faculty was led by Jakob Schegk (1511–87). This polymath had a distaste for Ramism and used Neo-Aristotelian arguments to defend Lutheran Christology.[15] The first noteworthy Orthodox Lutheran, Tübingen professor Jakob Heerbrand (1521–1600), studied under Luther and Melanchthon, but shared Brenz and Schegk's spirit. Heerbrand's *Compendium theologicae* (1573) was the first dogmatics authored during the Concord Project. It first explicitly stated the visible and invisible church distinction, and added a locus on Scripture by 1578 (albeit Johannes Wigand [1523–87] and Matthäus Judex's [1528–64] *Syntagma* (1558) did so already and spoke of true and false church). When Heerbrand and the faculty entered into dialogue with the Ecumenical Patriarchate (1573–81), a Greek translation of the Augustana was sent to support their orthodoxy. Matthias Hafenreffer's (1561–1619) *Loci theologici* (1601) extended Tübingen's influence. It was translated into French for Montbéliard (1610) and was well-received in Sweden (1612, 1686). The 1611 edition included a prolegomena that grounded theology in Luther's prayer, meditation, and cross. The book was divided into three parts: God, angels, and man.

Unlike his Stuttgart court preacher father, remembered for his annotated Bibles, the Tübingen professor Lukas Osiander II (1571–1638) was the duchy's main controversialist. Osiander was the chief opponent of Johann Arndt's *Wahres Christentum* (1605–10). His *Theologisches Bedenken* (1623) charged the devotional with false mysticism. Sensitivity about the errors of his own grandfather Andreas Osiander (1496/98–1552) likely factored into his indictment. Regardless, the university disagreed with Osiander, and Arndtian piety continued to capture Orthodox Lutheran hearts in Württemberg and everywhere. In fact, Hans Leube has long demonstrated the dead orthodox thesis is untenable because Arndtian-like reform had always been central theme of Lutheran Orthodoxy.[16] During the Crypto-Kenotic Controversy (1619–27), Osiander led the faculty's (Theodor Thumm [1586–1630] and Melchoir Nicolai [1578–1659]) opposition to Giessen University professors Balthasar Mentzer I (1565–1627) and Justus Feuerborn (1587–1656). This controversy concluded Tübingen's influence. The rival positions on Christ's humiliation threatened the Christological tension the Formula had maintained. To safeguard the integrity of Christ's person, Tübingen's omnipresence-oriented Christology spoke of the communication of divine majesty to Christ's human nature in the state of humiliation in hidden terms. To protect a real atonement, Giessen's Lower Saxon multivolipresent Christology describes it as a real emptying. The Electoral Saxon Oberhofprediger (Supreme Court Preacher) Matthias Hoë von Hoënegg (1580–1645) resolved the controversy with the *Decisio Saxonica* (1624), which recognized both sides' problems, but affirmed Giessen's stress on real atonement without an

---

15. For a reevaluation of Luther's relationship to Aristotle, see Theodor Dieter, *Der junge Luther und Aristoteles* (Berlin: Walter de Gruyter, 2001).
16. Hans Leube, *Die Reformideen in der deutschen Lutherischen Kirche zu Zeit der Orthodoxie* (Leipzig: Dörffling & Franke, 1924), 36 ff.

absolute renunciation of divine majesty. The duchy's champion of Arndtian piety was Johann Valentin Andreae (1586–1654), the enigmatic grandson of the formulator. Often associated with Utopianism and Rosicrucianism, he developed Arndtian insights into a Christian society. As court preacher and councilor, he revitalized the duchy, until he became Bebenhausen Abbot and engaged in a remarkable correspondence. The capstone of Württemberg Lutheran Orthodoxy was the *Summaria* (1659–72), a glossed Bible associated with vespers.

Saxon Orthodoxy

The center of Lutheran Orthodoxy was Electoral Saxony. After the second attempt to Calvinize it, Tübingen-trained theologians were largely called to Wittenberg University to establish Lutheran Orthodoxy. Beforehand, Aegidius Hunnius I (1550–1603) strove to establish Lutheran Orthodoxy at Marburg University, but his Swabian Christology revealed a split between Reformed Hesse-Kassel and Lutheran Hesse-Darmstadt was inevitable.[17] His *Saxon Visitation Articles* (1592) rooted out Crypto-Calvinists by committing the electorate to a Lutheran understanding of the Lord's Supper, the person of Christ, baptism, and election. Academic disputations, often on the Lutheran Confessions, were revitalized to cultivate consensus.[18] His writing included doctrinal treatises, polemics, a preaching manual, table of duties sermons, postils, many Biblical commentaries, etc. The latter approached the Old Testament in a highly Christological fashion as opposed to the Judaizing exegesis he attributed to John Calvin (1509–64). When Wittenberg professor, Samuel Huber (1547–1624), a former Calvinist turned Lutheran, argued for universal election, Hunnius maintained the universality of atonement and the particularity of election in Christ via the problematic formula: election "on the basis of foreseen faith" (*ex praevisa fidei* later *intuitu fidei*).[19] Leonhard Hütter (1563–1616) helped the electorate internalize the Book of Concord. The celebrated *Lutherus redonatus* arranged Scripture and the Confessions into a celebrated doctrinal compendium (1610), soon translated to enhance its accessibility. His *Concordia concors* (1614) defended the Formula from Rudolf Hospinian's (1547–1626) Calvinist charge that it brought discord. Unlike Chemnitz's *Loci theologici* (1591), which Polykarp Leyser I edited, Hütter's *Loci Communes Theologici* (1619) stopped commenting on Melanchthon and advised his writings be interpreted via the Book of Concord. It was the most comprehensive formulation of Scripture's self-

17. Markus Matthias, *Theologie und Konfession: Der Beitrag von Ägidius Hunnius (1550–1603) zur Enstehung einer lutherischen Religionskultur* (Leipzig: Evangelische Verlagsanstalt, 2004).
18. Kenneth Appold, *Orthodoxie als Konsensbildung: Das theologische Disputationswesen an der Universität Wittenberg zwischen 1570 und 1710* (Tübingen: Mohr Siebeck, 2004), 92.
19. Gottfried Adam, *Der Streit um die Prädestination im ausgehenden 16. Jahrhunderts: Eine Untersuchung zu den Entwürfen von Samuel Huber und Aegidius Hunnius* (Neukirchen-Vluyn: Neukirchener Verlag, 1970).

authenticating authority, perspicuity, perfection, and canon (as confessed by Chemnitz) yet. The Wittenberg-trained Saxon Friedrich Balduin (1575–1627) replaced Pomeranian David Runge (1564–1604) on the faculty. Like Hunnius, Balduin also provided pastors with many commentaries. His exegesis has been called dogmatic because after exegeting a pericope, the doctrines therein were gathered according to hermeneutical principles and then applied.[20] But his real significance was the posthumous-published *De casibus conscientiae* (1628). Despite earlier precedents, it was regarded as the earliest Lutheran casuistry. This systematic study of the application of God's word to concrete but unclear cases of consciousness was highly-prized.

Wittenberg theology now acquired a new interest in systematics and philosophy. Unlike the Roman Catholics and Reformed who often drove advancements in these fields, Lutherans were more exegetically and historically focused. The Padua logician Giacomo Zabarella's (1533–89) distinction between synthetic and analytical disciplines sparked the interest. After the Danzig theologian Bartholomäus Keckermann (1571/73–1608) first applied the analytical method to Reformed dogmatics in 1602, the Wittenberg professor Johann Förster (1576–1613) applied it to Lutheran dogmatics in 1608, albeit Calov popularized it. The synthetic method moved from cause to effect, implying theology was a theoretic science and remained more popular among Reformed. The analytical method moved from effect to cause, suggesting theology was a God-given practical habit and therefore became more popular among Lutherans. Meanwhile, Jacob Martini (1570–1649) and Balthasar Meisner (1587–1626) developed a Wittenberg philosophy that now included metaphysics in service of Lutheranism.[21] Still, Meisner's *Philosophia sobria* (1611) cautioned Lutherans to recognize philosophy's misuses and practice it prudently. The zenith of Meisner's piety and devotional writings were his deathbed admonitions about the church's defects. Philipp Jakob Spener (1635–1705) later published them as the *Pia desideria: Paulo ante beatum obitum* (1679).

The most significant Lutheran court preacher and the original Oberhofprediger (supreme court preacher) was the Austrian-born Matthias Hoë von Hoënegg (1580–1645). He and Saxon Elector Johann Georg I (1585–1656) shared a hostility to Calvinism and the historic Saxon fidelity to the emperor. After Hoë von Hoënegg and the Wittenbergers helped the Brandenburg Lutherans resist Calvinization, he was convinced of Reformed duplicitousness and with Polykarp Leyser I aligned Reformed theology with Islam. When Calvinist Elector Palatinate Friedrich V (1596–1632) assumed the Bohemia crown, initiating the Thirty Years' War, Electoral Saxony sided with the Habsburgs. The sole exception was when the Edit of Restitution (1629)

20. Benjamin Mayes, "Scripture and Exegesis in Early Modern Lutheranism," in *The Oxford Handbook of Early Modern Theology, 1600–1800*, ed. Ulrich Lehner et al. (Oxford: Oxford University Press, 2016), 283–97.
21. Walter Sparn, "Die Schulphilosophie in den lutherischen Territorien," in *Grundriss der Geschichte der Philosophie*, ed. Helmut Holzhey (Basel: Schwabe Verlag, 2001), 4:475–606.

prompted the short-lived Leipzig Colloquy (1631) with the Reformed, lest the Germans become Swedish vassals. Hoë von Hoënegg presided over a number of inter-Saxon conferences between 1621 and 1630 that helped developed the Saxon Elector's role as the Augustana's chief pillar and *Corpus evangelicorum* leader into the claim that the elector (and Wittenberg as *Cathedra Lutheri*) possessed oversight in Lutheranism.[22] This later exacerbated tensions between Electoral Saxons, Ducal Saxons, and Lutheran Irenicists. When the Danzig pastor Hermann Rathmann (1585–1628) distinguished between the living inner word and the dead external word of Scripture, the Oberhofprediger issued a refutation in the name of the Saxon theologians (1629).

The brilliant and prolific Prussian, Abraham Calov (1612–86), was chiefly an exegete and polemicist, who inaugurated Wittenberg Orthodoxy's second flowering. Called to counter Georg Calixt's (1586–1656) Lutheran Irenicism (dubbed syncretism by Orthodox Lutherans), his lectures drew crowds up to five hundred. His over-combativeness stemmed from the Great Elector Friedrich Wilhelm's (1620–88) employment of Lutheran Irenicism to undermine the Lutheranism of Calov's Brandenburg-Prussian compatriots.[23] Not unlike Luther, Calov's Christology challenged Aristotelian physics by arguing space and time are experienced reality (not necessarily part of reality itself) and his philosophical *Gnostologia* and *Noologia* anticipated Immanuel Kant (1724–1804).[24] His anti-Socinian writings made him the foremost defender of the Trinity. His pastoral formation writings and analytically-arranged *Systema locorum theologicorum* (1655–77) was the most thought-provoking after Gerhard's own. Buttressed with his anti-syncretistic writings and compendiums, the *Systema* produced the most complete prolegomena, bolstered the Scripture locus, explicated the symbols' functions, historically scrutinized the *consensus patrum*, defended the *genus maiestaticum*, exposed Helmstedt synergism, refuted the historicizing of Majorism, systematized the mystical union, advanced Lutheran ecclesiology, and coined dogmatic terminology like "eschatology." His greatest claim to fame was a massive Latin Bible commentary, the *Biblia illustrata* (1672–76). As syncretistism eroded Lutheran identity, Calov contributed to new Late Orthodox interest in Luther studies and devotional life with a glossed Bible, *Die Heilige Bibel* (1681–82), composed largely of Luther annotations. It was regarded as Luther's own and profoundly shaped the piety of J. S. Bach (1685–1750).[25] His catechisms, *Wittenbergisches Gesang-buch* (1671), and *Biblischer Calendar* (1671) edified the electorate as well.

---

22. Hans-Dieter Hertrampf, "Der kursächsische Oberhofprediger Matthias Hoë von Hoënegg—seine Theologie, Polemik und Kirchenpolitk" (Theol. Diss., Karl-Marx-Universität Leipzig, 1967), 156–76.
23. Martin Lackner, *Die Kirchenpolitik des Grossen Kurfürsten* (Wittenberg: Luther-Verlag, 1977).
24. Wernert Elert, *Structure of Lutheranism*, trans. Walter Hansen (St. Louis, MO: Concordia Publishing House, 1962), 250–51; Marco Sgarbi, *Kant and Aristotle: Epistemology, Logic, and Method* (Albany: State University of New York Press, 2016).
25. *The Oxford Encyclopedia of Martin Luther*, s.v. "Lutheran Orthodoxy."

The Syncretistic Controversy (ca. 1648–86) was without a doubt the most significant controversy of the seventeenth century. It officially began with the 1645 Colloquy of Thorn, but Calixt's theology had been disputed before joining the Helmstedt faculty. The Polish King Władysław IV (1595–1648) called the colloquy to reconcile Polish Lutherans and Reformed with Roman Catholicism. As a Polish vassal, the Great Elector hoped it could advance Calvinism in his Lutheran Ducal Prussian lands. Instead of sending his own Lutheran Königsberg professor Celestyn Myślenta (1588–1653) as a delegate, the Great Elector replaced him with Georg Calixt. The Great Elector then sent two delegations to Thorn that shared Calixt's irenicism—one Lutheran and the other Reformed. There Calixt was sidelined by Wittenberg theologian Johann Hülsemann (1602–61) and Danzig pastor Abraham Calov. Despite the colloquy's failure, the Great Elector appointed and fostered Calixtine theologians at Königsberg University which now embraced Lutheran Irenicism. The Saxon Elector and his theologians' synodical solution to syncretism was opposed by Johannes Musaeus (1613–81), Jena University, and the Saxon Dukes. They sought a third way between Lutheran Irenicism and Electoral Saxon Orthodoxy. After Calixtine theology spread, conversions to Roman Catholicism rose, and the Regensburg Diet (1653–54) expressed sympathy for Calixt; the Electoral Saxons drafted the *Consensus repetitus fidei vere lutheranae* (1655/64), a reaffirmation of the Augustana and Formula and refutation of syncretism. The fundamental doctrinal agreement reached at the Kassel Colloquy (1661) between Lutheran Rinteln University and Reformed Marburg University proved Lutheran Irenicism was advancing. The Great Elector hoped for the same outcome at his Berlin Colloquy (1662–63), but only succeeded in barring his subjects' attendance at Wittenberg, nullifying the Formula in his lands, and removing Lutherans (like Paul Gerhardt [1607–76]) who refused to comply with his religious edicts. This ensured that the *Consensus repetitus* got published in a collection of faculty *Gutachten*, asserting Wittenberg oversight in Lutheranism. Calov achieved a posthumous pyrrhic victory, but the controversy concluded with bitter polemics against Musaeus and the syncretists. The *Consensus repetitus* never became symbolic throughout Lutheranism. Wittenberg divided. The new Saxon Electors Johann Georg II (1613–80) and Johann Georg III (1647–91), lacking their predecessor's orthodoxy, marginalized Calov. Nevertheless, Calov's resistance to the Hohenzollerns and to his *Historia syncretistica*'s (1682) confiscation shows Lutherans were not mere tools of state.[26] Finally, this controversy showed that different hermeneutical approaches to the Confessions existed before the nineteenth century.

Johann Gerhard's nephew, Johann Andreas Quenstedt (1617–88), was the consensus builder amidst the aftermath. Educated at Helmstedt where Lutheran Irenicists befriended him, he was rehabilitated at Wittenberg and

26. Timothy Schmeling, "Slaying the Syncretistic Chimera: A Study of the *Consensus Repetitus* in Light of Confessionalization Theory" (PhD diss., Concordia Seminary, 2014).

joined the faculty. He lacked Calov's mind, but his *Theologia didactico-polemica, sive systema* (1685) was more complete and diplomatic. His writing shows Lutheran systematics bore fruit even beyond Lutheranism. To counter the Kiev Academy's acceptance of Jesuit theology, the Novgorod archbishop Theophan Prokopvich (1681–1738) ensured through his influence on Tsar Peter the Great (1672–1725) and other theologians that the systematics of Quenstedt and other Lutherans had a significant influence on Russian Orthodoxy.[27]

The earliest direct attack on Philipp Jakob Spener's (1635–1705) Lutheran Pietism came from the Calixtine Nordhausen pastor Georg Konrad Dilfeld (d. 1684) in 1679. Spener gave a powerful defense of his continuity with Luther and Orthodoxy in *Die allgemeine Gottesgelehrtheit* (1680). In fact, Johannes Wallmann rightly disputed the distinction between Lutheran Orthodoxy and a Proto-Pietistic "Reform Orthodoxy," showing that even the most polemic Orthodox Lutherans (like Dannhauer [1603–66] and Calov) supported early Spenerian reforms.[28] However, Radical Pietism, August Hermann Francke's (1663–1727) Leipzig conventicles controversy (1689), and Pietism's expansion into Württemberg and Hesse-Darmstadt invited scrutiny. The cultured Wittenberger Johann Friedrich Mayer (1650–1712) initially supported Spener in his inaugural speech (1684). But Mayer's marriage soon fell apart. When Spener criticized the moral ramifications of a theologian's divorce and prevented Mayer's assumption of the late Calov's faculty position, Mayer was filled with vitriol against Spener. Thus Mayer had to accept the Hamburg St. Jacobi pastorate in 1687, but he quickly accumulated positions and remained an influencer through the network he built. Here the bellicose Mayer attacked the Pietists in the ministerium (for example, Spener's brother-in-law Johann Heinrich Horb [1645–95]), but also faced pietism's enthusiastic and ascetic excesses. When he became Swedish-Pomeranian General superintendent and Greifswald professor in 1701, Halle entered his crosshairs. The Wittenberger Johann Deutschmann (1625–1706) attacked Spener for 284 deviations from the Confessions in his *Christ-Lutherische Vorstellung* (1695).

One of the last Orthodox Lutherans was Valentin Ernst Löscher (1673–1749). As Jüterbog superintendent, he started the first German Protestant theological journal, *Altes and Neues* (1701), later renamed *Unschuldige Nachrichten*. He was open to Spener initially. His *Elde Andachts-Früchte* (1702) sought to cultivate "mystical orthodox theology." But as Delitzsch superintendent, he started to address Pietism's extremes with his journal in 1705. He briefly served Wittenberg before becoming Dresden superintendent. His most complete critique of Spener's movement was the *Vollständiger Timotheus Verinus* (1718–22).[29]

---

27. George Maloney, *A History of Orthodox Theology Since 1453* (Boston: Nordland, 1976), 42–49.
28. Johannes Wallmann, *Pietismus-Studien: Gesammelte Aufsätze* II (Tübingen: Mohr Siebeck, 2008), 1–21.
29. Martin Brecht, ed., *Geschichte des Pietismus* (Göttingen: Vandenhoeck & Ruprecht, 1993–2004), 1:321–71, 507–11.

The Leipzig faculty lacked Wittenberg's dynamism, but Leipzig remained resolutely Orthodox as the last holdout against the Aufklärung. The learned Saxon Carpzovs played an important role here. The law professor Benedikt Carpzov II (1595–1666) was the "founder of German jurisprudence." Besides civil law, he penned the first system of Lutheran church law, the *Jurisprudentia ecclesiastica seu consistorialis* (1649). His half-brother, Johann Benedikt Carpzov I (1607–57), become the "father of Lutheran symbolics" because of his *Isagoge in libros ecclesiarum lutheranum symbolicos* (1665). The *Hodegeticum* (1652) shows he was also an influential homiletician. The East Friesian and former Wittenberger, Johann Hülsemann (1602–61), is known more for his churchmanship in the Syncretistic Controversy than his writings. However, the *Consensus repetitus* seems to derive more from Hülsemann's hand than Calov's, though Hieronymus Kromayer (1610–70) and Daniel Heinrici (1615–66) assisted. Briefly Hebrew professor, Martin Geier (1614–80) wrote edifying postils as Dresden Oberhofprediger and was milder than his predecessors. The greatest Leipziger systematics was Johann Adam Scherzer's (1628–83) *Systema theologiae* (1680). His temperament gained him the nickname "Leipzig Calov." He still felt the need to author the *Anti-Bellarminus* in 1681. Spener believed Leipzig favorable to his project. Johann Benedikt Carpzov II (1639–99), Valentin Alberti (1635–97), Johannes Olearius (1639–1713), and August Pfeiffer (1640–98) all seemed open to it. But after Francke's *Collegia Biblica* awoke a public pietistic disturbance, the Carpzov-led Leipzig faculty (save Olearius) called for investigations that prohibited Francke from lecturing on theology. Carpzov, Pfeiffer, and Alberti also got the Leipzig Enlightenment Jurist and Francke defender, Christian Thomasius (1655–1728), ousted for challenging the confessional state and its Christian metaphysical underpinnings. The secularizing Thomasius proceeded Francke at the new Hohenzollern Halle University.[30]

As the immediate heirs of the reformers' devotional writings, Electoral Saxon resources were rich. Johann Habermann's (1516–90) *Christliche Gebet* (1567) remained so influential that "taking up one's Habermann" became an idiom "for going to prayers." This lay breviary delivered a prayer regiment for each day of the week and special occasions.[31] Many famous church musicians served the electorate: Nuremberg and Dresden composer, Hans Leo Hassler (1564–1612); Wolfenbüttel and Dresden composer, Michael Praetorius (1571–1621); and Leipzig composer, Johann Hermann Schein (1586–1630). The best were the Dresden composer, Heinrich Schütz (1585–1672); and the Leipzig composer J. S. Bach (1685–1750). They enriched Saxon spirituality with their masses, passions, cantatas, etc. Lutheran artists absorbed Baroque art. The most famous Lutheran church built in this style was the Dresden Frauen-

30. Otto Kirn, *Die Leipziger Theologische Fakultät in Fünf Jahrhunderten* (Leipzig: S. Hirzel, 1909), 68–133.
31. Nicholas Hope, *German and Scandinavian Protestantism 1700 to 1918* (Oxford: Oxford University Press, 1999), 27.

kirche which provided a Lutheran conception of liturgical space. Dresden remained the most beautiful German Baroque city until it was firebombed in World War II.

Hessian-Darmstadt Orthodoxy

Hesse-Darmstadt Lutheranism eclipsed the early Swabian Orthodoxy at Tübingen and Wittenberg. The landgraviate's existence was forged in Calvinization. To counterbalance a now Reformed Marburg, Landgrave Ludwig V (1577–1626) founded the Lutheran Giessen University in 1607. Former Marburg professor Balthasar Mentzer I (1565–1627) moved to Giessen to staff it. His highly influential and insightful theology took the form of collected disputations and polemics, but are less polemic than they appear. This Hessian provided an assessable summary of Lutheran catholicity in the *Catholisch Handbüchlein* (1619). He became the earliest non-Braunschweiger to question Calixt's theology in 1620. Mentzer's Lower Saxon multivolipresent orientated Christology and articulation of Christ's humiliation against Calvinism brought him into loggerheads with Tübingen and marked Hesse-Darmstadt Lutheranism's ascendency. Mentzer left his stamp on Jena and Wittenberg via his students Johann Gerhard and Balthasar Meisner respectively.

Christoph Scheibler (1589–1653) was Giessen's preeminent philosopher. He came to be known as the "Protestant Suárez." His *Opus logicum* (1620) and *Opus metaphysium* (1617) drew international attention to Lutheran school philosophy. In 1676 the Hesse-Darmstadt court preacher Johannes Winckler (1642–1705) attempted to introduce conventicles. But Oberhofprediger Balthasar Mentzer II (1614–79) spoke out against the practice. Winckler later moved to Hamburg and contributed to its pietistic disputes with Mayer.

Orthodoxy in Urban Centers

In the urban centers, one can see that Luther's marriage of doctrinal fidelity, pastoral care, and piety continued in Lutheran Orthodoxy from the start. When Unna (Westphalia) needed a pastor to counter a Calvinist influx, they called Philipp Nicolai (1556–1608). He was not only a robust controversialist, but the earliest Orthodox Lutheran to devotionally explicate a sacramentally-grounded mystical union at length. The two were not mutually exclusive, but organically followed from Wittenberg's Christocentric theology which interpreted any attack on doctrine as an attack on Christ.[32] Earlier sermons aside, his richest expression of mystical union was his plague-prompted devotional, *Freuden Spiegel des ewigen Lebens* (1599), which included the king and queen of chorales, "Wake, Awake for Night is Flying" and "How Lovely Shines the Morning Star."

32. Elert rightly traced Nicolai's mystical union back to the Formula, Luther himself, and via Luther to medieval figures. See his *Structure*, 154–76, especially 154, n.1.

Friendship and pastoral care drove Georg Dedekenn (1564–1628). He ministered with Nicolai at the Hamburg St. Katharinen Church. There Dedekenn edited Nicolai's complete German and Latin works. He also gathered together one of the largest casuistry collections in the *Thesauri consilorum et decisionum* (1623). Johann Ernst Gerhard (1621–68) and Christian Grübel (1642–1715) expanded and reprinted it in 1671.[33] Near Hamburg is the town of Wedel. The polymath and poet laureate Johann Rist (1607–67) served as its pastor. He once claimed that the calamitous times brought forth his ponderous hymns. His additional stanzas to "O Darkest Woe" expressed Lutheranism's Cyrillian faith: "Our God is dead." Some of the greatest Lutheran musicians like Hamburg composers Jacob Praetorius (1586–1651), Johann Schop (ca. 1615–64/65), Georg Philipp Telemann (1681–1767), and Lübeck composer Dietrich Buxtehude (1637–1707), wedded tunes to his hymns.

Aegidius Hunnius's son, Nikolaus Hunnius (1585–1643), became Lübeck superintendent after a Wittenberg professorship. His *Diaskepsis theologica* (1626) refuted Reformed Irenicism, demonstrating that they were not in fundamental agreement. The earliest Lutheran articulation of fundamental (primary and secondary) and non-fundamental doctrine was articulated herein. His popular *Epitome Credendorum* (1628) laid out the first systematic treatment of an order of salvation. This feature became standard with the analytical method. In 1633 he organized Lübeck, Hamburg, and Lüneberg into the Ministerium Tripolitanum to combat false theological tendencies. He also suggested the formation of a *Collegium Irenicum* to function like a Lutheran supreme court. A Lübeck doctor named Peter Heyling (1607/8–52) decided to become a missionary to Ethiopia in 1634. After studying in Egypt, he served Ethiopian King Fasilides (1632–67), translated Biblical texts into Amharic, and spoke for reforms. He left in 1652, but was beheaded by a Turkish pasha.

Konrad Dieterich (1575–1639) served the Giessen *Paedagogium* before becoming Ulm Münsterprediger. Naturally this instilled in him the importance of solid catechesis. He developed tiered catechisms to help all ages internalize the faith. His *Institutiones Catecheticae* (1613) became a prevalent, concrete alternative to other compendiums. His Ulm catechetical sermons reveal how important Christian education was to him. Rothenburg ob der Tauber remains an idyllic town today. Spener's friend, Johann Ludwig Hartmann (1640–84) was its superintendent. In 1678 he authored the highly-consulted pastoral theology, the *Pastorale Evangelium*.

Evangelical monasteries remain a little explored loci of Lutheran spirituality. Lower Saxony had the highest concentration. If Luther's corrections to monasticism were accepted, they could continue and grow, albeit this arrangement had its distractors.[34] The daughters of Lutheran nobles ran the

33. Benjamin Mayes, *Counsel and Conscience: Lutheran Casuistry and Moral Reasoning After the Reformation* (Göttingen: Vandenhoeck & Ruprecht, 2011), 28–39.
34. Hans Otto, ed., *Evangelisches Klosterleben: Studien zur Geschichte der evangelischen Klöster und Stifte in Niedersachsen* (Göttingen: V&R unipress, 2013).

Quedlinburg imperial abbey. Abbess Anna Sophia of Hesse-Darmstadt (1638–83) (who resisted her blood sister's temptation to pope) defended the evangelical monastic life, wrote hymns, and published *Der treue Seelenfreund* (1658) devotional. Johann Gerhard and Johann Andreas Quenstedt grew up in this environment. Johann Arndt and Christian Scriver (1629–93) served abbey parishes. A friend of Spener, Scriver is known for uplifting sermons on the soul's progress, *Seelen-schatz* (1675–92), and emblematic devotions.

There was a time when Johann Arndt (1555–1621) was the most influential Orthodox Lutheran. His *Wahres Christentum* was reprinted more than any book except the Bible. Arndt published the first book in 1605 and three more in 1610. Two more and his *Paradiesgärtlein* prayer book were added posthumously. Committed to the Formula, he was dismissed from Anhalt for retaining the baptismal exorcism, published an early polemic against Rome, and repeatedly asked that any imprecision in his writings be understood according to the Lutheran Confessions. In contrast to Nicolai's comfort piety, a perceived lack of clerical godliness prompted Arndtian piety. He opposed unnecessary polemics and impious living, stating Luther taught an authentic faith is living and active. Just as Orthodox Lutherans were now going further than Luther to reclaim the best medieval theology, he sought to reclaim the best medieval mysticism to foster godliness. Often misinterpreted as challenging Lutheran Orthodoxy, most embraced him, albeit "correctly understood." Arndt eventually coupled mystical union to new obedience resulting in deeper interiorizing of the faith-life. Since he wrote *Wahres Christentum* as a Brauschweig city pastor (1599–1609), his initial target might actually be the cantankerous Helmstedt Gnesio-Lutherans and Philippists. He studied there in 1576.[35]

The well-read Duke August II of Braunschweig-Wolfenbüttel (1579–1666) (of *Herzog August Bibliothek* fame) tried to inject Arndtian piety into his Calixtine duchy. He took the Pomeranian devotional writer, Joachim Lütkemann (1608–55), as his court preacher instead of a Calixtiner. He attempted to reform the duchy's civil and ecclesial life, even trying to replace the lectionary with Biblical paraphrases. He conducted a fascinating correspondence with Johann Valentin Andreae.

Johann Gerhard and the Return of Saxon Orthodoxy

It was the archtheologian of Lutheranism, Johann Gerhard (1582–1637), who brought the star of Ducal Saxon Lutheranism back into ascendency. Spiritually mentored by Arndt as a sickly youth, he was a synthesis of Arndtian pastoral piety and Balthasar Mentzer I's penetrating theological acumen. No theologian shaped as many facets of Orthodox Lutheranism as Gerhard. Beginning as a youth, he wrote in many different devotional genres: meditations (1606), art of dying (1611), passion history (1611), prayer book

35. Johannes Wallmann, "Johann Arndt (1555–1621)," in *The Pietist Theologians*, ed. Carter Lindberg (Malden: Blackwell, 2005), 21–37.

(1612), Gospel postil (1613), and finally the *Scholia pietatis* (1622–23), a sort of corrected *Wahres Christentum*. Before being called to Jena University, he served as Heldburg superintendent and prepared the Saxony-Coburg church order (1626). Gerhard authored works on Biblical interpretation (1610) and a methodology for pastoral formation (1620). His *Loci theologici* (1610–22) was Lutheranism's *Summa theologia* and the most comprehensive rebuttal of Bellarmine. The preface to its supplement exegesis (1625) was the first Lutheran prolegomena in the strict sense. Both he and Meisner explicitly called theology a God-given practical habit in 1625. Gerhard bore this out when he provided a practical use for each locus. While the *Loci theologici* offered the most comprehensive Scripture commonplace yet, its relocation of the election commonplace has been criticized. Besides his own commentaries, Gerhard finished Chemnitz and Leyer's harmony of the gospels (1626–27). His *Confessio catholica* (1634–37) was the fullest expression of Lutheran Catholicity after Chemnitz's *Examen decretorum concilii tridentini* (1566–73). He also wrote the first critical patrology in 1653. Duke Ernst the Pious of Saxony-Gotha-Altenburg (1601–75) commissioned him to supervise the creation of the famed Weimar glossed Bible (1641). Gerhard was the very embodiment of an Orthodox theologian, churchman, pastor, and spiritual director.[36]

Due to a lack of Wittenberg, Jena, and Eisleben editions of Luther's writings, Duke Friedrich Wilhelm II of Saxony-Altenburg (1603–69) commissioned the new twelve-volume Altenburg edition (1661–64). His successor Ernst the Pious was celebrated as a reformer in his own day. He was cut out the same Arndtian cloth as Duke August of Braunschweig-Wolfenbüttel. Ernst focused all his efforts on his conception of the "reformation of life." This included pedagogical, socio-economic, and political reforms. His innovative Gotha Gymnasium provided asylum for the sons of Eastern European Lutherans. Ernst the Pious funded a Lutheran school in Moscow. He brought the Ethiopian priest Abba Gregorius (1595/1600–58) to Gotha to study his culture and initiate a mission to Ethiopia.[37]

Gerhard's handpicked successor was Salomo Glass (1593–1656) who completed Ernst the Pious's Weimar Bible. Glass added spiritual uses or applications to the pericopes therein. After Flacius's *Clavis scriptura sacrae* (1567), Glass's *Philologia sacra* remains a significant hermeneutic text. Herein he argues for a mystical sense in Scripture that must be distinguished from mere allegories and applications. He also provides rules for ferreting this out. Johannes Musaeus (1613–81) took the Jena theological faculty in a new direction, forging a third way between Helmstedt and Wittenberg. He was the earliest Lutheran to critically engage Enlightenment philosophy. He helped introduce natural theology, proposing a sort of unregenerate theology. Musaeus split

36. Markus Friedrich et al., eds., *Konfession, Politik und Gelehrsamkeit: Der Jenaer Theologe Johann Gerhard (1582–1637)* (Stuttgart: Franz Steiner Verlag, 2017).

37. Veronika Albrecht-Birkner, *Reformation des Lebens: Die Reformen Herzog Ernsts des Frommen von Sachsen-Gotha und ihre Auswirkung auf Frömmigkeit, Schule und Alltag im ländlichen Raum (1640–1675)* (Leipzig: Evangelische Verlagsanstalt, 2002).

the difference between Gerhard and Calixt by defining theology both as a God-given habit and as a practical science. He maintained that conversion is neither instantaneous nor purely passive. He historicized the Book of Concord, suggesting his new spiritually-deficient context permitted saying "good works are necessary for salvation." His son-in-law Johann Wilhelm Baier (1647–95) synthetized his theology in his *Compendium theologiae positivae* (1685).[38] It is interesting to speculate if Friedemann Bechmann's (1628–1703) *Annotationes uberiores in compendium theologicum Leonhardi Hutteri* (1690) is an attempt to realign Jena with Hütter over against Calov and Musaeus.

Alsatian Orthodoxy

Three theologians left their mark on Alsatian Lutheranism and its Strassbourg University. In 1651 Johann Georg Dorsche (1597–1659) wrote a remarkable defense of the Augustana with Thomas Aquinas, arguing the Angelic Doctor was more Lutheran than papist. He later assumed a post at Rostock University. Johann Conrad Dannhauer (1603–66) was the day's most voracious Luther reader. He organized his penetrating *Hodosophia Christiana* (1649) and polemics around emblematic themes. Known to be as pious as he was polemic, his Straßburg Cathedral catechetical sermons (1642–78) were highly prized and collected in ten volumes. Sebastian Schmidt (1617–96) was a premiere exegete of the age. He produced a Lutheran revision of the Vulgate (1696), a hybrid exegetical-dogmatics (1670), and numerous commentaries. Spener found his time here to be very fruitful.

Lutheran Orthodoxy in the North and East of the Empire

David Chytraeus left his stamp on early Mecklenburg Lutheranism. His student Paul Tarnov (1562–1633) carried forth his legacy at Rostock University. But he was also influenced by Johannes Caselius. When Tarnov's nephew was rebuked for deviations from the Lutheran divines, Tarnov counseled restraint on issues not impacting the fundamentals. When Calov earned his doctorate at Rostock, he lived with Johann Quistorp I (1584–1648), and the two remained close friends. Known for moderation, the Great Elector first recruited him for the Colloquy of Thorn. Quistorp declined, recognizing its intended purpose. But when the political theorist, Remonstrant Irenicist, and Swedish Ambassador Hugo Grotius (1583–1645) took ill traveling though Rostock, Quistorp afforded the Arminian pastoral care before he died. Johannes Quistorp II (1624–69), Theophil Großgebauer (1627–61), and Heinrich Müller (1631–75) conducted one of the most intensive Orthodox reforms of life. In the process they wrestled from the magistrates more control of the Rostock church than typical in the empire. Their sermons were voraciously consumed. Therein Müller warns his flock about the four dumb idols of Lu-

38. Schmeling, "Slaying," 115–31, 169–228, 296–338. See also Harry Mathias Albrecht, *Wesen und Einheit der Kirche nach der Lehre des Johannes Musäus (1613–1681)* (Mainz: Verlag Philipp von Zabern, 2003).

theranism: altar, pulpit, font, and confessional chair. This oft-misunderstood remark was directed against cheap-grace Christianity. He never intended to challenge the sacraments' efficaciousness.[39]

After the House of Greifen died out (1637) and the Thirty Years' War, Sweden took over Western Pomerania and Brandenburg took over Farther Pomerania. The Swedish-Pomeranian Greifswald University like Rostock transmitted Lutheran Orthodoxy to Scandinavian students. Unlike Pomerania itself, Greifswald accepted the Formula in 1623. Its Johann Friedrich König (1619–64) had to contend with an influx of Reformed that the Great Elector allowed into Farther Pomerania. When König moved to Rostock, the compendium he composed became the foundation for Quenstedt's *Systema*. In 1701 Mayer joined Greifswald. The Jakobshagen provost David Hollaz (1648–1713) wrote the last major Orthodox dogmatics (1707) without ever serving as a professor.

The Brandenburg Lutherans had a proud history of resisting Calvinization. But under the Great Elector this proved more difficult. In the heart of Berlin was the greatest hymnist after Luther, Paul Gerhardt (1607–76). His hymns are of the highest quality. His friend, the Nicolai Kirche cantor Johann Crüger (1598–62), wrote tunes for some them and collected many into the most widely used hymnal, the *Praxis pietatis melica* (1647), which was expanded in subsequent editions. After the Great Elector expelled him, Gerhardt assumed the Lübben parish in Electoral Saxony. An inscription therein captures the crosses that made him sing: "A theologian sifted in Satan's sieve."

LUTHERAN IRENICISM

Contrary to older scholarship, Georg Calixt (1586–1656) neither started as a Lutheran irenic, nor did he learn it from Reformed Irenicism. He was not really an Erasmian Irenic either. In the Helmstedt Philippist circle, Calixt had maintained that fundamental doctrinal agreement between the confessions did not exist. The real catalyst for his devotion to the path of Lutheran Irenicism was the Thirty Years' War as well as the Old Catholic Irenicists Georg Cassander (1513–66) and Marco Antoni de Dominis (1560–1624). Moreover Calixt became a Confessional Irenicist who advocated for mutual toleration between the confessions and hoped for a God-given reunion of Christendom on the basis of the fundamental doctrine encapsulated in the Apostles' Creed and its proper explication via the patristic consensus of the first five centuries. Since Calixt believed that the Augsburg Confession was the most faithful expression of this apostolic and catholic theology, he insisted that his project (which opposed the Formula on authority, Christology, ecclesiology, and soteriology) was not only catholic, but irrefutably Lutheran. Lutheran Irenicism soon spread throughout Helmstedt, the Braunschweig duchies, Königsberg

39. Jonathan Strom, *Orthodoxy and Reform: The Clergy in Seventeenth Century Rostock* (Tübingen: Mohr Siebeck, 1999).

University, Rinteln University, and Altdorf University. It was less hospitable to Pietism than Orthodoxy and sputtered out after Calov's death.[40]

Calixt was raised by a Philippist father in Danish-controlled Schleswig where the Formula was not accepted. Before becoming an irenicist, Calixt's theology deviated from the Braunschweig-Wolfenbüttel's *Corpus doctrinae julium* (1576) as well. Calixt maintained that only church teachers needed theology because it is a practical, intellectual aptitude acquired via natural means. His attacks on Lutheran "ubiquity" stem from a Calvinizing Christology. Calixt posited a state of pure nature. Original sin was a mere accident or lack of original righteousness. With his colleague Conrad Horneius (1590–1649), he made synergistic statements and taught that good works are necessary for salvation or at least are the *sine qua non* for it. Calixt produced the first Lutheran moral theology (1634) but used it to spread his ecumenical objectives.

The Great Elector appointed Calixt's student Johann Latermann (1620–62) to Königsberg University. He quickly caused a major controversy with his predestination disputation. Calov's former friend turned syncretist, Christian Dreier (1610–88), advocated for Calixt's attendance at the Colloquy of Thorn. Thus Königsberger's writings took syncretism into a Crypto-Roman Catholic direction. The Danzig Lutheran ministerium even claimed that they would sooner commune with the Reformed than Dreier. Johannes Musaeus's brother, Peter Musaeus (1620–74), studied at Helmstedt and lived with Calixt. As Rinteln professor, he helped craft the Kassel Colloquy with the Marburgers that affirmed Lutherans and Reformed were in fundamental doctrinal agreement.[41]

EARLY PIETISM

Lutheran Pietism was the last movement of the era, but its definition is the most contentious.[42] Not unlike Hans Leube, Martin Gierl has the most restricted definition. Pietism emerges from the late 1680s Leipzig conventicles controversy between Orthodox Lutherans and Pietists, when the term "Pietist" found resonance, and then expands to the northern parts of the empire. It was a new way of practical theological engagement within German Lutheranism. In contrast to Arndt's program, Wallmann begins Pietism, strictly speaking, with Spener and the 1670s Frankfurt lay conventicles and concludes it in the late eighteenth century. It unfolded around three generations of pietistic patriarchs, though Wallmann also recognizes Radical Pietists who challenged their confessions. It is distinguished from Arndt by three marks: conventicles of the pious, chiliastic hope for better times, and the centrality of lay Bible reading. Hartmut Lehmann argues for a more flexible, transconfessional, transatlan-

40. See also Hermann Schussler, *Georg Calixt: Theologie und Kirchenpolitik* (Wiesbaden: Franz Steiner Verlag, 1961).

41. Schmeling, "Slaying," 17–115, 132–68, 229–67.

42. *Dictionary of Luther and the Lutheran Traditions*, s.v. "Pietism"; *Encyclopedia of Martin Luther and the Reformation*, s.v. "Pietism in Northern Europe, The Descendants of"; *Religion Past & Present*, s.v. "Pietism"; *Theologische Realenzyklopädie*, s.v. "Pietismus."

tic, and social and cultural view of Pietism, one that emerged with Spener (if not Arndt) and continued into the twentieth century. Its four marks include devotional gatherings of the reborn, a new tradition of Biblical interpretation, ecumenical solidarity with all reborn and separation from the world, and chiliastic hope for better times. Fred van Lieburg builds off of Lehmann's work, maintaining that Pietism should not be essentialized in terms of origins, confession, epoch, or type, but defined functionally like a pattern or model.[43]

The Alsatian Philipp Jakob Spener (1635–1705) was the father of Lutheran Pietism. He came under the influence of Jean de Labadie (1610–74), a Reformed mystic who conducted conventicles. In 1666 Spener became the senior of the Frankfurt (am Main) ministerium. Unsatisfied with Lutheran Orthodoxy's more social, external, and top-down approach to piety, his more individualistic, internal, and bottom-up Lutheran Pietistic approach emerged when laymen encouraged (for example, later Radical Pietist Johann Jacob Schütz [1640–90]) him to found a conventicle (*collegium pietatis*) in 1670. These became lay-orientated small groups in congregations where religious texts were discussed to mutual edify and reform. He summarized his conception of Pietism in his *Pia desideria* (1675), a preface to an Arndt postil. When Spener lost control of the Radical Pietists who fostered separatism, he accepted a call as Dresden Oberhofprediger in 1686. He soon found life there insufferable. In 1691 he accepted a call as pastor of St. Nicolai in Berlin, Paul Gerhardt's former church, as well as serving as consistory member. There he called for tolerance, advocated for Lutheran Pietism, and reined in Radical Pietists. When Hohenzollerns founded Halle University in 1694, he lobbied to staff it with Pietists. He was obliged because Lutheran Pietism served Hohenzollern ends.[44]

August Hermann Francke (1663–1727) had been reared around Ernst the Pious's court. He and Paul Anton (1661–1730) founded an exegetical-oriented Collegium Philobiblicum for fellow Leipzig theology lecturers in 1686. Francke came under Spener's influence before his Lüneburg conversion experience (1687), something foreign to Spenerian Pietism. After returning to Leipzig, Francke's Collegium morphed into edifying public conventicles that incited enthusiasm among the general populace in 1689. Controversy followed him to Erfurt. In 1691 Spener got Francke the St. Georg Glaucha pastorate and a theology professorship at the soon-to-open Halle. Francke established a school for the poor in 1695. With donor support, he founded an orphanage by 1698 to which he eventually added a bookstore, publishing house, and training camp for missionaries, all of which profoundly impacted Lutheranism and society at large.[45]

43. Douglas H. Shantz, *An Introduction to German Pietism: Protestant Renewal at the Dawn of Modern Europe* (Baltimore: The John Hopkins University Press, 2013), 1–14.

44. Jonathan Strom and Hartmut Lehmann, "Early Modern Pietism," in *The Oxford Handbook of Early Modern Theology, 1600–1800*, ed. Ulrich Lehner, et al. (Oxford: Oxford University Press, 2016), 402–35.

45. Markus Matthias, "August Herrmann Francke (1663–1727)," in *The Pietist Theologians*, ed. Carter Lindberg (Malden: Blackwell, 2005), 100–114.

SEVENTEENTH CENTURY LUTHERANISM BEYOND THE HOLY ROMAN EMPIRE

Danish influence waned and Swedish power expanded at this time. The Saxon Elector August I tried to persuade his brother-in-law King Fredrik II (1534–88) of Denmark and Norway to remove his leading Philippist theologian Niels Hemmingsen (1513–1600) and subscribe to the Formula of Concord. In 1579 Hemmingsen was dismissed from Copenhagen University and reassigned as a Roskilde canon, but the king refused to subscribe and his lands never did. Under King Christian IV (1577–1648), Hans Poulsen Resen (1561–1638), Cort Aslakssøn (1564–1624), and Jesper Brochmand (1585–1652) strived to plant Lutheran Orthodoxy. The Copenhagen professor and later Zealand bishop Resen focused on rooting out Crypto-Calvinism and producing a Danish Bible translation (1607) from the original languages. The Norwegian Copenhagen professor Aslakssøn put aside Crypto-Calvinism for the Formula. He wrote on Christology and sought to reconcile Tycho Brahe's (1546–1609) astronomy with Genesis. Brochmand, who held both of Resen's posts, was the greatest Orthodox Scandinavian theologian. His *Universae Theologiae Systema* (1638) was so well-received that it was republished in the empire. Brochmand was a capable exegete and controversialist, but his treasured *Huuspostil* (1638) touched more lives than his other works. The Paul Gerhardt of Scandinavia was the Fyn bishop Thomas Kingo (1634–1703). The Kingo hymnbook (1699) endured for a century and his hymns remain classics. Beloved hymnists were found elsewhere in the realm. In Norway, Petter Dass (1647–1707) stands out, female hymnist Dorothe Engelbretsdatter (1634–1716) too. Hallgrímur Pétursson's (1614–74) passion hymns spoke to the soul of Iceland. Unlike the Germans, the Scandinavians could engage in colonialism and mission. The first Lutheran service in North America (1619) was celebrated in Canada by Rasmus Jensen (d. 1620), whose expedition sought the Northwest Passage. In 1663, Danes started a colony in the West Indies. While it engaged in the slave trade with its African Gold Coast colony, it eventually evangelized non-Europeans. The Danish Halle Mission to India was established in 1706. Norwegian pastor Hans Egede (1686–1757) established a mission to Greenland in 1721.[46]

King Johan III Vasa (1537–92) of Sweden and Finland was devoted to Georg Cassander's irenicism and tolerated Jesuits. When the Roman Catholic Sigismund III (1566–1632) was to assume the throne, the Uppsala Synod (1593) committed the church to the creeds and Augsburg Confession. Civil War ensued. But the Lutheran Karl IX (1550–1611) eventually took power and was succeeded by Gustav II Adolf. The latter made efforts to evangelize the Lapps. Whereas the Danish King Christian IV failed to drive back the Roman Catholic forces in the Thirty Years' War, Gustav II Adolf's dying victory was a stalemate that kept imperial Protestants from recatholization. The Uppsala

46. Martin Schwartz Lausten, *A Church History of Denmark*, trans. Frederick Cryer (Burlington: Ashgate, 2002), 127–78.

professor, Västernås bishop, and royal chaplain Johannes Rudbeckius (1581–1646) fostered Lutheran Orthodoxy in the realm. He produced a revision of the Swedish Bible (1618). Nowhere were Lutheran bishops as strong as Sweden. Gustav II Adolf's daughter Kristina (1626–89) was sympathetic to Lutheran Irenicism until her conversion to Roman Catholicism. The Orthodox Lutherans took umbrage with both her syncretism and Cartesianism. Her mentor and Strängnäs bishop Johannes Matthiæ Gothus (1592–1670) encouraged her syncretistic views. In opposition to him, the Wittenberg-educated Chancellor Axel Oxenstierna (1583–1654) and the diet asked that the Formula of Concord be adopted in 1647. Gothus's clear unionistic theology in his *Idea boni ordinis in ecclesia Christi* (1664) made the Formula's acceptance possible in 1663 and church law in 1686. Skara bishop Jasper Svedberg (1653–1735) produced a new Swedish Hymnal in 1695. Its chief hymnist was Linköping bishop Haquin Spegel (1645–1714) who imbibed Anglican spirituality. The chief Finnish hymnist was Hemminki Maskulainen (ca. 1550–1616). In contrast to Lund University, founded in 1666, the Livonian (Estland) Dorpat (Tartu) University and the Finnish Åbo (Turku) University were established in 1632 and in 1640 respectively. Many Baltic Lutherans were originally served by Germans, but gradually came to be served my non-Germans. At Dorpat, a Baltic German named Georg Mancelius (1593–1654) wrote the earliest Latvian book, his *Lettische lang-gewünschte Postill* (1654). A complete Latvian Bible was printed in 1685. In Finland, the Åbo bishop Isak Rothovius (1572–1652) favored Lutheran Orthodoxy, but Åbo professor and friend of Kristina, Johannes Elia Terserus (1605–78), favored Lutheran Irenicism. By 1638 Sweden founded New Sweden on the Delaware River in America. Its second pastor, Johannes Campanius (1601–83), translated the Small Catechism (1648) into a Native American tongue. The Dutch Republic absorbed New Sweden into its New Netherlands in 1655. New Netherlands had begun in the 1620s, but Dutch Lutherans first established New World free congregations in the 1640s. In 1650, the Swedes founded a colony on the African Gold Coast. The Danes captured it in 1663, and held it until 1850. After the Great Northern War (1700–21), the Russian Tsardom gained control of Swedish Livonia and Estonia, expanding their Lutheran population beyond Germans.[47]

In the Polish-Lithuania Commonwealth, Calvinism eventually outpaced Lutheranism. Lutherans were concentrated in the German-speaking areas of the former Prussian Teutonic knight lands and Greater Poland. Unlike Courland and Semigallia, much of the Polish Duchy of Livonia fell to the Swedes in 1629. Royal Prussia remained Polish until it fell to the Hohenzollerns in 1772. Ducal Prussia was a Hohenzollern Polish fief until 1657 when it came entirely under Hohenzollern control. Once the Hohenzollerns became Calvinist, Ducal Prussians Lutherans appealed to the 1569 Union of Lublin's desire for one Protestant church and their Polish citizenship to stem

47. Eric Lund, "Nordic and Baltic Lutheranism," in *Lutheran Ecclesiastical Culture, 1550–1675*, ed. Robert Kolb (Leiden: Brill, 2008), 411–54.

the tide of Calvinization. Greater Poland Lutherans increased because of emigration from German lands. There were certainly many ethnic German Lutherans in the commonwealth, but there were many ethnic Poles too. The Königberg professor Celestyn Myślenta (1588–1653), who molded Abraham Calov, was the most important ethnic Polish Lutheran theologian.

Lutherans were found in Austria, Hungary, and Silesia. Prior to the Council of Trent, Lutherans outnumbered Roman Catholics in Austria. The Hapsburg Counter-Reformation stemmed the Lutheran tide. The oppressive Emperor Ferdinand II (1578–1637) recatholisized in earnest after the 1620 Battle of White Mountain. Though the Wittenberg faculty missions *Gutachten* (1651), responding to the concerns of Baron Ehrhard Ferdinand Truchsess von Wetzhausen in Vienna, became infamous, it raised theological issues for ecclesiology and eschatology thereafter. Frustrated, the exiled Austrian Lutheran Baron Justinian von Welz (1621–68) set out to evangelize Suriname in South Africa in 1664, but died not long after without lasting results. Emperor Leopold I (1640–1705) brutally suppressed Protestantism in Hungary, but he could not completely extinguish it.[48] Despite persecution, Silesia was a center of Lutheran spirituality: Martin Moller's (1547–1606) 1601 *Praxis evangelicorum* was the most important devotional after Nicolai's and before Arndt's. After Roman Catholics stripped the Frauenstadt Jesus-preacher Valerius Herberger's (1562–1627) congregation of its building, they were able to turn two buildings into a new Lutheran church aptly-named "Christ's manger." He wrote very devout sermons, hymns, and devotional commentaries. The poet laureate Martin Opitz (1597–1639) revolutionized German Baroque poetry and hymnody. Opitz's new style was picked up by Johann Heermann (1585–1647). The only hymns to rival his sacred lyrics are Luther's and Gerhardt's.

Seventeenth century Lutheranism was many things. Monolithic, dead, and sterile are not among them. It certainly had its warts. But its theology and piety still impact Lutherans and non-Lutherans today. If new research institutes, scholarly studies, and translations are any indication, seventeenth century Lutheranism will only continue to do so.

TIMOTHY R. SCHMELING is professor of exegetical and historical theology at Bethany Lutheran Theological Seminary in Mankato, Minnesota.

---

48. Howard Louthan and Graeme Murdock, eds., *A Companion to the Reformation in Central Europe* (Brill Leiden, 2015).

BIBLIOGRAPHY

PRIMARY SOURCES

Arndt, Johann. *True Christianity.* Translated by Peter Erb. New York: Paulist Press, 1979.

Calixt, Georg. *Werke in Auswahl.* 4 vols. Vandenhoeck & Ruprecht, 1970–82.

Calov, Abraham. *I. N. J. Biblia . . . illustrata . . . locupletissimo.* 4 vols. Frankfurt am Main: Balthasar Christoph Wust, 1672–76.

Erb, Peter C., ed. *Pietists: Selected Writings.* New York: Paulist Press, 1983.

Dedekenn, Georg. *Thesauri consilorum et decisionum.* 3 vols. Hamburg: Paul Lange, Michael Hering, Hans Mose, 1623.

Die evangelischen Kirchenordnungen des XVI. *Jahrhunderts.* Edited by Emil Sehling et al. Leipzig and Tübingen: O. R. Reisland and J. C. B. Mohr [Paul Siebeck], 1902–.

Gerhard, Johann. *Theological Commonplaces.* Translated by Richard Dinda. Edited by Benjamin T. G. Mayes. St. Louis, MO: Concordia, 2006–.

________. *Confessio catholica . . . confirmatur.* Jena: Steinmann, 1634–37.

Gerhard, Johann, and Salomo Glass, ed. *Biblia, das ist: Die gantze H: Schrifft, Altes und Newes Testaments Teutsch / D. Martin Luthers.* Nürnberg: Wolfgang Enter, 1641.

Lund, Eric, ed. *Seventeenth-Century Lutheran Meditations and Hymns.* New York: Paulist Press, 2011.

Quenstedt, Johann Andreas. *Theologia didactico-polemica, sive systema theologicum . . . divisum.* Wittenberg: Johann Ludolph Quenstedt, Elert Schumacher, and Matthäus Henckel, 1685.

Steiger, Johann Anselm, ed. *Doctrinae et Pietas: Zwischen Reformation und Aufklärung.* Abteiling 1: Johann-Gerhard-Archiv. Abteilung 2: Varia. 14 vols. Stuttgart-Bad Cannstatt: Frommann-Holzboog, 1997–.

________. *Doctrinae et Pietas: Zwischen Reformation und Aufklärung.* Abteilung 2: Varia. 5 vols. Stuttgart-Bad Cannstatt: Frommann-Holzboog, 1997–.

SECONDARY SOURCES

Brecht, Martin, ed. *Geschichte des Pietismus.* 4 vols. Göttingen: Vandenhoeck & Ruprecht, 1993–2004.

Elert, Werner. *Morphologie des Luthertums.* 2 vols. Munich: C. H. Beck'sche Verlagsbuchhandlung, 1958. (The first volume is translated under the title *The Structure of Lutheranism*).

Headley, John M., Hans J. Hillerbrand, and Anthony J. Papalas, eds. *Confessionalization in Europe, 1555–1700.* London: Routledge, 2004.

Koch, Ernst. *Das konfessionelle Zeitalter—Katholizismus, Luthertum, Calvinismus (1563–1675)*. Leipzig: Evangelische Verlagsanstalt, 2000.

Kolb, Robert, ed. *Lutheran Ecclesiastical Culture, 1550–1675*. Brill: Leiden, 2008.

Lehner, Ulrich L., and Richard A. Muller, eds. *The Oxford Handbook Early Modern Theology, 1600–1800*. Oxford: Oxford University Press, 2016.

Preus, Robert. *Theology of Post-Reformation Lutheranism*. 2 vols. St. Louis: MO Concordia, 1970–72.

Schindling, Anton, and Walter Ziegler, eds. *Die Territorien des Reichs im Zeitalter der Reformation und Konfessionalisierung: Land und Konfession 1500–1650*. 7 vols. Münster: Aschendorf Verlag, 1989–99.

Schmeling, Timothy, ed. *Lives and Writings of the Great Fathers of the Lutheran Church*. St. Louis, MO: Concordia, 2016.

Sparn, Walter. "Die Schulphilosophie in den lutherischen Territorien." In *Grundriss der Geschichte der Philosophie*, edited by Helmut Holzhey, 4:475–606. Basel: Schwabe & CO AG Verlag, 2001.

Wallmann, Johannes. *Theologie und Frömmigkeit im Zeitalter des Barock*. Tübingen: Mohr Siebeck, 1995.

Lutheranism in the Eighteenth Century

Eric Lund

In the first half of the eighteenth century, Pietism was on the ascendancy within the Lutheran churches, sometimes aided by the support of kings in Germany and Scandinavia. There continued to be an Orthodox party within the churches that viewed these developments critically, but by mid-century both the Pietists and the Orthodox began to overlook some of their differences and direct more of their attention toward a common challenge: the growing influence of Rationalism. The German Enlightenment (*die Aufklärung*) was an intellectual revolution as significant for the Lutheran churches as the Reformation of the sixteenth century. While some church leaders argued that the new stress on the power of human reason undermined faith and that historical-critical study of texts was incompatible with Christian claims about revelation, others tried to reconcile philosophy and historical analysis with Lutheran theology. At the end of the century, there were more diverse interpretations of Lutheranism within the churches than there had been at the start. Germany continued to be the leading source of new ideas in theology and biblical studies, but the eighteenth century is also notable as the period in which Lutheranism truly became a global movement. Missionaries spread it to other regions of the non-western world, and widely scattered German and Scandinavian immigrants in North America took the first important steps towards forming durable, organized ecclesiastical communities.

SPENER AND HALLE PIETISM

In 1670 six men began to meet twice weekly in Frankfurt am Main in the home of the young senior minister, Philipp Jakob Spener (1635–1705), to deepen their spiritual lives through discussion of devotional books and study of the Bible. This conventicle, intended to supplement weekly worship in church, gradually expanded and, by 1677, involved around one hundred people, including some women. It also inspired similar *collegia pietatis* in other cities throughout Germany. Critics fearing separatism or fanatical enthusiasm derogatorily called the participants Pietists, but eventually Spener and his associates accepted this label to differentiate the reform movement that developed out of these gatherings from the traditional orientation of the Orthodox Lutherans. In 1675, Spener set forth an agenda for this movement in a booklet titled *Pia Desideria*. In it he protested against moral decay in German society and pointed out inadequacies in the Lutheran churches. He criticized the lack of true Christian living among those who professed allegiance to Lutheran doctrine and expressed dissatisfaction with theologians whose zeal for purity of doctrine, he claimed, had degenerated into a focus on subtle controversies remote from the essentials of practical Christian living. Without challenging the basic tenets of Lutheran theology, Spener sought to shift concerns away from the preservation of confessional purity toward the nurturing of purity of life.[1] Spener's voicing of these "heartfelt desires for improvement" was not entirely novel. Throughout the seventeenth century various Lutheran devotional writers had denounced the shortcomings of various social classes and contended that true faith should work a substantial change in people's lives. Foremost among them was Johann Arndt (1555–1621), whose major work, *Four Books of True Christianity*, stressed the importance of true repentance, rebirth (*Wiedergeburt*) and renewal (*Erneuerung*). The influence of Arndt on Spener is evident from the fact that *Pia Desideria* was first published as a preface to a new edition of Arndt's postil sermons. In addition, Spener's outlook was shaped by reading Puritan writers such as Lewis Bayly and by contact with the French Reformed preacher Jean de Labadie.[2] Spener added something to the message of the earlier devotional writers by suggesting concrete proposals for improving conditions in the churches. He called for a more extensive use of the Bible beyond the short passages favored by the liturgical lectionary, greater involvement of lay people in the church's ministries, increased emphasis on the cultivation of Christian love, and a shift in the focus of pastoral training away from the acquisition of disputational skills for polemical debating toward the study of theology as a practical discipline. After advocating these proposals for twenty years in Frankfurt, Spener served five years as court preacher for the Elector of Saxony in Dresden and then moved to Berlin where he spent the last fifteen years of his life as dean of the clergy and pastor of the St. Nikolai church.[3]

The Pietist reform movement initiated by Spener entered a new phase when August Hermann Francke (1663–1727) became a pastor and professor in Halle in 1692. While teaching as a *Privatdozent* in Leipzig in 1686, Francke participated in the Collegium Philobiblicum, a student group formed to read the Bible in its original languages. When Spener, then in Dresden, was invited to give advice to the participants, he encouraged them to incorporate a devo-

1. Stein, James, *Philipp Jakob Spener: Pietist Patriarch* (Chicago: Covenant Press, 1986), 74–106.
2. F. Ernest Stoeffler, *The Rise of Evangelical Pietism* (Leiden: E. J. Brill, 1971), 193–232.
3. Philip Jacob Spener, *Pia Desideria*, trans. Theodore Tappert (Philadelphia: Fortress Press, 1964), 8–28.

tional perspective into their study of the Bible. Francke and his friend Paul Anton favored this modification of the group's scholarly purpose and were deeply affected by the results. Francke felt, however, that something was missing in his life until he had a conversion experience while preparing a sermon in Lüneberg. He committed himself thereafter to amendment of life and service to others. Francke visited with Spener in late 1688 and then returned to Leipzig to lecture at the university. When his popular lectures sparked a spiritual revival among the students, Johann Benedikt Carpzov II (1639–99), an Orthodox theologian, accused him of teaching false doctrine and persuaded the authorities to dismiss him. For the same reason he lost his next position as a pastor in Erfurt. Francke again spent some time with Spener who used his influence as court preacher to secure Francke's appointments at a church in Glaucha and at the recently founded University of Halle in 1692.[4]

Glaucha was a poor district outside the city walls of Halle. The physical and spiritual condition of the people who came weekly to Francke's home, begging for alms, troubled him, so he introduced a poor box to gather funds for the needy. He also established a charity-school in 1695 to rectify the ignorance of indigent children. This school developed such a positive reputation that he decided to expand his reform programs to minister to other social classes. He set up a *Paedagogium* for the sons of the nobility, a Latin school to provide future lawyers, doctors and merchants, and German schools for the children of tradesmen. Some of the boys attending the *Armenschule* lived on the streets; to provide them with a more stable upbringing, Francke started an orphanage in 1698. This was expanded in 1709 to provide also for girls. By 1706, his growing foundation (*Stiftung*) enrolled 698 children in the schools, one hundred twenty-two of whom were orphans. By the time of his death in 1727, the number had risen to over two thousand.[5] Francke also built a seminarium to train teachers for his schools, homes for widows, a pharmacy and a publishing house. In 1702, he founded the Collegium Orientale, to teach biblical languages, and he also encouraged his influential supporter in Berlin, Baron Karl Hildebrand von Canstein (1667–1719), to fund an institute for the mass printing of inexpensive Bibles. By the end of the eighteenth century, this *Bibelanstalt* in Halle had published over 2.7 million Bibles.[6]

Throughout all those years, Francke also taught at the university, first in oriental languages and later in theology. His influence there was strengthened by like-minded colleagues, several of whom also owed their appointments to Spener's influence on Prussian King Friedrich I (ruled 1688–1713). These included Paul Anton (1661–1730) and Joachim Justus Breithaupt (1658–1732), who became the first systematic theologian of Pietism. After Spener's death in 1705, aristocratic sympathizers in the court of Friedrich Wilhelm I (1713–40) persuaded the king to provide additional support to the many endeavors

4. Douglas Shantz, *An Introduction to German Pietism* (Baltimore, MD: The Johns Hopkins University Press, 2013), 117–143.
5. Stoeffler, *German Pietism during the Eighteenth Century* (Leiden: E. J. Brill, 1973), 1–38.
6. Gary Sattler, *God's Glory, Neighbor's Good* (Chicago: Covenant Press, 1982), 83–89.

Francke had organized in Halle. Francke met with him after his coronation in 1713, and General Dubislav Gneomar von Natzmer (1654–1739) played an ongoing role as Francke's advocate in Berlin. The king was a devout Calvinist but felt a commonality with any who sought to follow God's commandments. His own stress on self-sacrificing service fit well with Francke's promotion of an intensely disciplined spirituality. The "Soldier King" organized a separate church for his expanded army in 1718 and filled its chaplaincy with Halle-trained pastors who stressed the importance of morality and the fulfillment of vocational duty. He also used Pietist pastors to develop the educational system in Prussia and to help him secure the loyalty of Lutherans in East Prussia and in Pomerania after it was annexed from Sweden in 1720. In 1717, the king decreed that all candidates for the ministry in Prussia obtain a recommendation from Halle's theological faculty. After 1729, all of them were required to study for at least two years in Halle. By the time of Francke's death, a kind of State Pietism prevailed in northern Germany. Some scholars see this as a reciprocal partnership of independent parties interested in the reform of society, while others think that Halle Pietism was co-opted and made a pliant instrument in the consolidation of Prussian absolutism.[7]

PIETISM OUTSIDE OF PRUSSIA

Pietism also flourished in the Duchy of Württemberg in southwest Germany, but there the movement tended to be more inward looking and less engaged with the government. Many conventicles developed in the region during the late seventeenth century, influenced in part by Spener but also by a local concern for spiritual renewal initiated earlier by Johann Valentin Andreae (1586–1640), a disciple of Arndt. The state grew more concerned when some conventicles developed chiliastic interests and became very critical of the Lutheran establishment. A series of edicts required pastoral supervision of these groups, but lenient treatment of dissenters and an inclination to tolerate inner-churchly gatherings kept most of the Pietists connected to the state church. Württemberg Pietism was primarily a peasant and middle-class movement, sustained throughout the century by conventicles such as the fellowships started by Johann Michael Hahn (1759–1819) in more than 200 communities. On the other hand, it also attracted some notable intellectuals such as Johann Albrecht Bengel (1687–1752) and Friedrich Christian Oetinger (1702–82).[8] Bengel was educated at Tübingen and spent most of his life as a pastor and teacher at a theological preparatory school in Denkendorf. He made impor-

7. Richard Gawthrop, *Pietism and the Making of Eighteenth-Century Prussia* (Cambridge: Cambridge U Press, 1993), 200–246; Mary Fulbrook, *Piety and Politics* (Cambridge: Cambridge U Press, 1983), 153–173; Terry Thompson, *God's Special Way: August Hermann Francke, Friedrich Wilhelm I and the Consolidation of Prussian Absolutism* (PhD diss., Ohio State University, 1996), 3–19, 255–270.

8. Hartmut Lehmann, *Pietismus und weltliche Ordnung in Württemberg von 17. bis zum 20. Jahrhundert* (Stuttgart: Kohlhammer, 1969).

tant contributions to textual criticism of the Bible (see below) and to the interpretation of salvation history. Oetinger, who served as a pastor and church superintendent in several localities, had a complex spiritual journey during which he developed interests in philosophy, science, Jewish Kabbalah, Jacob Böhme and the writings of Emanuel Swedenborg. He was a prolific writer whose influence would be greater after his death, on speculative theologians in the nineteenth and twentieth centuries.

The influence of Jakob Böhme and other mystical writers inspired some Pietists to express more radical criticisms of Lutheranism. Most notable among them was Gottfried Arnold (1666–1714), who had been educated at Wittenberg, an Orthodox stronghold, but became a Pietist after contact with Spener in Dresden. While teaching in Quedlinburg his thought moved in a more spiritualist direction, and he decided against both ordination and marriage. After a very brief stint as a professor of church history at Giessen, he returned to Quedlinburg where he began to write a series of controversial books. Most notable among them was his *Impartial History of the Church and Heretics* (1699), which traced the fall of the church away from the simple message of Christ. He also wrote *The Secret of the Divine Sophia* (1700), in which he argued that the soul must be purified before it can be joined in marriage with heavenly Wisdom or the spirit of Christ.[9] Arnold eventually reconciled with the Lutheran church and became a court pastor in Allstedt in 1701. After facing criticism for his refusal to endorse the Formula of Concord and for his additional writings on mystical theology, he had to leave that position. The protection of King Friedrich I, however, enabled him to spend the last seven years of his life as pastor and superintendent in Perleberg.[10] Another notable radical, Johann Konrad Dippel (1673–1734), the son of a Lutheran pastor, came under the influence of Arnold while studying in Giessen. His diatribes against the church, published under the pseudonym Christianus Democritus, destined him to a life of wandering: from the Netherlands to Denmark to Sweden, and finally back to Germany, where he found refuge in Berleburg. He practiced medicine there among other radicals who were protected by the Count of Sayn-Wittgenstein.[11] Less radical but still controversial, Count Nikolas von Zinzendorf (1700–60) was pushed to the periphery of Lutheranism because of his distinctive piety and his relations with the *Unitas Fratrum*, a group originating from the Hussite movement in Bohemia and Moravia. After attending Francke's school for the nobility in Halle, he studied law at the University of Wittenberg. During a grand tour of Europe from 1719 to 1720, he met with representatives of a variety of religious traditions and came to believe that each of the confessional groups had something to add to Christianity. He served for a number of

9. Gottfried Arnold, *Unparteyische Kirchen—und Ketzer-Historie* (Leipzig: Fritsch, 1699); *Das Geheimnis der göttlichen Sophia* (Leipzig: Fritsch, 1700).
10. Peter Erb, "Gottfried Arnold," in *The Pietist Theologians*, ed. Carter Lindberg (Oxford: Blackwell Publishing, 2005), 175–189.
11. Hans Schneider, *German Radical Pietism* (Lanham, MD: The Scarecrow Press, 2007).

years on the judicial council of Electoral Saxony in Dresden but increasingly became preoccupied with the plight of the Moravian refugees he had accommodated on his estate in Berthelsdorf in Upper Lusatia. Under his guidance, they formed a covenanted community at Herrnhut. Through the innovative use of small groups (choirs) they developed a method for spiritual development that would influence the English Methodists.[12]

Various issues such as Zinzendorf's relative indifference to confessional distinctions, his references to the Holy Spirit as mother, and his emotional emphasis on the blood and wounds of Christ stirred up opposition not only among Orthodox theologians but also from some Pietist leaders. Zinzendorf continued to value his ties to the Lutheran church and sought validation by passing theological exams in Stralsund. The theological faculty in Tübingen certified his ministry in 1734, but he was banned from Saxony between 1736 and 1747. The situation worsened when he agreed to be a bishop in the Moravian Church in 1737, even though he had persuaded them to accept the Augsburg Confession. For almost two decades, Zinzendorf traveled throughout Europe, the West Indies and North America, interacting with various religious groups and helping along the Moravian missionary activities that started in 1732. He worked to modify some of the controversial features of Moravian piety that were most pronounced during the Sifting Period from 1743 to 1750. Zinzendorf settled in London from 1749 to 1755, but after the Moravian Church was finally recognized as an approved church in Saxony, he returned to Germany to spend his final years in Herrnhut.[13]

ORTHODOX-PIETIST DEBATES

There were fewer Orthodox Lutheran university professors producing massive systematic theologies during the eighteenth century. *Examination of Academic Theology*, usually considered the last of the old-style dogmatic textbooks, was published in 1707 by David Hollaz, a pastor in Pomerania. Nevertheless, some universities, like Wittenberg and Leipzig, continued to be bastions of Orthodoxy, notwithstanding the growing influence of the Pietists at the University of Halle. A number of influential pastors and professors defended the doctrinal tradition that prevailed in the previous century by writing polemical treatises against the Pietists.[14] Foremost among them was Valentin Ernst Löscher (1673–1749) who studied and taught at the University of Wittenberg before serving for forty years

12. Arthur Freeman, *An Ecumenical Theology of the Heart: The Theology of Count Nicholas von Zinzendorf* (Bethlehem, PA: Moravian Church of America, 1998).

13. Martin Brecht, "Zinzendorf in der Sicht seiner kirchlichen und theologischen Kritiker," in *Neue Aspekte der Zinzendorf-Forschung*, ed. Martin Brecht & Paul Peucker (Göttingen: Vandenhoeck & Ruprecht, 2006), 207–228.

14. Vernon Kleinig, "Confessional Lutheranism in Eighteenth Century Germany," *Concordia Theological Monthly* 6:1–2 (Jan–Apr 1996): 97–125. Other notable anti-pietist writers were Johann Friedrich Mayer (1650–1712) and Erdmann Neumeister (1671–1745) in Hamburg, Johannes Fecht (1636–1716) in Rostock, and Johann Georg Neumann (1661–1716) in Wittenberg.

as court preacher and church superintendent in Dresden. Starting in 1701, Löscher published the first theological magazine in Germany, *Innocent News* (*Unschuldige Nachrichten*), in which he criticized rival confessional groups, mystical Pietists, and atheistic rationalists. While intent on defending pure doctrine, Löscher also showed interest in practical pastoral issues through another periodical, *Evangelical Tithes* (*Evangelische Zehnten*). He respected the devotional writers who prepared the way for the development of Pietism, but also stated that "the sainted Johann Arndt" had spoken carelessly about the means and fruits of salvation, and that others such as Heinrich Müller and Theophilus Großgebauer had spoken too harshly about the ministry and the universities. At first, Löscher faulted the Halle Pietists primarily for failing to distance themselves from more radical enthusiasts. Joachim Lange, the combative successor to Joachim Justus Breithaupt on the theological faculty in Halle, defended the Pietists in a counter-publication, *Upright News* (*Aufrichtige Nachrichten*), and then in a 1709 book, *Against the Barbarians*. He portrayed Halle Pietism as "the true middle way" between the "pseudo-orthodox" and the fanatical enthusiasts. This, in turn, prompted Löscher to publish his master work, *Timotheus Verinus* (1718–22), in which he dissected fourteen problematic characteristics of the "pietistic evil."[15] Löscher stopped short of calling Pietism a heresy, and sometimes spoke of Spener as a gifted and honorable man. However, he felt that the divisions in the church caused by the Pietists created a *status confessionis* that compelled him to present a vigorous refutation of their ideas. Although he theoretically distinguished between types of Pietism, his charges were based on incriminating citations from Pietists as varied as Francke, Lange, Arnold and Dippel. He saw "indifferentism" manifested in both their dismissal of some doctrines as secondary teachings and in their mystical stress on Christ's indwelling more than external means of grace. They extolled conventicles to the neglect of regular communal worship and scorned the legitimacy of the clergy unless they are perfectly holy. In their emphasis on regeneration they mixed the righteousness of faith and works, making works necessary, in contradiction to the Formula of Concord. Löscher argued that the Pietists inordinately stressed asceticism and, in their condemnation of practices such as dancing and other moderately enjoyed entertainments, eliminated any concept of *adiaphora*. They preached a dangerous perfectionism and engaged in fanciful chiliastic speculations. Despite the harshness of these criticisms, Löscher, with the help of a young Zinzendorf, met with Francke and his associates at Merseburg in 1719. When he refused to confess that he had treated Pietism unfairly, the parties departed unreconciled.[16]

---

15. Joachim Lange, *Antibarbarus orthodoxiae* (Berlin/Halle: J. G. Meyer, 1709); Valentin Löscher, *The Complete Timotheus Verinus*, trans. James Langebartels & Robert Koester (Milwaukee: Northwestern Publishing House, 1998).
16. Martin Greschat, *Zwischen Tradition und neuem Anfang: V. E. Löscher und die Ausgang der lutherischen Orthodoxie* (Witten: Luther Verlag, 1971), 275–282.

RESPONSES TO RATIONALISM

After 1722, both Löscher and Lange became alarmed by the spread of rationalism in Germany.[17] This development was made most evident by the growing popularity of Christian Wolff (1679–1754) at the same academic center which had been so closely identified with Pietism. Wolff, who was appointed professor of mathematics and natural philosophy at the University of Halle in 1706, was influenced by Gottfried Leibniz (1646–1716), the first major German to be involved in the new debates about metaphysics, epistemology, physics and religion that had originated abroad in the work of Descartes, Spinoza, Newton and Locke. Raised a Lutheran, Leibniz argued in *Theodicy* (1710) that belief in an all-powerful, benevolent God was not incompatible with the existence of evil in the world. His concern for religious matters was also evident in his life-long efforts to promote rapprochement between Protestants and Catholics.[18] Leibniz recognized a place for assent to revelation by faith, so long as it did not contradict reason. Questions remained, however, about his actual conception of God and his stress on the principle of sufficient reason.

Christian Wolff attempted to apply Leibniz's method at Halle to a wide range of disciplines and held up mathematics as the model of demonstration. In his 1719 book, *Rational Thoughts on God, the World and the Soul,* he stated that God created the world like a machine and that God's omniscience is more evident in the regularity of nature than in supernatural occurrences such as miracles. Wolff was a church-going Lutheran, but also taught that atheists were capable of recognizing the good. He provoked a great controversy in 1721 when, in a public lecture, he argued that the Chinese, whom many thought to be atheists, had ethical views that were compatible with his own.[19]

Joachim Lange immediately attacked Wolff and began a campaign to have him dismissed from Halle. In a series of writings, Lange claimed that Wolff espoused a deterministic view of the world and subordinated the Holy Scriptures to the principles of reason. After being censured by the Halle theologians, Wolff appealed to King Friedrich Wilhelm I. To his surprise, the king supported the Pietists and ordered Wolff to leave Prussian territory within forty-eight hours or face hanging. The king apparently had been persuaded that, if Wolff's deterministic views became known among his soldiers, deserters would claim that they could not have acted otherwise. Wolff taught for the next seventeen years at the University of Marburg until he was recalled to Halle in 1740 by the

17. Löscher wrote against rationalism in *Nöthige Reflexiones* (1724) and *Quo Ruitis?* (1735).
18. Ursula Goldenbaum, "Leibniz as a Lutheran," in *Leibniz, Mysticism and Religion*, ed. Allison Coudert, Richard Popkin & Gordon Weiner (Boston/Dordrecht: Kluwer Academic, 1998), 169–192.
19. Charles Corr, "Christian Wolff and Leibniz," *Journal of the History of Ideas*, 36:2 (1975): 241–262; Tore Frängsmyr, "Christian Wolff's Mathematical Method and Its Impact on the Eighteenth Century," *Journal of the History of Ideas*, 36:4 (1975): 653–668; Christian Wolff, *Gedancken von Gott, der Welt und der Seele des Menschen* (Halle: Renger, 1719).

next king, Friedrich the Great, whose own religious views were Deistic.[20] Despite the initial victory of the Halle Pietists in their fight against Wolff, the influence of his philosophical ideas gradually seeped into the universities throughout Germany. Scholars differ about how best to categorize the spread of the Enlightenment in theological circles, but one of the most common approaches is to differentiate between three degrees of influence: Transitional Theology (*Übergangstheologie*), Neology, and skeptical Rationalism.[21] The most notable representative of the first group was Siegmund Jacob Baumgarten (1706–57) who studied at Francke's *Paedagogium* and became a theological professor at the University of Halle in 1734. Sympathetic to a scholarly, non-mystical Pietism, he gradually came to feel that many of his theological colleagues at the university lacked intellectual rigor. He sought to present a mediating option between defensive conservatism and dangerous forms of new thought such as Deism or atheism. In numerous writings culminating in his 1760 systematic theology, he sought to utilize Wolff's method and analytical categories in support of traditional Christian articles of faith. He thought that natural theology could prove many important beliefs, but that there were other important truths that were above, but not opposed to, reason. Revelation about the atoning work of Christ was necessary to attain salvation.[22] Joachim Lange called for an investigation of Baumgarten after his popularity among students surged, but the Prussian government supported him, as long as he promised to teach "a true active Christianity" and to refrain from the use of "incomprehensible philosophical terms." Baumgarten continued to teach that theology must be grounded in Scripture but also found fault with the subjective exegesis of some Pietists as well as Orthodox claims that the very words of the Bible were from God. He called for historical attention to the intentions of the human authors and was also one of the first scholars to suggest that the biblical writers accommodated their message to what their readers could understand.[23] Other professors often associated with this transitional category are Johann Franz Buddeus (1667–1729) and Johann Georg Walch (1693–1775) in Jena, Christoph Matthäus Pfaff (1686–1760) in Tübingen, and Johann Lorenz von Mosheim (1694–1755) in Göttingen.

The Neologists went beyond the Transitional theologians in their efforts to use reason in defense of Christianity. They focused on natural theology in their apologetic writings against atheism and viewed revelation as a necessary supplement provided by God for the sake of the unlearned who are

20. Albrecht Beutel, "Causa Wolffiana: die Vertreibung Christian Wolffs aus Preussen 1723," in *Wissentschaftliche Theologie und Kirchenleitung*, ed. Ulrich Köpf (Tübingen: Mohr Siebeck, 2001), 159–202; *A Documentary History of Lutheranism*, ed. Eric Lund, vol. 2 (Minneapolis:, MN Fortress Press, 2017), 1–10.
21. Beutel, *Kirchengeschichte im Zeitalter der Aufklärung* (Göttingen: Vandenhoeck & Ruprecht, 2009), 24–33; Emanuel Hirsch, *Geschichte der neuern evangelischen Theologie*, vol. 3 (Waltrop: H. Spenner, 2000), 318–390.
22. Siegmund Baumgarten, *Evangelische Glaubenslehre* (Halle, Johann Justinus Gebauer, 1760).
23. David Sorkin, *The Religious Enlightenment* (Princeton, NJ: Princeton University Press, 2008), 115–163. Voltaire called Baumgarten "the jewel in the crown of German scholarship."

slow to comprehend the necessary truths of reason. While accepting the possibilities of miracles, they were also interested in finding natural explanations for their occurrence. Eschewing metaphysical speculation, they sought to shape a practical philosophy of life that supported morality and gave hope for a future life. The core of Christian teachings that interested them tended to be smaller than what traditional Lutheranism had emphasized. For example, they stressed the moral pre-eminence of Jesus but said less about his death as a salvific act. Their general optimism about human capabilities led to a downplaying of the doctrine of original sin. Some of the most influential Neologians were pastors, rather than professors, who disseminated their perspectives in sermons as well as books. Johann Joachim Spalding (1714–1804) served for twenty-four years as pastor of the St. Nikolai Church in Berlin and as a member of the Prussian Upper Consistory. He translated English refutations of Deism, such as Bishop Joseph Butler's *Analogy of Religion*, and published *Reflections on the Determination of Man* in 1748, a book of popular philosophy that went through eleven editions up to 1794. Instead of offering philosophical proofs, it presented a somewhat subjective defense of religion, celebrating the order and beauty of the world, evaluating the pleasures offered by the senses, the mind and religion, and making a case for the immortality of the soul. In keeping with his new, more literary approach to apologetics, Spalding also sought to integrate head and heart in his 1761 book, *Thoughts Concerning the Value of Feelings in Christianity*.[24] Johann Friedrich Wilhelm Jerusalem (1709–89), court preacher and advisor for the Duke of Braunschweig-Wolfenbüttel, also interjected warm feeling into his three part *Reflections on the Noble Truths of Religion* in 1768. Concerned to nurture a practical religion that edified and comforted, he concentrated on teachings about God, morality and immortality in the first volume. The second volume pointed out the limits of reason, noted the value of divine revelation for the education of the human race, and traced God's providential dealings with humanity from creation to the end of the Old Testament era. Although Jerusalem never finished the third volume, which was meant to focus on the period from Jesus to the present, his work was a best-seller and was translated into French, Danish, Swedish and Dutch. Other Neologians of note were Wilhelm Abraham Teller (1703–50), Johann Salomo Semler (1725–91), Johann Gottlieb Toellner (1724–74) and Johann Georg Rosenmüller (1736–1815).[25] The more skeptical Rationalists commonly experienced a gradual alienation from traditional Lutheranism and frequently faced persecution because of

24. Michael Printy, "The Determination of Man: Johann Joachim Spalding and the Protestant Enlightenment," *Journal of the History of Ideas* 74:2 (2013): 189–212; Johann Joachim Spalding, *Betrachtung über die Bestimmung des Menschen* (Greifswald: Weitbrecht.1748); *Gedanken über den Werth der Gefühle* (Leipzig: Weidmann, 1764).

25. Andreas Sommer, "Neologische Geschichtsphilosophie: Johann Friedrich Wilhelm Jerusalems Betrachtungen," *Zeitschrift für neuere Theologiegeschichte* 9:2 (2002): 169–217; Johann Friedrich Wilhelm Jerusalem, *Betrachtungen über die vornehmsten Wahrheiten der Religion* (Braunschweig: Waisenhaus Buchhandlung, 1768).

their radical views, especially about the interpretation of the Bible. Emanuel Hirsch called Johann Lorenz Schmidt (1702–49) "the first clear and decisive rationalist among German theologians."[26] He is best known for his 1735 translation of the Pentateuch, the so-called *Wertheimer Bible*, which offered a scientific description of natural processes in its translation of the creation account in Genesis and rationalistic explanations of miracle stories and prophecies. Joachim Lange led a campaign against Schmidt, whose book was banned and confiscated. He was imprisoned in 1737, but after escaping, went on to translate English Deist books and Spinoza's *Ethics* into German. The most provocative of the skeptical rationalists was Carl Friedrich Bahrdt (1740–92), the son of a Lutheran pastor, who taught theology in succession at Leipzig, Erfurt and Giessen. He repeatedly lost positions because of the increasing radicalism of his views and the profligacy of his personal life. Nevertheless, he later served as general superintendent of the churches in Dürkheim and returned to teaching at Halle in 1778, where he attracted up to 900 students to his lectures. Bahrdt was a prolific writer and, like Schmidt, especially triggered outrages by his work on biblical translation. In 1774, he published a paraphrase of the New Testament that downplayed the divinity of Jesus. In his personal confession of faith published in 1779, he doubted that humans came into the world with a tendency towards evil and stated that any interpretation of how God is in Christ should be left to individual judgment, not dictated by any church authority. In the face of hostility from the Prussian government, Bahrdt resigned from his position in Halle and ended his life as an innkeeper.[27] Hermann Samuel Reimarus, a professor in Hamburg, also developed a radical critique of biblical revelation, which he did not dare publish during his lifetime.

BIBLICAL STUDIES

Traditional views of the Bible had already been challenged in the seventeenth century by Baruch Spinoza, a Jew who suggested reasons why Moses was not the author of the whole Pentateuch; Hugo Grotius, a Protestant who pointed out problems in the transmission of the received text; and Richard Simon, a Catholic who raised questions about biblical translation and chronology. When the skeptical rationalists built on these early efforts in textual and historical criticism to raise doubts about the inspiration and general reliability of Scripture, eighteenth century Lutheran scholars undertook extensive efforts to rehabilitate the Bible.

Johann Albrecht Bengel, working primarily on textual criticism, was the most important of the Pietist biblical scholars. Assessing a wide collection of ancient manuscripts, he produced a more reliable version of the Greek

26. Hirsch, *Geschichte der neuern evangelischen Theologie*, vol. 2, 418; Paul Spalding, "Noble Patrons and Religious Innovators in Eighteenth-Century Germany: The Case of Johann Lorenz Schmidt," *Church History* 65:3 (1996): 376–388.
27. Douglas Shantz, "Karl Friedrich Bahrdt: Pietism, Enlightenment and the Autonomous Self in Early Modern Germany," *Historical Papers: Canadian Society of Church History* (Waterloo: May 2012), 53–68.

New Testament in 1734 with an *apparatus criticus* that listed all variant readings. This formed the basis for his 1752 updating of Luther's German translation. In *Gnomon of the New Testament* (1742), he categorized manuscripts into several families and offered seventeen principles to use in determining the most reliable version of a disputed text. Bengel's confidence that the Bible contained divine revelation also prompted him to investigate the relation between the prophecies of the book of Revelation and the course of history. He speculated that the angels in chapter fourteen were Arndt and Spener. After undertaking a complicated series of calculations, he concluded that the thousand year reign of Christ would begin in 1836.[28] By the 1760s, after moderate rationalism had become more prominent in the German universities, several Lutheran scholars took further steps towards the development of modern higher criticism through detailed philological and historical studies of the Bible. Johann August Ernesti (1707–81) first taught ancient literature at the university in Leipzig and later became a professor of theology in 1756.[29] His major book was the eight-volume *Principles of New Testament Interpretation* (1761–69), which established some of the rules of analysis that would become common in modern biblical exegesis. Although he continued to believe that God empowered the biblical writers, his approach to the texts was no different from the method he used in analyzing any other ancient document written from human experience. Johann David Michaelis (1717–91), who taught at Göttingen, is best known for a major work on *The Law of Moses* (1770–75) and a six volume *Introduction to the New Testament.* He was one of the first scholars to use extra-biblical materials to understand the context in which the biblical writers were working. He was succeeded at Göttingen by Johann Gottfried Eichorn (1752–1827) who broke new ground with his theory that the Pentateuch was assembled from various sources. In New Testament studies, Johann Jacob Griesbach (1745–1812) a professor at Jena for thirty-seven years, is notable for discerning the synoptic relationship between the gospels of Matthew, Mark and Luke. Johann Gottfried Herder (1744–1803), general superintendent of the churches in Saxe-Weimar, was never a professor but also made major contributions to the field of biblical interpretation. In *The Spirit of Hebrew Poetry* (1782), he drew attention to the different literary forms in the Old Testament and suggested that these writings should be appreciated for their cultural particularity. Although the Bible contained myths or archaic conceptions of the world, he still considered it edifying. He thought that it was not surprising that the Bible contained errors of history and science because God spoke through humans and not instead of them. Herder also contributed to New Testament stud-

28. Donald McKim, *Dictionary of Major Biblical Interpreters* (Downer's Grove, IL: InterVarsity Press, 2007), 45–65.
29. John Salhammer, "Johann August Ernesti: The Role of History in Biblical Interpretation," *Journal of the Evangelical Theological Society* 44:2, (2001): 193–206.

ies as one of the first scholars to argue that Mark was the earliest gospel.[30] Baumgarten's innovative work at Halle was continued by his student, Johann Salomo Semler (1725–91), who is best known for his reevaluation of the biblical canon. In his 1771 book, a *Treatise on the Free Investigation of the Canon,* he argued that not all of the biblical books were equally useful or edifying.[31] Some parts had diminished significance because they contained ideas particular to a certain time or addressed circumstances that were no longer relevant. Like Herder, he had a strong sense of historical development and stressed the importance of determining the original intent of the biblical writers. He also believed that Jesus adjusted his teachings to his audience because they were not yet capable of understanding certain things. Although Semler distinguished between Holy Scripture and the Word of God and also sought to separate the kernel of value from the husk of outmoded ideas, he continued to defend the basic historicity of the gospels and the relevance of the teachings of Jesus in opposition to more radical scholars such as Hermann Reimarus (1694–1768). After studying at Jena, Reimarus had traveled to England where he was exposed to the writings of the Deists. While teaching oriental languages in Hamburg, he published a treatise on *The Most Noble Truths of Natural Religion* (1755) but circulated his more controversial thoughts about the historicity of the Bible only among friends. In 1774, Gotthold Ephraim Lessing (1729–81), a noted playwright who also served as librarian for the Duke of Braunschweig-Wolfenbüttel, began to publish them as *Fragments of an Anonymous Writer,* apparently to raise questions about neological attempts to reconcile faith and reason. In addition to calling for toleration of Deism, the Reimarus essays attacked the historical credibility of various biblical events, most notably the resurrection of Jesus. In a piece on the intention of Jesus and his disciples, which Lessing published in 1778, Reimarus argued that Jesus was a Jewish teacher of a simple, practical religion who had no notion of the Trinity and did not think of himself as divine. The New Testament books, written years after the events of Jesus' life, thus presented a more mysterious set of beliefs fabricated by his disciples.[32] Johann Melchior Goeze (1717–86), Orthodox chief pastor in Hamburg, attacked Lessing for publishing the *Fragments* and focused especially on the axioms that Lessing himself had written and attached to the *Fragments.* Goeze objected especially to the distinctions Lessing made between the letter of the Bible and the spirit of religion and between the religion of Jesus and the religion about Jesus. Goeze argued that the truth of Christianity depends on the Bible alone, which he considered to be infallible. After Goeze and Lessing had exchanged several pamphlets, the Duke of Braunschweig-Wolfenbüttel inter-

---

30. William Baird, *History of New Testament Research*, vol. 1. (Minneapolis, MN: Fortress Press, 1992), 108–165.
31. Semler, Johann Salomo, *Abhandlung von freier Untersuchung des Canon* (Halle: C H Hemmerde, 1772).
32. Hermann Reimarus, *Fragments*, ed. Charles Talbert (Philadelphia: Fortress Press, 1970).

vened and required Lessing to submit his writings to an ecclesiastical censor. In response, Lessing turned his attention back to the theater and wrote a play about religious toleration titled *Nathan the Wise* (1779). He expressed his personal religious perspective most fully in *The Education of the Human Race*, published in 1780. Lessing acknowledged that Christianity had contributed to the development of humanity, but just as it had surpassed the teachings of the Old Testament, he thought it would someday be replaced by a new eternal gospel, which would bring the human race closer to perfection. Johann David Michaelis also prepared a refutation of Reimarus. Goeze wrote additional critiques of Carl Friedrich Bahrdt and Johann Salomo Semler.[33]

RESPONSES TO THE CRITICAL PHILOSOPHY OF KANT

Orthodoxy, Pietism, Neology and even Deism all faced a new challenge in the thought of Immanuel Kant (1724–1804), who began to publish his three critiques of reason in 1781, the year of Lessing's death. Kant, who spent his whole teaching career at the University of Königsberg, praised the Enlightenment for releasing humans from self-incurred ignorance and for giving them the courage to think for themselves, but he also had a strong sense of the limits of reason in resolving perennial metaphysical questions. Since it is not possible to have unmediated intellectual access to the noumenal world (that is, "things in themselves") and since knowledge of the sensible world is actively filtered by the human mind, pure reason cannot prove the existence of God, the soul, or an afterlife. His *Critique of Pure Reason*, however, was followed in 1788 by a *Critique of Practical Reason* in which Kant sought to establish a firm ground for living morally. Although his thought was far removed from the Pietism he had been exposed to while growing up, he perpetuated Pietism's concern for morality and sought to establish a new basis for religion within the limits of reason. In his second critique, he argued that beliefs in God's existence, human freedom and the immortality of the soul have a practical usefulness as "postulates" that support the sense of moral obligation or duty that is a universal element of human experience. They are legitimate convictions (*Überzeugung*) because they motivate human commitment to "the Highest Good."[34] Kant said in the preface of the *Critique of Pure Reason* that he was inquiring about the limits of knowledge (*Wissen*) "in order to make room for faith (*Glaube*)." What a practical rational faith or moral religion might look like was explored in his 1793 treatise, *Religion within the Limits of Reason Alone*. He rejected any notion of a vicarious atonement by a savior and talked of saving faith as a hope that one could become pleas-

33. Toshimasa Yasukata, *Lessing's Philosophy of Religion and the German Enlightenment* (Oxford: Oxford University Press, 2002), 41–55; Gotthold Lessing, *Die Erziehung des Menschengeschlechts* (Berlin: Voss, 1780): Lund, vol. 2, 13–17, 72–75.

34. Lawrence Pasternack, Philip Rossi, "Kant's Philosophy of Religion" in *Stanford Encyclopedia of Philosophy*, accessed October 2019, https://plato.stanford.edu/entries/kant-religion/.

ing to God by pursuing a moral course of life. He also repurposed a number of practices familiar to his Lutheran upbringing, seeing prayer as an act that awakened the disposition to goodness, church-going as a way to share and propagate moral goodness, and holy communion as a possible rite to maintain fellowship among members of an ethical body.[35] Some of the most effective responses to Kant's critical philosophy came from his Lutheran friends or students. Johann Georg Hamann (1730–88), who also lived in Königsberg, had a very unconventional life and wrote in a rather eccentric style. He left university before completing his studies and never held a teaching position. Kant found him a position as a Prussian civil servant, but the foremost interest of his life was a series of philosophical writings he produced in his spare time. Hamann had a transformative spiritual experience while on a trip to London in 1758 and developed a deep appreciation of the Bible. He continued to believe that God is revealed in both nature and "his word." Hamann was not an irrationalist but faulted Kant for making reason the only way to procure knowledge. In his 1784 *Metacritique on the Purism of Reason*, he argued that Kant had produced an indefensible dichotomy between pure reason and the content of experience. For Hamann, human knowledge before or beyond all perception is an impossibility. He also suggested that Kant failed to appreciate how thought is enmeshed in language. Since all language is formed by personal experience, it is part of a stream of custom and tradition. Experience cannot be transcended nor can the nuances of language be totally reduced to pure logic. In his more theological writings, Hamann emphasized how God had condescended to make himself known in the incarnation of Christ and in the Holy Spirit's use of human authors to write the Scriptures.[36] Johann Gottfried Herder, previously cited for his work on the Bible, studied philosophy with Kant in Königsberg but also came to see Hamann as his mentor. In 1798, he produced *Understanding and Experience*, his own metacritique of Kant's *Critique of Pure Reason*. In this he argued that it is not possible to separate oneself from the particularity of received ideas in order to inspect the functioning of pure reason. Like Hamann, he noted how reason operates through language, which cannot be divorced from the experiences out of which words evolved. Herder was more interested in an empirically focused analysis of the development of humanity than in abstract reasoning or philosophical system building. In addition to their interests in language, Hamann and Herder also both appreciated individual subjectivity and objected to the bifurcating of thought and feeling.[37]

35. Immanuel Kant, *Religion within the Boundaries of Mere Reason and Other Writings*, ed. Allen Wood, George di Giovanni (Cambridge: Cambridge University Press, 2018), 37–230; See *Critique of Pure Reason*, trans. Max Müller (Garden City, NJ: Doubleday Anchor Books, 1966), xxxix.
36. John Betz, "Enlightenment Revisited: Hamann as the First and Best Critic of Kant's Philosophy," *Modern Theology* 20:2 (2004): 291–301; Lund, vol. 2, 18–26.
37. Sonia Sikka, "Herder's Critique of Pure Reason," *The Review of Metaphysics* 61:1 (2007): 31–50; Johann Gottfried Herder, *Verstand und Erfahrung* (Leipzig: Hartnoch, 1799).

THE IMPACT OF THE ENLIGHTENMENT ON CHURCH LIFE

It is important to investigate whether the new currents of thought filtered down to ordinary believers. It is possible to gain an impression by considering the way Christianity was encountered in the parishes through sermons, hymnbooks and in liturgies or church rites. The content of sermons varied depending on the inclinations of the preacher toward Orthodoxy, Pietism or Rationalism. This can be illustrated by some examples from the latter decades of the century. Johann Jacob Rambach II (1737–1818), who served as pastor of St. Michael's Church in Hamburg for almost forty years, was typical of the more conservative preachers who continued to proclaim traditional Lutheran doctrine. In his sermons he often expressed dismay at the growing neglect of church practice by those who saw Christianity as a "burdensome yoke." He declared that these prideful "scorners of religion" were a danger to themselves and others and would find no consolation at the end of life unless they experienced a renewal of heart and mind through faith in Christ. Rambach strongly affirmed the importance of the reconciling death of Christ and the historicity of the resurrection.[38] Several of the Neologians were famous for their preaching, and they too often made note of a growing indifference (*Gleichgültigkeit*) to religion in Germany. However, they concentrated on different themes in their defense of Christianity. While they too expressed belief in the resurrection of Jesus, they tended to present Jesus as the true bearer of enlightenment whose intention was to gather a society of good and upright people from all nations.[39] J. F. W. Jerusalem was concerned about the persistence of superstition (*Aberglaube*) as well as the rise of disbelief (*Unglaube*). For Johann Joachim Spalding, it seemed important to focus on what was understandably true and effectively fruitful (*Verständlichkeit und Fruchtbarkeit*) for the growth of goodness in human souls.[40] There were other rationalist pastors whose sermons were almost devoid of doctrinal content. For example, Günther Gottlieb Ernesti (1759–97), a court preacher in Thuringia, proclaimed that it was God's will that humans should be opened to new blessings for themselves through the use of their reason. He asserted that nothing dishonors a Christian more than a blind faith. Traugott Günther Röller, a pastor in Schönfels, preached a series of sermons for "villagers" in which he noted the wholesome effect of thunderstorms on the earth and "our hearts" and the harm-

38. Johann Jacob Rambach, *Predigten über die Sonn- und Festtäglichen Evangelia zur häuslichen Erbauung*, (Hamburg: Gottlieb Friedrich Schniebes, 1796). See especially the sermon for *Judica* Sunday, 493–511. He was named after his relative, a Pietist theologian (1693–1735) who taught at Halle and Giessen earlier in the century.

39. Johann Georg Rosenmüller, *Predigten gehalten in der Thomaskirche zu Leipzig*, Bd. 2. (Leipzig: Siegfried Lebrecht Crusius, 1788), see especially 3–26.

40. J. F. W. Jerusalem. *Sammlung einiger Predigten* (Braunschweig: Verlag der Schulbuchhandlung, 1788), Sermon 5, 141–178; Johann Joachim Spalding. *Neue Predigten* (Berlin: Voss, 1784), Sermon 4: Was erbaulich ist, 87–122.

ful custom of consulting quack doctors (*Quacksalber*) to treat illnesses.[41] There was no liturgical uniformity across the more than ninety different Protestant territories, so it is difficult to make generalizations about trends in worship life for all of Germany. A few examples from Leipzig and Berlin must suffice for this overview. At the start of the century, cities like Leipzig, Dresden and Berlin needed to build new churches to accommodate the growing number of people coming to worship. Every Sunday there were multiple services, supplemented during the week by additional gatherings for prayer and religious instruction. Leipzig was a traditional center of Lutheran Orthodoxy and had a conservative liturgy, which was more like Luther's 1523 *Formula Missae* than his 1526 *Deutsche Messe*. It retained Latin antiphons and made extensive use of trained musicians. Organs were often supplemented by brass and string instruments, and a boys' choir performed cantatas in addition to hymn singing by the congregation. This contrasted greatly with services in rural parishes where a verger often led the congregation in singing memorized hymns. Since many of the country folk were illiterate, they rarely used the hymnbooks common in city parishes.[42] Many consider the Baroque era the high point of Lutheran church music. Outstanding musicians such as Johann Sebastian Bach (1685–1750) in Leipzig and Georg Philipp Telemann (1681–1767) in Hamburg composed cantatas that were performed in an annual cycle before the weekly sermon. However, both the Pietists and the Rationalists were critical of this rich musical tradition. Christian Gerber (1660–1731), a Pietist pastor who wrote a 1732 book about church ceremonies in Saxony, thought that elaborate music distracted from true worship. Bach also quarreled with Johann August Ernesti, the biblical scholar, with whom he had to work for over a decade at the Thomasschule in Leipzig. Like many of the rationalists, Ernesti preferred simple, word-centered didactic worship and was disinterested in musical embellishments. He refused to support Bach's effort to appoint qualified assistants to help rehearse the boys' choir.

The impact of rationalism on Leipzig church life became even greater after Bach's death, while the Neologian Johann Georg Rosenmüller (1736–1815) was superintendent of the clergy. He shortened the liturgy, dropped the use of Latin antiphons, and freed the clergy from the need to wear traditional vestments or preach from the set lectionary. He introduced a new hymnbook, which excluded many time-honored hymns, and in 1787 ended the practice of requiring private confession before participation in the Lord's Supper. From mid-century to 1790, the average number of people communing at the two main churches in Leipzig dropped from 27,774 to

41. Günther Gottlieb Ernesti, *Predigten* (Hildburghausen: Hanisch, 1798). 857–868; Traugott Gottfried Röller. *Dorfpredigten für gemeine Leute besonders Handwerksleute und Bauern* (Greiz: Henning, 1797), l: 195–214, 2:326–356. See also Lund, 31–36, 43–46.

42. Tanya Kevorkian, *Baroque Piety: Religion, Society and Music in Leipzig 1650–1750* (Aldershot: Ashgate Publishing, 2007); Nicholas Hope, *German and Scandinavian Protestantism 1700–1850* (Oxford: Clarendon Press, 1995), 99–187, 256–315.

17,012. Rosenmüller apparently hoped that the substitution of a less intrusive group confession would remove a barrier to church participation.[43] Hymnbooks were used for both public worship and private devotion, so when the Neologians introduced new hymnbooks in many of the Lutheran states they often faced opposition from more traditional believers. One of the most successful resistance movements took place in 1781 when Johann Joachim Spalding led the effort to create a new hymnbook for Prussia. This new *Mylius* hymnbook excluded half of the Reformation era hymns found in the pietistic *Porstsche Gesangbuch* of 1713, among them Luther's "A Mighty Fortress." It decreased the number of hymns concerned with doctrine, and increased the number focusing on ethical themes. Throughout Brandenburg-Prussia groups of parishioners resisted pastors when they tried to introduce the new hymnbook, and a tradesman in Berlin, Samuel Lobegott Apitzsch (d.1786), started a protest petition which was presented to King Friedrich the Great. The king was scornful of traditional Christianity but was also a supporter of tolerance. He allowed individual parishes to opt out of the hymnbook change and, in the end, only three of Berlin's eleven Lutheran parishes accepted it.[44] The innovators were set back more decisively when King Friedrich Wilhelm II (ruled 1786–97), nephew of Friedrich the Great, came to the throne in 1786. He was strongly influenced by Johann Christoph von Wöllner (1732–1800), his former tutor, a pastor serving as Minister of Religious Affairs, who thought that the new forms of theology and biblical studies were "entirely contrary to the spirit of Christianity." They issued an edict in 1788 that required clergy and professors to repudiate the "delusions of new-fangled teachers." Semler supported the *Wöllnerscher Religionsedikt* because it continued to tolerate multiple confessional groups and promoted civic peace by maintaining a balance between them. Spalding resigned from his preaching position in protest against it. Kant had to pledge to the king that he would no longer write about religion.[45]

SCANDINAVIA

Both Denmark-Norway and Sweden-Finland were absolute monarchies, so the religious dispositions of the kings had a significant impact on developments within their state Lutheran churches. The clergy were viewed as servants of the king and as a result had various civic duties to perform in addition to guiding spiritual life. Church records served as population registers, and pastors played an important role in administering poor relief and local schools. Pietism had a strong influence on church life throughout Scandinavia in the first half of the eighteenth century, though there were some significant regional differences. A kind of State Pietism developed in Denmark, as it

43. Jeffrey Sposato, *Leipzig after Bach: Church and Concert Life in a German City* (Oxford: Oxford University Press, 2018), 160–172.
44. Christina Rathgeber, "The Reception of Brandenburg-Prussia's New Lutheran Hymnal of 1781," *The Historical Journal* 36:1 (1993): 115–136.
45. Uta Wiggermann, *Woellner und das Religionsedikt* (Tübingen: Mohr Siebeck, 2010).

had in Prussia, but this was not the case in Sweden. Less religiously interested monarchs in the second half of the century in both Denmark and Sweden permitted Rationalism to make greater inroads into church life, though fewer radical freethinkers made an impact in Scandinavia as compared to Germany. Danish Pietism first appeared in Jutland around 1700 through the influence of students returning from Germany. It entered the court of King Frederik IV (ruled 1699–1730) and shortly thereafter through the German court preacher, Franz Julius Lütkens (1650–1712). The king's personal life was not always consistent with Pietist moral values, but in 1705, through Lütkens, he invited Halle to supply missionaries for Tranquebar, the Danish colony on the southeastern coast of India. Joachim Lange recruited Bartholomäus Ziegenbalg (1682–1719) and Heinrich Plütschau (1677–1742), who thereby became the first Lutheran missionaries to work outside of Europe. Hans Bartholin (1665–1739), a professor of theology, led an Orthodox campaign against foreign mission work, but Frederik went on to create a missionary college in 1714 and support the establishment of a mission in Greenland in 1721, led by Norwegian pastor Hans Egede (1686–1758).

Pietism found even greater support from Frederik's son, Christian VI (ruled 1730–46). In 1732, he was persuaded by Count Zinzendorf to support Moravian mission work in the Danish West Indies. In 1735, he required all citizens to attend church and, in 1736, made confirmation obligatory. To prepare children for this rite every parish was required, in 1739, to establish a school. Erik Pontoppidan (1698–1764), a pastor who later served as bishop of Bergen in Norway, was commissioned to produce an explanation of Luther's small catechism for use in these schools. This book, *Truth unto Godliness,* and his major devotional work, *Mirror of Faith* (1740), greatly shaped Danish and Norwegian piety well into the next century. Christian VI also appointed several Pietists as bishops, the most notable of whom was Hans Adolf Brorson (1694–1764), the composer of 82 hymns, which were widely admired within the Danish church. Finally, to ensure that Pietism remained under the control of the state church, King Christian ordered in the Conventicle Act of 1741 that all lay religious gatherings get the approval of local pastors.[46] When Pietism was no longer favored by the state after the death of Christian VI, rationalist thought spread more freely among Danish intellectuals and the clergy. Ludwig Holberg (1684–1754), the most prominent literary figure of the day, had been influenced by Deism while visiting France and wrote against superstition and intolerance. At the end of the century, there continued to be battles between defenders of traditional Lutheran theology such as Bishop Nicolai Edinger Balle (1744–1816) and doctrinal skeptics such as Otto Horrebow (1769–1823). As was the case in Denmark, students returning from study in Halle were the

46. Martin Schwarz Lausten. *A Church History of Denmark* (Burlington, VT: Ashgate, 2002), 161–196; Erik Pontoppidan, *Sandhed til Gudfrygtighed* (Copenhagen, 1737); The Norwegian lay preacher Hans Nielsen Hauge (1771–1824) was first imprisoned in 1797 under a later version of this Act.

first to bring Pietist reform concerns to Sweden. King Karl XII (ruled 1692–1718) was suspicious of any movement that might threaten the religious uniformity of his kingdom and issued an edict in 1706 requiring all students who had been abroad to be examined by the authorities before receiving any position in the church. Pietism gained strength, however, from five thousand Swedish prisoners of war who returned from Russia at the end of the Great Northern War in 1721. Many of them had been influenced by Halle Pietists who had aided them during their captivity. King Fredrik I (ruled 1720–51) and many of the Swedish bishops viewed Pietist conventicles as "a dangerous novelty" and took further measures to control them through the Conventicle Decree of 1726. This prohibition of unsupervised lay religious gatherings remained in effect until 1858.[47]

A form of churchly Pietism was nurtured by Henrik Schartau (1757–1825) especially in southwest Sweden. Thore Odelhius (1705–77) advanced the work of Moravian missionaries who had been allowed to enter Sweden because they accepted the Augsburg Confession. Later, however, the Moravians faced opposition from some of the Swedish bishops when concerns about more radical Pietism increased. Johann Konrad Dippel had lived in Sweden from 1727 to 1728 and influenced harsh critics of the clergy such as Erik Tolstadius (1693–1759). Dippel also initially influenced Immanuel Swedenborg (1688–1772), the son of Lutheran bishop Jesper Swedberg (1653–1735) who was a crucial early supporter of Swedish settlers in North America. Swedenborg began to talk about founding a new Christian church after experiencing a series of visions in 1745, but he avoided prosecution by authorities because his books were published in Latin outside of Sweden. Interest in the philosophy of Christian Wolff was already evident in some of the Swedish universities in the 1720s, and this too prompted a royal decree in 1749. Philosophers were prohibited from disputing articles of the Christian faith during the reign of Fredrik I, but when Gustav III (ruled 1771–92) came to the throne, the situation changed. The new king was a nephew of King Friedrich the Great of Prussia and had been exposed by his tutors to French thought. He visited France in 1771 and expressed admiration for Voltaire and Rousseau.[48] In this new intellectual climate, Catholicism was granted limited toleration, and rationalism also began to influence some clergy within the Swedish church.

NORTH AMERICA

At the start of the eighteenth century, small groups of German, Dutch and Swedish-Finnish Lutherans were living primarily in the Hudson and Delaware river valleys. They were joined after 1708 by German refugees who fled the Palatinate region when Elector Johann Wilhelm pressured them to

47. Todd Green, "Swedish Pietism (1700–1727) as Resistance and Popular Religion," *Lutheran Quarterly* 21 (2007): 59–77.
48. H. Arnold Barton, "King Christian III and the Enlightenment," *Eighteenth Century Studies* 6:1 (1972): 1–34.

convert to Catholicism. An initial group of around two thousand settled in New York, but later waves, coming after 1720, mostly settled as indentured servants or redemptioners in the colony of Pennsylvania or further south in Virginia and the Carolinas. In 1731, another group of Lutherans, forced to leave the region around Salzburg because of religious persecution, accepted an invitation to settle in the new colony of Georgia.[49] Supported by the English Society for the Promotion of Christian Knowledge, guided by Augsburg senior pastor Samuel Urlsperger (1728–1806), and accompanied by two Halle-trained Pietist pastors, Johann Boltzius (1703–65) and Israel Gronau (c. 1706–45) they created the Lutheran settlement of Ebenezer, twenty-five miles northwest of Savannah.

There were no formal connections between the scattered Lutheran communities, and many of them had to function without pastoral leadership for months at a time. The first Lutheran minister to be ordained in North America (1703) was Justus Falckner (1672–1723), who had studied theology with Francke in Halle. He spent twenty years traveling throughout the middle colonies, preaching in German and Dutch, establishing new congregations, and training lay leaders. His work was continued by William Christopher Berkenmeyer (1687–1751) who arrived from Hamburg in 1725. He made the first attempt to create a synodical structure among some New York area congregations in 1735, but this collapsed because of tensions between Dutch and German factions, Orthodox-Pietist differences, and interference by "pretenders" (unauthorized vagabond preachers).[50] Facing their own troubles of this sort, some Pennsylvania Lutherans appealed once again to Halle for help. In 1742, they were sent Henry Melchior Muhlenberg (1711–87), a young pastor who had hoped to go to India as a missionary. When he arrived in Philadelphia after a stop at the Ebenezer community in Georgia, he discovered that a pretender had usurped his position in one of the congregations he had been sent to serve and others had fallen under the influence of the Moravians. He managed to establish the legitimacy of his call but still faced a rival in Nicholas von Zinzendorf who had arrived in Philadelphia in 1741. The ecumenically minded count presented himself as a legitimate inspector of the Lutheran churches but also held forth the vision of forming a new "Congregation of God in the Spirit" that would unite the various denominations in America. Muhlenberg questioned whether Zinzendorf was a Lutheran, although the count had renounced his position as Moravian bishop in 1739. The conflict subsided when Zinzendorf returned to England in 1743, and Muhlenberg went on with his efforts to bring unity and order to the Lutheran churches.[51] He pursued a

49. Thomas Tappert, "The Church's Infancy 1650–1790" in *The Lutherans in North America*, ed. E. Clifford Nelson (Philadelphia, PA: Fortress Press, 1975), 3–77.
50. Mark Granquist, *Lutherans in America* (Minneapolis, MN: Fortress Press, 2015), 61–84.
51. Walter Wagner. "A Key Episode in American Lutheranism: Muhlenberg's and Zinzendorf's Encounter," *Concordia Historical Institute Quarterly*, 71:2 (1998): 72–85.

middle path between the somewhat rigid Orthodoxy of Berkenmeyer and the permissive ecclesiology of Count Zinzendorf. His efforts culminated in the formation of the Ministerium of Pennsylvania in 1748, which regularized the appointment of ministers and agreed upon a common form of worship.[52] In 1778, John Christopher Kunze (1744–1807) began a similar effort to form a ministerium in New York but that process was not completed until 1792. Synodical organizations also started to take shape in South Carolina (1787), North Carolina (1791) and Virginia (1793). The first formal seminary for the training of ministers was established in New York state in 1797 from an endowment provided by pastor John Christopher Hartwick (1714–96). At first, Lutherans tried to stay out of the fray when the American Revolution began, but in 1778 Muhlenberg finally signed an oath of allegiance to the emerging republic. Two of his sons served as soldiers during the Revolutionary War and one of them, Frederick (1750–1801), was chosen in 1789 to be the first Speaker of the House of Representatives. Some of the important leaders of the American Revolution were influenced by the Enlightenment, but its new perspectives had minimal impact within the American Lutheran churches until the early part of the nineteenth century.[53]

At the start of the 1700s, America had been like a mission field since the Lutheran churches were undeveloped and dependent on leadership from Europe. In 1720, there were probably no more than eight thousand Lutherans in America. It required a lot of adjustment to survive in an American religious milieu where, unlike Europe, churches were voluntary societies unsupported by the state. Eventually, however, the churches learned to cope with this reality. By 1790, there were 314 active congregations, and, although links to Europe remained strong, they had managed to become self-governing and self-supporting.

Eric Lund is professor emeritus of religion at St. Olaf College.

---

52. George Handley, "A Look at Henry Melchior Muhlenberg, the Ministerium of Pennsylvania, and the Development of Lutheranism in the Northeast," *Lutheran Historical Conference* 18 (1998): 15–38.
53. Paul Baglyos. "The Muhlenbergs become American," *Lutheran Quarterly* 19 (2005): 43–62.

BIBLIOGRAPHY

DOCUMENT COLLECTIONS

Greschat, Martin, ed. *Kirchen- und Theologiegeschichte in Quellen: Von Konfessionalismus zur Moderne.* 5th edition. Neukirchen: Neukirchener Verlagsgesellschaft, 2015.

Lund, Eric, ed. *A Documentary History of Lutheranism*, vols. 1 and 2. Minneapolis: Fortress Press, 2017.

PRIMARY SOURCES

Bengel, Johann Albrecht. *Gnomon of the New Testament.* Translated by Andrew Fausset. Edinburgh: T & T. Clark, 1877. Reprint: Eugene, OR: Wipf & Stock, 2004.

Goeze, Johan Melchior. *Etwas Vorläufiges gegen des Herrn Hofraths Lessings . . . feindselige Angriffe auf unsre allerheiligste Religion* (1776). In *Gotthold Ephraim Lessing Werke Bd. 8 Theologiekritische Schriften* III, edited by Helmut Göbel. München: Carl Hanser Verlag, 1979.

Hamann, Johann Georg. *Metacritique of the Purism of Reason* (1784). In *Hamann: Writings on Philosophy and Language*, translated and edited by Kenneth Haynes, 205–218. Cambridge: Cambridge University Press, 2007.

Jerusalem, Johann Friedrich Wilhelm. *Betrachtungen über die vornehmsten Wahrheiten der Religion.* Braunschweig: Waisenhaus Buchhandlung, 1768.

Lange, Joachim. *Antibarbarus orthodoxiae dogmatico-hermeneuticus.* Berlin/Halle: J. G. Meyer, 1709.

Loescher, Valentin. *The Complete Timotheus Verinus.* Translated by James Langebartels and Robert Koester. Milwaukee: Northwestern Publishing House, 1998.

Pontoppidan, Erik. *Explanation of Luther's Small Catechism based on Dr. Erick Pontoppidan.* Translated by E. G. Lund. Minneapolis, MN: Augsburg Publishing House, 1949.

Semler, Johann Salomo. *Abhandlung von freier Untersuchung des Canon* (1772). Edited by Heinz Scheible. Gütersloh: Gerd Mohn, 1967.

Spalding, Johann Joachim. *Betrachtung über die Bestimmung des Menschen* (*1748*). Edited by Wolfgang Erich Müller. Waltrop: Spenner 1997.

Spener, Philip Jacob. *Pia Desideria.* Translated by Theodore Tappert. Philadelphia, PA: Fortress Press, 1964.

SECONDARY SOURCES

Beutel, Albrecht. *Kirchengeschichte im Zeitalter der Aufklärung.* Göttingen: Vandenhoeck & Ruprecht, 2009.

Gawthrop, Richard. *Pietism and the Making of Eighteenth-Century Prussia.* Cambridge: Cambridge University Press, 1993.

Granquist, Mark. *Lutherans in America*. Minneapolis: Fortress Press, 2015.

Hirsch, Emanuel. *Geschichte der neuern evangelischen Theologie*, vols. 2 and 3. Waltrop: H. Spenner, 2000.

Hope, Nicholas. *German and Scandinavian Protestantism 1700–1850*. Oxford: Clarendon Press, 1995.

Kleinig, Vernon. "Confessional Lutheranism in Eighteenth Century Germany," *Concordia Theological Monthly* 6:1–2 (1996): 97–125.

Lindberg, Carter, ed. *The Pietist Theologians*. Oxford: Blackwell Publishing, 2005.

Salo, Timothy. "Joachim Lange: Lutheran Pietist Theologian and Halle Apologist." In *The Pietist Impulse in Christianity*, edited by Christian Collins Winn, William Carlson, Christopher Gehrz & Eric Holst, 82–93. Eugene, OR: Pickwick Publications, 2011.

Schwarz Lausten, Martin. *A Church History of Denmark*. Burlington, VT: Ashgate Publishing, 2002.

Sattler, Gary. *God's Glory, Neighbor's Good: A Brief Introduction to the Life and Writings of August Hermann Francke*. Chicago: Covenant Press, 1982.

Shantz, Douglas. *An Introduction to German Pietism*. Baltimore, MD: The Johns Hopkins University Press, 2013.

Stoeffler, F. Ernest. *German Pietism during the Eighteenth Century*. Leiden: E. J. Brill, 1973.

Nineteenth-Century Lutheran Missions

KLAUS DETLEV SCHULZ

THE NINETEENTH CENTURY IS HAILED as the Great Century of Missions because Protestantism experienced a worldwide expansion of the Gospel as it had never seen before. During this century, three types of mission approaches emerged, each represented by mission societies: (1) the parachurch, ecumenical missions which served a number of constituents or church bodies of different theological traditions; (2) the confessional church mission affiliated with a particular church body, with an emphasis on confessional identity and doctrinal agreement with partners; and (3) the non-ecclesial faith mission concentrating on the personal faith and fervor of the missionary with a message that had a strong eschatological orientation towards Christ's second return. Of these three approaches, type two, in particular, showed a strong Lutheran commitment, while type one often shared Lutheran interests but merged these at times with elements of type three.[1]

BEGINNINGS IN ENGLAND AND GERMANY

The nineteenth century's rise in interest for mission took its beginning in England with the cobbler William Carey (1761–1834). In his sermon on Isaiah 54:2–3 preached in May 1792 at Nottingham at the annual gathering of Baptist preachers and in his previously published essay, *An Enquiry into the Obligations of Christians to Use Means for the Conversion of the Heathens*, (1792), Carey made a sober yet earnest call against a hyper Calvinism for the validity and continuation of the Great Commission. This led to the formation

1. Werner Raupp, ed., *Mission in Quellentexten* (Bad Liebenzell: Verlag der Liebenzeller Mission, 1990), Raupp divides nineteenth century mission endeavors into similar three categories: 1. the "überkonfessionelle, ökumenische Ausrichtung (243); 2. Kirchlich-konfessionelle Mission (270); 3. Mission der 'radikalen' Erweckung (Glaubensmission) (287)." Some endeavors of type one, like the Basel Mission, can also be driven by category three tenets such as "einem romantisch-pietistischen und eschatologischen Drang, aufgrund der individuellen Heilserfahrung und Gewißheit des 'göttlichen Rufes in die Mission,'" 243-244.

of the Baptist Missionary Society in 1792, the first modern mission society.[2] Other societies soon came into existence such as The London Missionary Society (1795), the Anglican Church Missionary Society (1799), the Religious Tract Society (1799) and the British and Foreign Bible Society (1804).

The surge in awareness for mission spilled across the English Channel to Europe and was taken up by the Evangelical Awakening (*Erweckungsbewegung*) that was happening all across Europe, including Germany and Scandinavia. Conventicles, mission and tract societies emerged within the state churches and assumed the tasks of missions and human care which till then had been done either by the territorial authorities or committed individuals. Now, these societies were able to avoid compromises with commercial elements in their mission efforts.

Johann Heinrich Jung Stilling (1740–1817), a patriarch of the German Evangelical Awakening, and an arch defender of Christianity against German rationalism, planned a seminary for preachers and missionaries. His proposed approach was characteristic of the Evangelical Awakening or neo-Pietist missions, which was to concentrate on only the fundamental elements of the Christian faith with the motivation to remain both ecumenically minded and eschatologically focused. Included in that approach was also the motif of the individual believer's suffering from the burden of sin and God's judgment, which was followed by the typical emphasis on reestablishing and keeping a personal commitment to God.[3] This "pectoral theology," named after August Neander's (1789–1850) phrase "the heart makes a theologian" (*pectus est, quod facit theologum*) and perpetuated by Neander's scholar, August Tholuck (1799–1877), is indicative of the Awakening's criticism of rationalism, such as Georg Wilhelm Friedrich Hegel's (1770–1831) concept of reason.[4]

On 1 February 1800, Johann Jänicke (1748–1827) formed in Berlin the first mission seminary with an initial student body of seven "God fearing" students. During his lifetime, over eighty students had graduated and served as missionaries among whom its most famous candidate was Karl Gützlaff (1803–51), the missionary to China, whose faith mission was continued later by the legendary missionary Hudson Taylor (1832–1905) and his China Inland Mission (CIM).[5] Though Jänicke was a pastor of the Bohemian Lutheran congregation at the Bethlehem Church, he was greatly influenced by Moravian Pietism which included an ecumenical outlook that allowed the graduates from his seminary to go on and serve either the Danish Halle Mission, the Mission Society of the Netherlands, the London Mission Society (LMS) or the Anglican Church Mission Society.[6]

2. Ruth Tucker, *From Jerusalem to Irian Jaya: A Biographical History of Christian Missions* (Grand Rapids, MI: Zondervan, 2004), 123.
3. Werner Raupp, *Mission in Quellentexten*, 235–237.
4. Oswald Bayer, *Theology the Lutheran Way* (Grand Rapids, MI/Cambridge, U.K.: Eerdmans, 2007), 34, 224.
5. Tucker, *From Jerusalem to Irian Jaya*, 184–186.
6. Raupp, *Mission in Quellentexten*, 240–243.

In 1824, under Jänicke's successor and son-in-law, Johann Wilhelm Rückert, the mission seminary became the Berlin Mission Society (*Berliner Missionsgesellschaft* or in full *Gesellschaft zur Förderung der Evangelischen Missionen unter den Heiden*). This Berlin Mission Society (known as Berlin I) was supported by a Prussian group consisting of laity, noblemen, high ranked citizens and professors, among whom was also the aforementioned church historian August Neander. For a number of years its main purpose was to support other mission societies in Basel, Barmen, London, and Paris, before it started in 1833 to send its own graduates to the mission field, mainly to South Africa, East Africa and China.[7] In contrast to the rise of confessional Lutheran mission in Prussia under the Breslau Lutherans, first with the pastor and Professor Johann Scheibel (1783–1843) and then the lawyer, Eduard Huschke (1801–86), the Berlin Mission Society sided with unionism. However, under its long serving director (1865–94), Hermann Theodor Wangemann (1818–94), known for his prolific writing such as the publication on the history of the Lutheran Church in Prussia and a handbook on Luther's Small Catechism (*Biblisches Hand- und Hülfsbuch zu Luther's Kleinem Katechismus*, 1855), the Berlin Mission Society took on a distinct Lutheran character. Wangemann's Lutheran convictions motivated him to offer a major investigation into the Lutheran Church and her relation to the Prussian Church Union and it made him also wary of cooperative mission efforts.[8] As director, he conducted a mission trip to Southern Africa, his favorite mission field.[9] Wangemann was married to Helene Merensky, the sister of the pioneer missionary Alexander Merensky (1830–1918) who was a graduate of the Berlin Mission Society and founder of the fortress mission station, Botshabelo, in South Africa.[10]

The Goßner Mission Society (GMS) was directly related to the abovementioned Berlin Mission Society, since the former Roman Catholic priest and Awakening preacher, Johannes Evangelista Goßner (1773–1858) had been a member of the Berlin Mission Society but left it to form his own society, the Goßner Society (known as Berlin II). This society followed the model of the Moravian mission by sending men with simple tradesmen skills for a humble service on the field, providing their own means for existence like the Apostle Paul once did, and submitting themselves to their one and only

7. Raupp, *Mission in Quellentexten*, 250.
8. See Hermann Theodor Wangemann, *Die preußische Union in ihrem Verhältnis zur Una Sancta*, 3 vols. (Berlin, 1883–84); for further details on the Berlin Mission Society, see Hellmut Lehmann, *150 Jahre Berliner Mission* (Erlangen: Verlag der Ev.-Luth. Mission, 1974), 9–22; Wilhelm Oehler, *Geschichte der Deutschen Evangelischen Mission*, (Baden-Baden: Im Verlag Wilhelm Fehrholz and Co., 1949), 1:193–203.
9. This visit gave rise to an extensive report, Hermann Theodor Wangemann, *Ein Reise-Jahr in Süd-Afrika: asuführliches Tagebuch über eine in den Jahren 1866 und 1867 ausgeführte Inspectionsreise durch die Missions-Stationen der Berliner Missions-Gesellschaft* (Berlin: Verlag des Missionshauses in Berlin; zu beziehen durch J. A. Wohlgemuth, 1868).
10. Klaus Detlev Schulz, "Pioneer Missionaries: Putting Merensky to the Test," *Logia* 17, no. 1 (Epiphany 2008): 51–56.

Lord and Master, Jesus Christ.[11] From their work in North India emerged in 1919 The Goßner Evangelical Lutheran Church of Chotanagpur and Assam (GELC). This effort goes back to the year 1845 when its four missionaries Emil Satz, August Brandt, Fredrick Basch and Theodore Yankey reached Kolkata in 1845.[12]

The first German mission society that resulted from the Evangelical Awakening movement and which was strongly influenced and supported from England was the Basel Mission Society. It formed in September 1815 under Reverend Nikolaus von Brunn (1766–1849) as a joint venture between the Reformed Calvinists in Basel and Württemberg Lutherans. It operated as a parachurch and non-denominational society of the first kind that focused on a romantic-pietistic conversion experience with an eschatological view on the coming judgment day.[13] Its mission school, founded in 1816 under its first director Christian Gottlieb Blumhardt (1779–1838), served other mission societies especially the English Anglican Church Mission Society (CMS) before Basel started sending her own missionaries directly to the fields in 1822. Between 1815 and 1882 the Basel Mission Society had trained over a thousand (1,112) mission candidates.[14]

Among the older mission societies formed out of the Evangelical Awakening was the North German Mission Society (*Norddeutsche Missionsgesellschaft*) which was established in 1836 in Hamburg. This society pursued a trans-confessional interest that united both Lutheran and Reformed believers, and consequently, incurred a lot of criticism from the emerging confessional neo-Lutheran movement.[15] Another ecumenically minded mission society was the Rhenish Mission Society (*Rheinische Missionsgesellschaft*), established in 1828, which though Lutheran was influenced by the Reformed Pietism of that region along the Rhine.[16] From it came the famous Lutheran missionary Ludwig Ingwer Nommenson (1834–1918), often referred to as the Apostle of the Batak. He served among the Batak from 1864 to 1918 (fifty-four years), and should be noted for his translations of the New Testament and Martin Luther's Small Catechism (1877) into Batak.[17] The Evangelical-Lutheran Breklumer Mission Society or Schleswig Holstein

11. Raupp, *Mission in Quellentexten*, 258–261.
12. Jochen Teuffel, *Gossner Evangelical Lutheran Church in Chotanagpur and Assam* (GELC), 26 April 2010, https://jochenteuffel.com/2010/04/26/gossner-evangelical-lutheran-church-in-chotanagpur-and-assam/.
13. Raupp, *Mission in Quellentexten*, 243–244.
14. John Talbot Gracey, *The Missionary Year-Book for 1889–90: Containing Historical and Statistical Accounts of the Principal Protestant Missionary Societies in America, Great Britain, and the Continent of Europe*. Section III (New York, Chicago: Fleming H. Revell, 1889), 265–270; Raupp, *Mission in Quellentexten*, 243–250.
15. Raupp, *Mission in Quellentexten*, 262–265.
16. Raupp, *Mission in Quellentexten*, 255–258.
17. For an extensive biography of Nommenson, see Johannes Warneck, *D.J. Nommenson: Ein Lebensbild* (Barmen: Verlag des Rheinischen Missionshauses, 1919); Lothar Schreiner, "The Legacy of Ingwer Ludwig Nommenson," *International Bulletin* 24, no. 2 (April 2000): 81–85.

Society, founded on 19 September 1876, by the Lutheran pastor Christian Jensen (1839–1900), had her own mission seminary which, on 16 April 1877, began to educate her missionaries. On 24 November 1881, she sent out her first four missionaries to British India among whom was also the famous missionary Ernst Pohl (1860–1935), who came to Breklum Mission from the Evangelical Lutheran Immanuel Synod of Prussia. This was a confessional Lutheran synod founded in 1864 in Magdeburg on the principle that the pastors alone had the oversight over the church's constitution and not the laity.[18] The Breklum Mission expanded her fields to countries like Tanzania, China and German New Guinea. Christian Jensen's interest for mission was born out of his occupation with the Moravian Count Zinzendorf (1700–60) and like the nobleman, his motivation for mission was strongly shaped by the concept of the love (*agape*) of Christ as the Apostle Paul had laid it out in 2 Corinthians 5:14–15. Because he embraced a number of theological influences and forged alliances, Jensen would define himself as a mild Lutheran or a Lutheran Pietist.[19]

SCANDINAVIAN MISSION

The Scandinavian countries of Denmark, Norway, Sweden and Finland were all predominantly Lutheran territories with Lutheran state churches. Here the mission movement started through revival movements mostly of a Pietistic character that focused on bringing new life to the formalism and lethargy in the churches. This led to the formation of conventicles and many mission societies that operated within the larger church bodies.[20] Of note also is the influence of the Moravian (Halle) Pietism in Denmark and Scandinavia on the whole. This goes as far back as the Danish-Halle Mission, a joint venture started in 1706 between Halle, Germany and the Danish King Frederick IV (1671–1730). Through visits by Count Zinzendorf to Copenhagen and other Moravian missionaries to Scandinavia, the Moravian influence was kept alive throughout the century. An additional influence on missions was the Norwegian preacher Hans Nielsen Hauge (1771–1824) who greatly impacted the Scandinavian revivalist movement with what became known as the Haugean movement.

The Danish (Lutheran Foreign) Missionary Society was founded on 17 June 1821 by Bone Falck Rønne (1764–1833) in Lyngby, north of Copenhagen. It collaborated with the Basel Mission Society from 1828 onward for the training of her missionaries who would be sent to work in the Danish Gold coast. This territory was on the Guinea coast, west of today's Accra,

18. Ernst Henschen, *Die dem Ruf folgten: Lebensbilder Breklumer Missionare* (Breklum: Breklumer Verlag, 1980), 22.
19. Martin Pörksen, *Die Weite eines engen Pietisten* (Breklum: Christian Jensen Verlag, 1956), 9 and 96. He would also be called "ein überzeugter Lutheraner, doch ein weitherziger und warmer Allianzmann" (p. 13).
20. For a complete list of the Scandinavian mission societies, see John Talbot Gracey, *The Missionary Year-Book for 1889–90*, 289–305.

Ghana, located around Fort Christiansborg. Though it was affiliated with the Evangelical Lutheran Church in Denmark, it operated as a voluntary society that supported many auxiliary societies such as the Danish Lutheran New Greenland Mission, and in 1862 the Danish Lutheran New Tamil Mission associated with the missionary Carl Ernst Christoph Ochs (1812–73). Ochs had left the Leipzig Mission Society over the caste controversy and founded the mission Bethanien (Bethany) in Pattambakam in South Arcot near Madras (today Chennai), India. His work and that of other missionaries led in 1892 to the formation of the Arcot Lutheran Church.[21] In 1896, the Danish Missionary Society also began work in Manchuria, northeast China. Other societies in Denmark pursued particular regional interests such as the Danish Lutheran Loventhal Mission in Velore, south of Madras, India, founded in 1872, named after its first missionary Eduard Loventhal (d. 1917). This mission was supported by the Grundtvigian Church party, or the Danish Lutheran Red-Karen Mission in North East India founded in 1884 by Hans Poulsen (d. 1886) and Hans Jensen (d. 1888), and later in 1886 continued by missionary I. K. Knudsen.[22]

The revivalist movement in Norway began with the lay Lutheran preacher Hans Nielsen Hauge. This Pietistic, low church, Haugean movement occurred during the time of the immigration of many Norwegians to North America and resulted in the formation of the Hauge Synod Mission in North America, known also as the Hauge's Norwegian Evangelical Lutheran Synod. It had a strong influence on American Lutheranism for decades, and started its own mission to China in 1891 in the Hubei province.[23] The Norwegian (Lutheran Foreign) Missionary Society (*Det Norske Misjonsselskap*, NMS) is the first and oldest mission organization in Norway having formed in 1842 with South Africa (1843) and Madagascar (1867) being her oldest fields.[24] It was started by a group of approximately 180 people in the town of Stavanger in Norway in August 1842, and functions as a parent society of other auxiliary societies. The goal was to spread the Christian religion to other peoples, mainly in Africa. Hans Paludan Smith Schreuder (1817–82) became Norway's first missionary to Africa, leaving for Zululand in 1843, who then in 1873 broke away from the Norwegian Mission Society and formed the Schreuder Mission, which became the official mission of the Norwegian state church.

---

21. Gracey, *The Missionary Year-Book for 1889–90*, 290–291.
22. Gracey, *The Missionary Year-Book for 1889–90*, 291–292.
23. John Nicholas Lenker, *Lutherans in all Lands: The Wonderful Works of God*, 2 vols., 4th ed. (Milwaukee, WI: Lutherans in all lands Company, 1894), 819; Tore Hjalmer Saevik, "Hans Nielsen Hauge: An Early Norwegian Entrepreneur Evangelist Revered from Oslo to Minnesota," 30 May 2019, https://religionunplugged.com/news/2019/5/29/hans-nielsen-hauge-an-early-norwegian-entrepreneur-evangelist-revered-from-oslo-to-minnesota.
24. Jan Martin Berrensen, "Background and Emergence of Norwegian Missions: Historical Sketch and Brief Outlook," in *Mission to the World: Communicating the Gospel in the Twenty-First Century, Essays in Honor of Knud Jorgensen*, edited by Tormod Engelsviken, et al. (Eugene, OR: Wipf&Stock, 2009), 39–50; Gracey, *The Missionary Year-Book for 1889–90*, 293–296.

Schreuder was consecrated as Bishop of the Mission Field of the Church of Norway in 1866. Though not well known in the recordings of Protestant missions, he must be hailed as one of South Africa's greatest missionaries for a number of reasons. He produced the first written grammar book of the Zulu language. He translated Luther's Small Catechism into Zulu and introduced the Zulus into the Norwegian liturgy. He became a personal friend and served as "prime minister" to the Zulu King Mpande, and later he acted as intermediary between the Zulu king, Cetshwayo, Mpande's son and successor, and the British authorities, never forsaking his loyalty to the Zulu nation and promoting their cause.[25] A statue in honor of Schreuder now stands at his former mission station, Untunjambili, Natal, South Africa. Schreuder committed himself to a mission concept that was ecclesial, the church and mission should not be separated. Though "a Lutheran churchman of strong convictions, Schreuder placed his own work as a missionary in its true context of the entire church's obedience to mission." Hence he "rejoiced in the fact of ecumenicity" and "strictly adhered to the apostolic principle 'not to build on foundations laid by others' (Rom 15:20)."[26]

The Norwegian Lutheran Mission (NLM) was founded in 1891. It was formerly known as the Norwegian Lutheran China Mission or China Federation, having been inspired to look at that region by a visit from Hudson Taylor. It functioned as an independent organization within the Norwegian Lutheran Church which was evident by her consecrating her missionaries instead of having them ordained through the official church.[27] The revival movement led to its emergence, particularly through the work of Gisle Johnson (1822–94), a theology professor who combined confessional Lutheranism and Orthodoxy with subjective, pietistic elements. He became the torch bearer of the revivalist movement and the founder of the diaconal welfare organization, the Christiana Inner Mission (*Christiania Indremissionsforening*). One of Gisle Johnson's students at the Royal Frederik's University in Kristiana was Hermann Amberg Preus (1825–94), who later became one of the founding fathers of the Norwegian Synod in America and led it for the first thirty years of its existence. Not only did the NLM work in foreign lands such as Tanzania, Ethiopia, Kenya and Japan, it also continued the revivalist tradition of Norway. The Norwegian state church supported the Norwegian Santal Mission (*Den norske Santalmisjon*) that was mainly active in India, particularly among the Santal people, and founded in 1867 by the Norwegian missionary Lars Olsen Skrefsrud (1840–1910) and the Danish missionary Hans Peter Boerresen (1825–1901).[28]

25. Olaf Guttorm Myklebust, "The Legacy of H. P. S. Schreuder," *The International Bulletin of Missionary Research* (April 1984): 70–74, 71.
26. Myklebust, "The Legacy of H. P. S. Schreuder," 72.
27. Berrensen, "Background and Emergence of Norwegian Missions," 47.
28. "Den Norske Santalmisjon," accessed 31 May 2020, https://snl.no/Den_norske_Santalmisjon; Berrensen, "Background and emergence of Norwegian Missions," 45–46.

In Sweden a number of Lutheran mission organizations were established.[29] The Swedish Lutheran Missionary Society formed in 1835 as a mother organization of many smaller societies. It kept a close connection with the Swedish state church and sent its first missionary Carl Ludwig Tellström (1811–62) who worked more as a Methodist than a Lutheran with the Lapps, from 1836 to 1862.[30] Later in 1845 in cooperation with the Basel Mission Society, it sent missionary Theodore Hamberg (1819–54) to the Hakka Chinese to fill in for Karl Gützlaff. Together with the German Rudolph Lechler (1824–1908), Hamberg, who himself was influenced by the Methodist mission to Sweden, founded the Tsung Tsin Mission Church, a church that expanded in the eastern Guangdong-province and which still exists in Hong Kong.[31] The Swedish Mission Board was founded in 1874 and two years later the Sweden state church, at the behest of the King of Sweden, formed the Church of Sweden Mission (CSM) which absorbed the Lund Lutheran Mission Society (LuMS) that had been established in 1849 to promote confessional Lutheranism in China and which was supporting missionary Hamberg and the Leipzig Mission Society.[32]

In 1878, CSM bought a farm at Rorke's Drift in Natal, South Africa, to which it sent its first and chief missionary Peter Otto Helger Witt (1848–1923) who established the mission station among the Zulus named Oscarsberg, in honor of King Oscar II. Oscarsberg became the site of one of the most famous battles in the Anglo-Zulu War, which led to its destruction in 1879 and subsequent reconstruction through missionary Witt. Oscarsberg *redivivus* became a flourishing station under Witt. Unfortunately, because of his neo-Pietistic and Pentecostal affinities for tenets such as millenarianism, he no longer desired to serve under the centralized authority of the organization nor to have his missionary strategy confined to a mission station approach. He was prohibited to engage in an itinerant evangelism strategy visiting also individual Zulu kraals. CSM went on to establish other missions in Natal and Zululand (KwaZulu-Natal).[33]

The most important organization is the Swedish Evangelical National or Fatherland Society (*Evangeliska Fosterlands Stiftelsens*) born out of the revivalist movement. It formed in 1856 under the pale of the state church and set as its goal to become the "organ of all free and spontaneous mission movements which may arise among the Swedish people."[34] In 1865, it chose as its field the Oromo people of Abyssinia (Ethiopia), Africa, at the sugges-

29. Tore Furberg, *Kyrka och mission i Sverige 1868–1901* (Uppsala: Almqvist & Wiksells Boktryckeri AB, 1962).
30. Lenker, *Lutherans in all Lands*, 380.
31. Tobias Brandner, "Der Basler Missionar Theodor Hamberg in China," *Interkulturelle Theologie: Zeitschrift für Missionswissenschaft* (3/2013), 232–251, 235.
32. Rolf Gerhard Tiedemann, *Reference Guide to Christian Mission Societies to China: From the Sixteenth to the Twentieth Centuries* (London, England / Armonk, NY.: M. E. Sharpe, Inc., 2009), 177.
33. Frederick Hale, "The crisis of the Church of Sweden Mission among the Zulus during the 1880s," *Studia Historiae Ecclesiasticae*, 34, no. 2 (December 2008): 1–18.
34. Lenker, *Lutherans in all Lands*, 382.

tion of Ludwig Harms (1808–65) who himself had received information from the missionary Johann Ludwig Krapf (1810–88) and had made several failed attempts (1854 and 1857) at reaching them with his colonists. The Swedish missionaries, too, failed to penetrate the wall into the Oromo region. After two unsuccessful attempts, at which one missionary was killed, the missionaries of the Swedish National Society changed their strategy by purchasing Oromo slaves who were then educated by the missionaries and sent back to their own people. Among them was the native Oromo, Onesimus Nesib (1856–1931). Baptized in 1872, he translated the whole Bible into the Oromo language and wrote various Christian books as well as a large dictionary.[35]

The Lutheran missionary enterprises emerging in Finland, a country which had a number of revivals, should be noted for their valued contribution to worldwide Christianization. The first revivalism was the Later Awakening, whose leading representative was the layman Paavo Ruotsalainen (1777–1852). It was characterized by typical Pietistic elements that included a subjective experience, a struggle with repentance, personal faith, conventicles and large, yearly gatherings. The second was the Evangelical Movement founded by Fredrik Gabriel Hedberg (1811–93), therefore also known as Hedbergianism. His connection to Moravianism was complemented by his discovery of Luther as a source of comfort in his spiritual struggles, particularly the emphasis on the objective character of grace mediated through word and sacrament. Finally, there was the third revival pietistic movement called Laestadianism, taking its name from Lars Laestadius (1800–61), a pastor among the Lapps and Finns in Northern Sweden.[36]

The revival in the years 1820–30 particularly gave birth to an interest for missions. Thus, after contributing to the missionary work of other societies such as Hermannsburg, Leipzig and the Goßner societies, the Lutheran Foreign Missionary Society of Finland or the Finnish Lutheran Missionary Society (*Finska Missionssällskapet*) (FMS) with headquarters at Helsingfors was established in 1859, on the occasion of the seven hundredth anniversary of the conversion of Finland to Christianity. The FMS's confession was Evangelical Lutheran and it explicitly committed itself in its constitution of 1865 "to spread the Evangelical Lutheran doctrines among the non-Christian peoples."[37] It is one of seven organizations of the Evangelical Lutheran Church of Finland (ELCF) that conducted missionary work. The FMS was organized by Klemens Johan Gabriel Sirelius (1818–88), who first worked as the society's secretary and during 1864–72 as its first mission director. The FMS mission school was also founded during his term. Interest for mission work in Southern Africa was roused by a German missionary from

35. Ernst Bauerochse, *Ihr Ziel was das Oromoland* (Münster: Lit-Verlag, 2006), 106–114.

36. Clifford E. Nelson, *The Lutherans in North America* (Minneapolis, MN: Fortress Press, 1980), 272–273. For an overall view of Scandinavian revivalism, see Mark A. Granquist, ed., *Scandinavian Pietists: Spiritual Writings for Nineteenth Century Norway, Denmark, Sweden and Finland* (Mahwah, NJ: Paulist Press, 2015).

37. Lenker, *Lutherans in all Lands*, 417.

the Rhenish Mission Society, Carl Hugo Hahn (1818–95) who had visited Finland in 1867.[38] When the first missionaries from the FMS mission school graduated in 1868, they were deployed to establish a mission among the Ovambo people in the vicinity of the mission station Otjimbingwe of the Rhenish Society, associated with missionaries Hahn and Franz Heinrich Kleinschmidt (1812–64). The group's (six ordained and two laymen) journey took them first to Germany to meet with representatives of the Rhenish Mission. It seemed that FMS's missionaries were suspicious of the theological orientation of the Rhenish Mission because its backers were both Reformed and Lutheran, and because their Lutheran convictions aligned themselves more with Harms and Hermannsburg. Sirelius's response to their letter of query seemed to have assuaged their concerns, since they were told that they were not to be working under the authority and supervision of the Rhenish Mission Society.[39]

For thirteen years FMS missionaries labored without a single convert. Success, in the form of first baptisms, in 1883 came only when the native rulers ceased to oppose mission work. Of the nine stations, the mission station at Omandongo, today in the Onayena Constituency of Oshikoto region, is best known and was proclaimed a national monument in 2014. The most famous Finnish missionary in Namibia was Martti Rautanen (1845–1926) who toiled among the Ovambo people for more than fifty years. He was nicknamed Nakambale, which is Oshivambo for *the one who wears the hat.* Rautanen often suffered from severe headaches and thus wore a skullcap which the Ovambos thought was a basket woven out of palm leaves. From 1880, Rautanen worked in Olukonda at one of the first mission stations among the Ovambo people. He initiated the first church building in Ovamboland in 1889, and he translated the Bible into Oshindonga, a dialect of Oshivambo.[40]

In 1873 the Lutheran Evangelical Association of Finland (LEAF) was formed, indebted to Hedberg's influence, and which works inside the Evangelical Lutheran Church of Finland. This association combined Swedish and Finnish members, both lay and pastors. In 1922, the Swedish speaking group formed its own organization, the Swedish Lutheran Evangelical Association in Finland (*Svenska Lutherska Evangeliföreningen i Finland*). Both organizations should be noted for their foreign mission work which began first in Japan in 1900 and then spread to Kenya, Africa in the 1970s and then Ingria, Russia.[41]

The above references to a number of mission societies serve to illustrate how, in the nineteenth century, the first initial mission activity in Europe (especially in Germany) generally pursued mission of the first kind, as an

38. Matti Peltola, *Nakambale: The Life of Dr. Martin Rautanen*, trans. Lahja Lehtonen (Pietermaritzburg: Finnish Evangelical Lutheran Mission, 2002), 41.
39. Peltola, *Nakambale,* 30.
40. Peltola, *Nakambale,* 98, 67; 330–339; Gracey, *The Missionary Year-Book for 1889–90,* 304–305.
41. See "The Lutheran Evangelical Association of Finland, accessed 31 May 2020, https://www.sley.fi/in-english/.

ecumenical and trans-confessional endeavor, that also, as a result of the Evangelical Awakening in Germany, or revivalism in Scandinavia, embraced elements of the third kind, particularly pietistic tenets often coming from Moravianism or important individuals in a specific region. Historical recordings of these events used, at times generously, the term "Lutheran" to define either some of the societies, its leaders or its missionaries, to a degree that would be justified. Lutheran influences were definitely present in various ways, either in how a society defined its purpose and direction, or the theological formation and commitment of its founders and missionaries. Often, through the work of certain missionaries, such as the Goßner Mission Society and Ludwig Nommenson's work in Sumatra, Lutheran churches formed on the field. All these societies operated largely parallel to or within the church bodies themselves, and not against them, thereby enabling to keep a wider ecumenical unity and cooperation with other societies through an exchange of missionaries and in sharing mission fields.

THE LUTHERAN CONFESSIONAL CHURCH MISSION

In the 1830s the mission endeavor of the second type emerged where societies pursued an intentional, confessional Lutheran focus. It was a restorative, neo-confessional Lutheranism, also born out of the Evangelical Awakening but now in addition strongly committing itself to the Lutheran Confessions. The prelude to this movement, and partly a cause for its rise, was the Prussian Union. In October 1817, on the three hundredth anniversary of Martin Luther's Ninety-five Theses in Wittenberg, a decree of King Frederick William III (1779–1840) ended the inter-Protestant division between the Reformed Christian Unions and the Lutherans. In 1821, this ecclesiastical union also received a new liturgy drafted by none other than the king himself and was introduced in Prussia and regions annexed to it.

Whereas the former mission societies of the first kind were ecumenical in orientation and a direct result of the Evangelical Awakening, the mission societies of the confessional-ecclesial kind focused on ensuring that mission and the church came closer together. They succeeded in that effort, only in part, by having to overcome serious challenges with state churches of their region, such as who would assume responsibility for the education of the missionaries and their ordination and commissioning to the field. Often tensions arose among pastors of state churches which led to the formation of independent Lutheran churches which in turn became patrons of their own mission society.[42] In distinction to the first kind of mission societies which claimed immediate access to the Gospel and to the third kind, the

42. For a detailed study on the emergence of Lutheran Free Churches in numerous regions of Germany, see Wilhelm Wöhling, *Geschichte der Evangelisch-Lutherischen Freikirche in Sachsen u.a. Saint* (Zwickau: Verlag des Schriftenvereins, 1925). The connection of these churches to mission is traced by Volker Stolle, *Wer seine Hand an den Pflug legt: Die missionarische Wirksamkeit der selbständigen evangelisch-lutherischen Kirchen in Deutschland im 19. Jahrhundert* (Gross-Oesingen: Lutherische Buchhandlung Harms, 1992).

faith missions, where missionaries felt an immediate calling from Christ, the confessional-church societies obliged their missionaries to profess not their personal faith but the confession of the church to which the society was connected. The leaders of these societies held the firm belief that proper mission work emanated from the church and her confession and not from a mission society itself or alone, and that view also determined the relationship of the sending church with the young emerging churches on the field namely that they, too, had to adopt the particular confession of the mother church. Thus, the Confession was not a negotiable entity in mission but an indispensable requirement for both the mission enterprise, its missionaries and those on the receiving end, on the mission field. This exclusive and intentional particularism would not accept cooperation with the first and third kind of societies, but operated in distinct separation from them.

The leading supporter of this neo-Lutheran surge was the Hanoverian Pastor, Ludwig Adolf Petri (1803–76). Though he and his supporters' interest in mission was still a result of the Evangelical Awakening, he turned to the confessio-ecclesiological dimension of missions by drawing in Martin Luther and the Lutheran Confessions. Petri's treatise, *The Mission and the Church* (*Die Mission und die Kirche*) is a critical response to Friedrich Lücke's (1791–1855) presentation, "On the relationship of confessional differences among churches in their relationship to their mission societies" (*Über das Verhältnis der confessionellen Verschiedenheiten der Kirchen zu ihrem Missionswerke*).[43] In his 1848 speech to representatives of the Göttinger Mission Society (*Göttinger Missionsverein*), a society founded in 1837 to support the Leipzig Mission Society, Lücke made his case for missionary enterprises and societies supporting unionism. This was also a defense of the *modus operandi* of the previously mentioned trans-confessional mission society in Hamburg, the North German Mission Society (*Norddeutsche Missionsgesellschaft*). Though Lücke agreed that mission should emerge from the churches, he claimed that mission societies should preserve some independence and operate alongside these churches. The commissioning of missionaries to foreign lands should occur in the name of all churches of various confessions, which meant that mission itself should not be bound to a particular confession and church.[44]

Petri took a different position than Lücke. He opened his response in the tract *The Mission and the Church* with the self-posed question, "And what relationship to the church do I mean, into which mission is rightly, naturally, and necessarily to enter?"[45] He answered thus: "Mission . . . must have an ec-

43. Ludwig Adolph Petri, *Mission and the Church: a letter to a friend*, translated by David Buchs (Fort Wayne, IN: Concordia Theological Seminary Bookstore Reprint, 2012).

44. Hans-Walter Krumwiede, *Vom Deutschen Bund 1815 bis zur Gründung der Evangelischen Kirche*, vol. 2 of *Kirchengeschichte Niedersachsens* (Göttingen: Vandenhoek & Ruprecht, 1996), 328; Hartwig Harms, *Hamburg und die Mission des 19. Jahrhunderts: Kirchlich-missionarische Vereine 1814 bis 1836* (Hamburg: Friedrich Wittig Verlag, 1973), 156.

45. Petri, *Mission and the Church*, 2.

clesial character. It must proceed from the church and abide in the church. It must be nothing other than the church itself in its mission activity."[46] With this position, Petri would look favorably, for example, upon Ludwig Harms and the Hermannsburg Mission Society's separation from the unionistic North German Mission Society, and much less favorably on the Moravian Missions (*Brüdergemeinde*) that would operate with hardly any ecclesial connection.[47] To Petri the essence of the church, and that became the *proprium* of neo-Lutheran ecclesiology, was that the church functions and expands as an organism (*Organismus*). According to this concept, taken from Romanticism and German Idealism, mission must come out of the church. Petri would point out, "as such an organism, the church increases through times and lands. It takes in every individual as well as whole people groups who believe and are baptized. It appropriates the truth and eternal life in Christ ever more completely and seeks always more aptly to describe its inner essence."[48] This focus on expansion makes mission an ecclesial reality, the mission societies serve only as the "temporary or emergency solution," for a time when the Christian faith was still *innocent*.

Petri states that as an organism, the church takes her existence from the word and sacrament:

> All advanced education in the church must be organic if it is to be natural and beneficial. That is, it must proceed from the innermost foundations of life and never forcefully and capriciously break the connection to them . . . But this innermost foundation of life is the Word and the embodied Word, the Sacraments.[49]

An important discussion point for Petri was the relationship of church and the missionary. Petri argued for the missionary's commitment to preach not his own personal convictions, but what the church believes and confesses, and when on the field, the missionary should not withhold from his audience any theological position and ruling that the church had passed against heresies. Petri argues this point at length:

> But now the question arises: what posture toward the confessions, customs, and structure of the church shall these individuals take in their Christian activity? Shall they continue completely free and unrestrained by the church in their mission activity? Shall they not preach to the heathen Christendom as defined by the church? Shall the commissioned missionaries teach only the immediate content of the Scriptures without consideration for the development process of the past eighteen centuries? Shall they bring no form of the church to the heathen? . . . Shall we transmit dogma to the heathen so vaguely that they and

46. Petri, *Mission and the Church*, 9.
47. Petri, *Mission and the Church*, 2.
48. Petri, *Mission and the Church*, 5.
49. Petri, *Mission and the Church*, 6.

> Christianity with them must once again endure all the controversies in which we have bled: the Arian, Pelagian, Sacramentarian and others likewise? That appears to me equally foolish and unjust. If in our doctrine we have the truth and the correct understanding of the Scriptures, then we owe it to the heathen. If we have something good in our ecclesial nature, for example in our divine services or in our principle concerning the relative freedom of ceremony and structure, why should we withhold it from them? In any case there will remain so many battles for the heathen that we might well spare them the avoidable ones as much as we can.[50]

Finally, to ensure the commitment of the missionaries to the confession of the church and to underscore the ecclesial connection of the mission, Petri pushes one further important *proprium* of the confessional-ecclesial missions, the call and ordination of missionaries into the office of the church. By emphasizing that office and its ordination, mission takes on an ecclesial character that is non-sectarian:

> Mission takes its right of activity only from the church, it exercises it in the name of the church. It cannot go without the church . . . It desires for its activity recognition, protection, and the support of the church in order to show itself to be a justified, Christian activity and to protect itself from every suspicion of unchristian, sectarian, or outright worldly endeavor. It desires to give the right emphasis to all of its activity wherever possible through common prayer and work. It desires ordination for its missionaries, and it desires the prayer of the church.[51]

Petri's tract *Die Mission und die Kirche* is not only a tract shaping confessional missions, it is also a compelling "programmatic script for the formation of the Lutheran churches in the nineteenth century," according to Wilhelm Maurer, which was especially influential for Ludwig Harms and Wilhelm Löhe.

The first confessional Lutheran society was the Leipzig Mission Society (LELM) founded in 1836 (*Evangelisch-Lutherische Missionsgesellschaft in Sachsen*). Its roots go back to the Dresdner Society (*Dresdner Hilfsverein*) that was formed in 1819 to help the Basel Mission Society. Later a theological shift occurred in the 1830s through the influence of Huschke and Scheibel in Dresden and the LELM became more devoted to confessional Lutheranism. In a tract on the relationship of the Lutheran church to mission societies such as Basel, Scheibel brought out the confessional and ecclesial character of Dresden's mission by pointing out the fact that missionaries are ordained which makes mission a churchly confessional act (*kirchliche Konfessionshandlung*) and not a private affair. Thus Dresden's missionaries cannot ignore

50. Petri, *Mission and the Church*, 3.
51. Petri, *Mission and the Church*, 10.

the confessional distinctions and must teach on the Sacrament of the Altar in the Lutheran way.[52]

The Dresdner period of this society is strongly associated with Pastor Johann Georg Wermelskirch (1803–72) who served as its director from 1836–42. Its founding statutes from 1840 reflect its intentional confessional line with a purpose statement to uphold the entire Book of Concord so that its missionaries will bring the biblical truth to the field in accordance with the Lutheran Confessions.[53] In 1848 it relocated from Dresden to Leipzig. Karl Graul, its director from 1814–64, insisted on their missionaries' education at the University of Leipzig, and he hoped to boost the Leipzig society's trans-regional appeal by making it *the* Lutheran society in Germany. His aspirations were dashed with the emergence of another Lutheran society at Hermannsburg. Graul would have been the first German missiologist in Erlangen if it were not for his untimely passing. With the sending of the first missionary Heinrich Codes (1813–92) on 2 March 1840 to Tranquebar in South India and in 1842 Carl Ochs (1812–73), the Leipzig Mission Society took over officially the Danish-Halle Mission (1706).

In his treatise *Die evangelisch-lutherische Mission zu Dresden an die evangelisch-lutherische Kirche aller Lande: Vorwärts oder Rückwärts* (1845) (*The Evangelical-Lutheran Mission of Dresden to the Evangelical-Lutheran Churches of All Lands: Forward or Retreat*), Graul reiterates the Leipzig society's commitment to the entire Confessions (*Gesammtbekenntniß der Kirche*) so that the missionaries bring the word in its full and unadulterated form:

> That is the understanding with which we conduct our mission: that it is the apostolic way . . . not that a missionary selfishly brings a confession of one of his teachers or his own . . . or that he fails to bring the congregations gathered from the heathen . . . together as one member with the mother church.[54]

In this treatise, Graul further bemoans the lack of support in congregations for those "young men, who avail themselves for missionary service . . . who 'decides for himself to go into mission.'" Such a comment revealed some uncertainty on the status of the missionary as either a volunteer for missions who fends for himself, (go-lings or *Gehlinge*, as Graul described them), or someone who is sent and supported by the sending church (*Sendlinge*). Adolf von Harless (1806–79), a professor at Erlangen and a member of the society's board (*Missionskollegium*), settled that question by insisting on the latter:

52. See reference to "Wie verhält sich die lutherische Kirche zu den Missionsgesellschaften und den dazugehörigen Instituten in unserer Zeit?", in Peter Hauptmann, ed., *Johann Gottfried Scheibel: Vom innersten Wesen des Christentums* (Göttingen: V&R unipress, 2009), 363.
53. Raupp, *Mission in Quellentexten*, 274.
54. Karl Graul, *Die evangelisch-lutherische Mission zu Dresden an die evangelisch-lutherische Kirche aller Lande: Vorwärts oder Rückwärts?* (Leipzig, 1845), quoted in Raupp, *Mission in Quellentexten*, 275.

> As far as their (missionaries') status is concerned, it would be difficult to dismiss the fact that it bears all marks of a proper, Christian and apostolic call. They are placed in the call of the Lord to the Apostles: Go ye to the world. They did not go on their own accord, but have been found fit for their office and have been placed into it by those who in the Evangelical Lutheran Church have the right to do so. The church is the community of believers, that keep themselves to the pure Word and Sacrament and such a community has sent them out with a loyal pledge to their confession.[55]

Thus, Harless concludes: "We cannot find anything amiss here that would prevent us from considering them *rite vocatus* in the sense of Article 14 of the Augsburg Confession."[56]

In close proximity to Hanover, in the town of Hermannsburg, located in an area called the Lüneburger Heide because of its heather landscape, another confessional mission society was founded in 1849 (*Evangelisch-Lutherisches Missionswerkes in Niedersachsen*) by the Lutheran St. Peter Paul congregation and its pastor, Ludwig Harms (1808–65). In his theology and work, Harms combined both elements of the pietistic-Awakening such as the personal faith, reading of Scripture and prayer with his subscription to the Lutheran Confessions. Harms' influence, through his preaching especially, contributed to a neo-Lutheran awakening in that region and a widespread interest for mission that impacted countries like Ethiopia and India, as well as Southern Africa and North and Latin America. From his own reporting in the mission publication *Hermannsburger Missionsblatt* (HBL) the reasons for his motivation to start a mission come to light:

> When in the [year 1848] one by one twelve young men came to me with the intentions of becoming missionaries to the heathen . . . I wrote to a number of mission societies and asked them to receive these young men and prepare them for service . . . Alas, my request was turned down. Then one evening when all twelve were in my room . . . They said to me . . . .'why don't you teach us and send us off?' This gave me no peace day and night, and so I finally decided, with God's help to buy a mission house (*Missionshaus*).[57]

Harms found in his brother Theodor Harms (1819–85) a loyal friend and compatriot serving at his side as the teacher of the *Missionshaus*, preparing the young candidates for what became known as the "farmer- and colonist mission," inspired and modelled after the medieval-Irish-Scottish mission.

55. Johannes Aagaard, *Mission, Konfession, Kirche,* (Gleerups, Denmark: Clemenstrykkeriet, 1967), 2:719.
56. Aagaard, *Mission, Konfession, Kirche,* 2:719. In contrast, the Director of the Leipzig mission, Karl Graul proposed that the church, which would emerge from the missionaries' work, should take over responsibility and not the home church, including ordination and salary; Aagaard, *Mission, Konfession, Kirche,* 718; Stolle, *Wer seine Hand an den Pflug legt,* 39 and 102.
57. Raupp, *Mission in Quellentexten,* 279.

The colonists and their pastor would build a colony in the land to which they were sent and through them, new converts would be assimilated. In 1851, Harms laid out his strategic plans in the HBL:

> For it is my burning desire to accomplish the conversion of the heathen in such a way that after every three to four years . . . a number of twelve are sent into the heathen world. The first twelve must stay together at one and the same location and settle there, so as to be strong enough to work in a joint effort among the heathen and earn their living, since they are skilled in agriculture and all other needed crafts . . . similar to what the Anglo Saxons did in Germany . . . Once a congregation from the heathens is formed, two or three will remain behind with them . . . and the others move on one, two or three miles away and begin their work once again.[58]

The target area was initially Ethiopia (at that time Abyssinia) and its people were the Oromo, a large tribe who, according to the reports of missionary Johann Ludwig Krapf (1810–88),[59] which Harms had read, was still surrounded by Islamic slave traders that made its borders impenetrable. With the help of donors, Harms purchased a ship called Candace and launched his first colonist mission to the East coast of Africa which reached the ports of Mombasa and Zanzibar in 1854 and 1857 respectively. On both occasions, however, the mission attempts failed because of the regional Sultan who prohibited their entry. This bust became the boon for South Africa, a mission field to which the colonists then turned. They reached the harbor of Port Natal and there, after being warmly received by missionary Karl Ludwig Posselt (1815–85), from the Berlin Mission Society, they established a colony called Hermannsburg in the Natal Province to work among the Zulu tribe.[60] In the end, the colonist strategy, shaped by their shared communalism and social cohesion as a group, failed since widespread lands were available for farming. That crumbling of strategy may be attributed largely to Harms' co-director August Hardeland, who had served as missionary to Borneo for the Rhenish Mission Society (1839–45 and 1849–58) and briefly in the Cape Colony (1845–48). His older brother was (Hermann Emil) Julius Hardeland (1828–1903), the director of the Leipzig Mission Society's director.[61] Hardeland himself had no interest in continuing Harms' community of property and colonization model or making it a success, and consequently through his authoritarian style enforced a strategy that arguably would have emerged anyway, being at variance with the southern African situation. Over time,

58. Raupp, *Mission in Quellentexten,* 280.
59. Rune Imberg, "Dr. Krapf-the (Almost) Forgotten Missionary Pioneer," *Swedish Missiological Themes*, 98, no. 1 (2010): 49–67.
60. Friedrich Speckmann, *Die Hermannsburger Mission in Afrika* (Hermannsburg: Verlag der Missionshausdruckerei, 1876), 12–54, 179.
61. Karl Böhmer, *August Hardeland and the "Rheinische" and "Hermannsburger" Missions in Borneo and Southeran Africa (1839–1870): The History of a Paradigm Shift and its Impact on South African Lutheran Churches* (Göttingen: Dr. Reinhilde Ruprecht e.K., 2016), 37, 74, 98.

the communal existence between missionaries and colonists broke apart. Mission stations rapidly emerged at which one or two missionaries resided while the colonists purchased lands and formed their own German speaking congregations. The missionaries, originally instructed to remain celibate, were allowed to marry and received a salary from HMS.[62]

Lutheran mission work through the Hermannsburg Society itself was successful and gave Lutheranism in southern Africa, the Republic of South Africa and Botswana, a strong foothold. In the span of eleven years, between 20 October 1853 and 24 August 1864, Harms had dispatched colonists nine times to South Africa, which totaled to a respectable number of 170 people: forty-four missionaries, forty-one colonists, nine women, approximately forty brides, sixteen girls and twenty-one children.[63]

For Harms, like Petri, mission could only be done by the church. For him mission was not the private enterprise of individual awakened souls, but God's work through the church which obeys His call and shows mercy for the unbeliever. This applies to the one, holy, Christian church in general, but Harms gave the Lutheran church preferential treatment. The Lutheran church is the true mission church (*rechte Missionskirche*) because she brings the pure word and sacrament to the heathen world from whose midst a Lutheran church will rise. Thus, he placed the mission work not only on the church but also on her confession: "We want to bring to the heathens the Lutheran church."[64] In an 1857 post in the HBL, he presents his case:

> If you were to ask what church should it be that we wish to bring to the heathen . . . then I respond, that I do not fully understand your question. For, you fool, one can only bring that what one has and because we are members of the Lutheran church, we of course can and want only to bring the heathen no other church than the Lutheran church . . . And we do so also for the reason that we have in the Lutheran church the Word of God taught purely and unadulterated, and [because] we have in our church baptism and the Lord's Supper administered purely and unadulterated in accordance with the institution of the Lord Jesus. That is why we want to do Lutheran mission, as we have done it thus far. I believe that those belonging to the Greek, Roman, Union or Reformed churches can also become members of the church of Christ and be saved . . . However in this universal, large church of Christ we Lutherans have the purest and most unadulterated teaching and the true sacraments, therefore we want to do uncompromising, Lutheran mission, but also willingly serve and help and pray for others, and walk fraternally alongside them, even when we cannot walk together with them.[65]

62. Böhmer, *August Hardeland and the "Rheinische" and "Hermannsburger" Missions in Borneo and Southeran Africa*, 292–293.
63. Böhmer, *August Hardeland and the "Rheinische" and "Hermannsburger" Missions in Borneo and Southeran Africa*, 341–347.
64. Raupp, *Mission in Quellentexten*, 279.
65. Raupp, *Mission in Quellentexten*, 279.

Harms vigorously pursued ecclesial recognition from the Hanoverian state church. He would call his mission organization also the institute of the Hanoverian Lutheran state church, and he pleaded for the ordination and commissioning of his candidates by the church's consistory. Because of its initial reluctance to do so, Harms took matters in his own hands and ordained and commissioned them himself as director of the organization, pointing out that the call of the heathen and their spiritual plight was good enough a reason to act in this extraordinary manner. A sense of urgency comes across in his appeal to the church:

> They [the heathen] are dying without God's word. And we have it, but we refuse to bring it to them? Six hundred million heathen, who are without the word of God, and cannot be saved without this word of God, six hundred million heathen are stretching their hands out to you Christians and call: come hither and help us! Do you have a heart made of stone, that you are so idle in helping them? . . . Have pity on them.[66]

Looking back in his *History of the Hanoverian Mission*, Georg Haccius (1847–1926), the Director of the Hermannsburg Mission, never had any doubt on the validity of the ordination of the first mission candidates performed by Harms: "Thus, they were duly and lawfully called and ordained and could therefore on the foundation of article fourteen of the Augsburg Confession move out confidently and joyfully."[67] On 19 October 1857, the HBL reports through an article published by Nieman, a member of the consistory, that the ordination of the next twelve missionaries was performed by the Hanoverian Lutheran Church, at which Harms preached.[68] Harms succeeded in his wish to imprint on the Hermannsburg Mission society an ecclesial character.

The third Lutheran mission society was established in 1849 in a town called Neuendettelsau located in the north Bavarian region of Franconia. It was named the "*Gesellschaft für Innere Mission im Sinne der lutherischen Kirche*," (in 1888 the title was expanded to include foreign mission, "*äußere Mission*") and became widely known because of its founder and director Pastor Wilhelm Löhe (1808–72), who as a churchman and prolific author and theologian, chose a mission that created and influenced Lutheranism worldwide, including North America. Löhe shared similar situations with Harms and the Hermannsburg Mission Society. For one, Löhe had to contend with the Bavarian Lutheran church, which he never left, and second, he also followed a similar strategy of colonist mission, this time among the Ojibwa (Chippewa) Indians along the Cass River in the Saginaw valley of Michigan. Colonists were sent

66. Raupp, *Mission in Quellentexten*, 279–280.
67. Georg Haccius, *Hannoverische Missionsgeschichte*, (Hermannsburg: Verlag der Missionshandlung, 1910), 2:217.
68. See the witness' report, in *Hermannsburger Missionsblatt* (HMB), No.10 (October 1857): 150–155.

out to colonize in short distances from one another. First, Frankenmuth was established in 1845 and then other colonies followed Frankentrost (1846), Frankenlust (1847) and Frankenhilf (1849). Strategically, Löhe operated with an understanding that mission flowed out of and back to the local congregation. For it served as the base for mission where the priesthood of all believers reached outsiders and assimilated them under the preaching and teaching office. To that end, at Frankenmuth, the colonists were instructed to assimilate the Indians into the St. Lorenz congregation, named after the main cathedral in Nuremberg, Germany. That well-intentioned strategy failed so that in 1847, at the request of Pastor August Crämer (1812–91), the missionary Ernst Baierlein (1819–1901) from the Leipzig Mission Society came to his assistance. Baierlein was a nobleman who had been disowned by his Roman Catholic parents for becoming Lutheran, and because of ill health was given temporary reprieve from being sent to India. Instead of staying with the community of colonists at Frankenmuth, Baierlein chose to serve as a pioneer missionary and settled among the Indians. According to his own autobiography, *In the Wilderness with the Red Indians: German Missionary to the Michigan Indians,*[69] Baierlein achieved modest success so that, at the time of his departure for India in 1853, he left behind at Bethany a community of Lutheran Indians that bid him farewell with great grief and sorrow. The Leipzig missionary Ernst G. H. Miessler (1826–1916) came in 1851 as an aid to Baierlein and continued the work among the Chippewa Indians from 1853 until 1869, when the mission came to an end and Miessler moved on to practice medicine in Chicago.[70]

Löhe should also be mentioned for coming to the assistance of immigrants in North America with emergency helpers and for the establishment of seminaries: Concordia Theological Seminary, Fort Wayne, Indiana and Wartburg Seminary, Dubuque, Iowa. His response to the North American German immigrant spiritual crisis came in 1841 after reading the appeal of the distress of pastors serving the Germans in America. Moved by the report, he published a summons to help in the local weekly newspaper, the *Nördlingen Sonntagsblatt*, and he himself began assisting the Ohio Synod by sending his first two emergency helpers, Johann Adam Ernst (1815–95) and Johann Georg Burger (1816–47).[71] From there a brief, yet fruitful relationship emerged with the Missouri Lutherans and its founding father C. F. W. Walther. However, that relationship was short-lived because of Missouri's disagreement with Löhe's theological position on ministry and eschatology. In 1853, Löhe thereupon turned to a region further west and with a remnant of loyal supporters. He founded the Iowa Synod, and the Wartburg seminary in Dubuque, Iowa the following year. The founders and senior officials of the Iowa Synod were graduates of the Neuendettelsau seminary: Georg Gross-

69. Ernst R. Baierlein, *In the Wilderness with the Red Indians: German Missionary to the Michigan Indians, 1847–1853*, trans. Anita Z. Boldt (Detroit: Wayne state University Press, 1996).
70. Baierlein, *In the Wilderness with the Red Indians*, 16; Paul M. Heerboth, "Missouri Synod Approach to Mission in the Early Period," *Missio Apostolica* 1, no. 1 (May 1993): 19–26.
71. Heerboth, "Missouri Synod Approach to Mission in the Early Period," 19.

mann (1823–97), Johannes Deindörfer (1828–1907), Dr. Sigmund Fritschel (1833–1900) and Gottfried Fritschel (1836–89).[72]

Löhe's final move in North America came in 1858 with the plan to begin mission to the Indians. In Detroit, the experienced missionary Johann Jakob Schmidt (b. 1838) met the U.S. government commissioner of Indian Affairs of the Upper Missouri, Alexander Redfield (1805–69) who invited Schmidt to accompany him on a visit to the Absarokee (Upsaroka or Crow) Indians and suggested to him that he should establish among them a mission presence. The mission committee of the Iowa Synod, together with the supporting mission agency of Nuremberg (*Nürnberger Zentralmissionsverein*) and the Neuendettelsau Society for Inner Mission (*Neuendettelsauer Gesellschaft für innere Mission*), looked at this invitation as an opportunity to begin mission among the Native American population which for Löhe was of particular importance. Also the Evangelical-Lutheran Mission Society of Lübeck, under the director of Lutheran pastor Johann Carl Lindenberg (1798–1892), provided monetary support for the project. Early in 1858, Schmidt requested a helper and the choice fell on Moritz Bräuninger (1836–60) who, after arriving from Neuendettelsau, Germany, had just completed his theological training at Wartburg seminary. On May 1858, he arrived in St. Louis and met Schmidt and Redfield with whom he boarded the schooner *Twilight*, chartered from Frost, Todd, & Company. Together they left St. Louis on 23 May 1858 to embark on a 2,386 mile journey up the Missouri River. Redfield had obtained a license for both missionaries to reside among the Crow for a year, and managed to persuade Captain Shaw to reduce their travel expenses on the schooner. After an arduous journey up and along the Yellowstone River, the two missionaries eventually met the Crow Indians, won over the friendship of two chiefs of the Crow, and accompanied the Crow tribe for two months from 17 August to 1 October 1858. The missionaries then decided to return to Saint Sebald, Iowa, and make arrangements for a sedentary lifestyle for the Indians and themselves. Having gained the necessary support and equipped with supplies, they returned with three ox wagons to the Powder River to create a model colony as was arranged for Frankenmuth, Michigan. Johann Jakob Schmidt had fallen ill and stayed behind in Iowa so that Moritz Bräuninger assumed leadership and took on the task together with helpers Beck, Bunge und Seyler to erect a mission station on the farm in 1860 at the Powder River in Wyoming. Unfortunately, the location of the mission farm was unwisely chosen for it was not in the territory of the Crow Indians but on a strip of land where the Sioux, Crow and Blackfoot were feuding. On 23 July 1860, Bräuninger was murdered by a party of six Indians, most probably consisting of Hunkpapa and Oglala, outside of the mission station when, in search of strayed cattle, he had stumbled upon the party. Löhe received the news of Bräuninger's death a few weeks later, and wrote about it early 1861 in

72. Hermann Vorländer, *Church in Motion: The History of the Evangelical Lutheran Mission in Bavaria* (Eugene, OR: Pickwick Publications, 2018), 114–15.

the first edition of the newspaper on church affairs in America (*Kirchlichen Mittheilungen aus und über Nordamerika*) concluding from the facts of his death, which to this day are uncertain, that the death of Bräuninger at the hands of the party was a martyr's death: "The circumstances of his death are of the kind that we can feel happy: our mission is consecrated with martyr's blood."[73] With that came the end of Löhe's mission to America and he devoted his attention to the diaconal work at home in Neuendettelsau.

In addition to its service to North America, other regions soon received missionaries from Neuendettelsau, beginning at Sattelberg, Papua New Guinea and among the Aranda and Loritja people on the Hermannsburg mission station—Australia's oldest—at the Finke River, Australia. The names Johannes Flierl (1858–1947) is the most well-known missionary to the former whereas Carl Strehlow (1871–1922) is the most well-known for the latter region.[74] That expansion of Neuendettelsau Mission took place under Johannes Deinzer (1842–97), who had taken over the leadership from Friedrich Bauer (1812–74), a loyal compatriot of Löhe's mission. During Löhe's directorship, Bauer had been responsible for teaching the candidates at the mission seminary and then succeeded Löhe as Director of Neuendettelsau. In 1897, in collaboration with the Lutheran Treasury of God for Beleaguered Co-believers (*Lutherischer Gotteskasten für bedrängte Glaubensgenossen;* called today *Martin-Luther-Verein in Bayern*), a support group for diaspora Christians in distress founded in Hersbruck, near Nuremberg in 1860, Neuendettelsau also assumed the responsibility to educate pastors for Brazil. Otto Kuhr (1864–1938) was the mission seminary's first emissary to Brazil who founded the Lutheran Synod which he led from 1905–23.

Löhe's understanding of mission was greatly influenced by the sixteenth and seventeenth century Lutheran Orthodoxy's understanding of mission, in that he was reluctant to break away from the parochialism that tied all ordained servants to the congregation to which they were called. The colonist idea helped him to circumvent the problem of ordaining and sending individuals as missionaries. Also the "emergency helpers" (*geistliche Nothelfer*) which he "sent" to North America went as lay helpers to help gather and serve spiritually neglected German immigrants. They were going as volunteers to a church that would receive them, teach them at the seminary in Fort Wayne, Indiana, or Wartburg, Iowa, and then call and ordain them to a congregation. Löhe's missionary outlook is captured best in his *Three Books about the Church,* (1845) (*Drei Bücher von der Kirche*), in which he not only provides an ecclesial foundation for his mission, but an ecclesiology that is embedded in a missionary framework. Church and confession are connected to the universal, catholic call of the Gospel. In this treatise he formulates his famous definition of mission as the movement of the one, church universal:

73. Hermann Vorländer, *Church in Motion*, 12.

74. Wighard Strehlow, *Wüstentanz: Australien spirituell erleben* (Allensbach am Bodensee: Strehlow, 1996), 19–30.

> It is the one flock of the one shepherd, called out of many folds (John 10:16), the universal—truly catholic—church which flows through all time and into which all people pour. [. . .] This is the thought which must permeate the mission of the church or it will not know what it is or what it should do. For mission is nothing but the one church of God in motion, the actualization of the one universal, catholic church. Wherever mission enters in, the barriers which separate nation from nation fall down. Wherever it comes it brings together what previously was far off and widely separated. [. . .] Mission is the life of the catholic church. [. . .] The catholic church and mission—these two no one can separate without killing both, and that is impossible.[75]

Löhe kept a wider ecumenical perspective that acknowledged the missionary contribution of particular churches of non-Lutheran tradition. "We know," he says, "that all other confessions which preach to the heathen bring them the possibility of salvation."[76] Yet he also drew attention to the Lutheran Church: "If the Lutheran Church has the pure Word and sacrament in a pure confession, it obviously has the highest treasures of the church unperverted."[77] Since the Lutheran Church is in possession of the truest and purest word of God preserved in her Confession and her sacraments, she would through her mission further the one catholic church, and become a blessing to the heathen carrying "the torch of the pure truth to all people."[78] "To bear this cleansing, purifying witness in the midst of the confessions is the chief calling of the church of God which is called Lutheran."[79]

Lutheran confessional mission reached its apex in 1892 when the Mission of the Hanoverian Evangelical-Lutheran Free Church (*Mission der Hannoverschen evangelisch-lutherischen Freikirche*" was founded. It later was continued under the name "*Mission Evangelisch-Lutherischer Freikirchen*" (Bleckmarer Mission) in 1973, as the mission arm for the newly formed *Selbständige Evangelisch Lutherische Kirche* (SELK). Today it is called the Lutheran Church Mission (*Lutherische Kirchenmission*), located in a small town called Bleckmar near Hermannsburg, Germany. The *Hannoversche evangelisch-Lutherische Freikirche* was founded on 30 April 1878 in Hermannsburg around the brother of Ludwig Harms, (Carl Friedrich) Theodor Harms who assumed the leadership as her superintendent.[80] Harms was one of a group of four pastors, who had been deposed as pastors by the Hanoverian state church in 1878 because they claimed that the Hanoverian state church was compromising her confessional Lutheran character in view of the encroaching Prussian union. They also opposed both the introduction of a new edi-

75. Wilhelm Löhe, *Three Books about the Church*, trans. James L. Schaaf (Philadelphia, PA: Fortress Press, 1969), 59.
76. Löhe, *Three Books about the Church*, 162.
77. Löhe, *Three Books about the Church*, 113.
78. Löhe, *Three Books about the Church*, 162.
79. Löhe, *Three Books about the Church*, 162.
80. Johannes Ehlers, *Ohne Kreuz keine Krone* (Hermannsburg: Missionshandlung, 1912), 12–17.

tion of a Catechism that was to replace the old catechism (1653) of the General Superintendent Michael Walther (1593–1662) and the new, revised marriage formula which the Hanoverian state church enforced on all her pastors. This deposition and cessation temporarily allowed the Hermannsburg Mission to operate independently of the Hanoverian state church which included the task of raising its own funds. However, that changed in 15 April 1890. Under Theodor Harms' son, Egmont Harms (1859–1916) the Hermannsburg Mission Society's neutral status ended when an official communion fellowship was declared between it and the Hanoverian state church. Representatives of the Hanoverian Evangelical Lutheran Free Church saw therein an attempt to drag the Hermannsburg Mission into unionism and thus decided at their Synodical conference on 14 June 1892 to establish their own mission society. The two resolutions passed that day would shape the mission of the Hanoverian Evangelical Lutheran Free Church from then on. First, they would see it as their duty of continuing the "old" Lutheran mission of the sainted Ludwig Harms, with priority on Africa, and, second, this mission society would run as a churchly organization, as the enterprise of the Hanoverian Evangelical Lutheran Free Church.[81]

Already the year before at the Synod of 1889, the Hanoverian Lutheran Free Church accepted two principle statements for her mission formulated by Heinrich (Wilhelm) Gerhold (1838–99): The Lutheran church can pursue only Lutheran mission, and Lutheran mission can only be pursued by the Lutheran church. These two principles looked closely at the relationship between the mission society and the sending church. The question about the relationship with an emerging church on the field came much later when in 1953 its director Friedrich Wilhelm Hopf (1910–82) added a third principle: Lutheran mission must lead to a Lutheran church. Thereby not only the mission enterprise but also the emerging churches on the field would define themselves from their base, the sending church.[82] In 1897 the local congregation in Bleckmar, the Ev. Lutherische St. Johannisgemeinde built a mission house (*Missionshaus*) at which candidates for the mission field in Africa were educated mainly by Pastor Friedrich Wolff (1841–1920). In 1899 Conrad Dreves (1837–1917), the director, published the official journal, the *Missionsblatt der Hannoverischen Ev.-Luth. Freikirche*. In South Africa, German speaking congregations formed their own Synod in 1897, The Free Evangelical Lutheran Synod in South Africa (FELSISA, *Freie Evangelisch Lutherische Synod in Südafrika*) while the Bleckmar missionaries operated parallel and independent of that Synod, even when some simultaneously served also as the Synod's pastor and president. By the outbreak of World War I, the Bleckmar Mission had sent out fourteen missionaries and pastors to South Africa to work among the German settlers and the Zulu and Tswana people.

81. Hans Peter Mahlke, ed., *Saint-Johannis-Gemeinde Bleckmar: Gemeindegeschichte 1878–2011* (Groß Oesingen: Lutherische Buchhandlung Harms, 2012), 53.
82. Volker Stolle, *Wer seine Hand an den Pflug legt*, 17–18.

By then the Bleckmar Mission had nine mission stations, 6500 baptized Zulu and Tswana Christians and twenty-one schools with a thousand children. Missionary Heinrich Prigge (1831–1920), who had left the Hermannsburg Mission in South Africa became the first superintendent on the field over the emerging congregations and missionaries.[83]

The above description of missions of the second type demonstrates that within the nineteenth century mission movement a neo-Lutheranism movement emerged that showed interest in missions but sought for it a confessional ecclesiological character, even when the institutional connection itself to a particular church did not always work out. The brothers Harms, Petri, Graul, and Löhe embraced an ecclesiology with her confession as her central core and which motivated the church to become involved in mission. With this approach to mission in the second type, they navigated between the first type that adopted unionism and the third mission type that focused on individual faith and internal motivation for missions.[84]

Nineteenth-century Lutheran mission must also be understood in the context of the large Lutheran emigrations that took place from Europe, mainly to North America and Australia, which reached their zenith between 1830 and 1850. Most Lutheran emigrants in this period came from confessional-minded Lutheran circles of which some were in territories that were affected by the Prussian union. In those years, nine out ten German Lutherans who emigrated went to North America. The emigration of Scandinavian Lutherans to North America also occurred in that period. In 1838 the first group of 665 German Lutherans came from the Margraviate of Brandenburg, Posen and Silesia and emigrated to South Australia under the leadership of Pastor August (Ludwig Christian) Kavel (1798–1860). In 1839 a group of 1,239 Lutherans mostly from Pomerania, but then also from the province of Saxony, Silesia and Berlin under the leadership of Carl Georg Heinrich von Rohr (1797–1874), and accompanied by Pastor Johann Andreas August Grabau (1804–79), left for Buffalo, New York and Wisconsin in North America. The cause for the immigration of these "old Lutheran" (*Altlutheraner*) parties was due to their stance towards unionism and Prussia's initial ban of their separatist movement of wanting to start free churches. Though that ban was eventually lifted, emigration to both continents continued well into the 1840s, so that in a ten year span, between the years 1835 and 1845, their number exceeded five thousand.

Parallel to the emigration of those who were connected to the Old Lutheran movement, was the emigration of another group from Saxony. In 1838 under the leadership of Pastor Martin Stephan (1777–1846), 800 Saxons emigrated from Germany to North America. Upon arriving at their destination, they separated with Stephan and their new leader became Carl

83. Hans Peter Mahlke, *Saint-Johannis-Gemeinde Bleckmar.* 12–15.57.

84. Scherer sees in their theology a dynamic relationship between mission, confession and office (ministry), see James Scherer, "The Triumph of Confessionalism in Nineteenth-Century German Lutheran Missions", *Missio Apostolica* 1, no. 2, (November 1993): 71–81.

Ferdinand Wilhelm Walther (1811–87). The theological direction Walther provided was the Saxons' unconditional subscription to the Lutheran Confessions. In 1847 they formed the Missouri Synod which had a polity and structure that affirmed both lay and ordained representation. Given the lack of pastors, the Missouri Synod reached out to fellow confessional Lutherans back in Germany for the provision of helpers. Such was the case in 1841, when Friedrich Wyneken (1810–76), known for being an itinerant Lutheran evangelist in North America, came to Germany bringing with him the letter, often called the *Notruf*, "The Distress of the German Lutherans in North America: Enjoined on their Fellow-Believers in the Native Country" (*Die Not der deutschen Lutheraner in Nordamerika. Ihren Glaubensgenossen ans Herz gelegt*), calling for the need of pastors to provide the German settlers with spiritual care. Wyneken attended meetings with Lutherans in Breslau (Huschke), Dresden (Trautmann), Neuendettelsau (Löhe) and Hanover (through correspondence with Petri). In a letter to Petri, dated 22 May 1842, which was read out loud to the leading confessional Lutheran participants of the Hanoverian Pentecost Conference (*Die Hannoverische Pfingstkonferenz*), Wyneken acknowledges that he is also familiar with Petri's missiological position and applying it to America he pleads that the help provided must go against ecclesial indifferentism. Mission "must be given by the entire Lutheran Community and from within it must rise preachers who are focused, churchly, vibrant in faith, sober, yet burning with love."[85] The most concerted and energetic response for this diaspora mission came from Wilhelm Löhe, first through his support group in Nuremberg and then later through his society in Neuendettelsau. Until the relationship with the Missouri Synod broke in 1853, Löhe had provided a substantial number of candidates to North America.[86] For a number of years the Hermannsburg Mission and its leader Ludwig Harms provided Missouri with preachers, forty-four in total, until the Missouri Synod and the Synodical Conference severed their ties with Hermannsburg in 1875 because of a disagreement over the doctrine of predestination. In 1860, C. F. W. Walther visited Hermannsburg to meet the Harms brothers. The Hermannsburg Mission had provided preachers for a number of Synods in North America. The Ohio Synod received the highest number, a total of sixty-nine preachers.[87] The continuation of providing helpers for North America then fell on Pastor Friedrich (August) Brunn (1819–95) in Steeden or Nassau to whom C. F. W. Walther paid a personal visit in July 1860.[88] In 1861 Friedrich Brunn, after confirming his doctrinal agreement with the Missouri Synod, began his pre-seminary school (*Proseminar*) in Steeden by preparing his first group of seven students as preach-

85. E. Petri, *D. Ludwig Adolf Petri: Ein Lebensbild* (Hannover: Verlag von Heinr. Feesche, 1888), 280.
86. Stolle, *Wer seine Hand an den Pflug legt*, 57–61.
87. Reinhard Müller, *Die vergessenen Söhne Hermannsburgs in Nordamerika* (Hermannsburg: Verlag der Missionshandlung Hermannsburg, 1989), 77–85, 186.
88. Wöhling, *Geschichte der Evangelisch-Lutherischen Freikirche in Sachsen u.a. Saint*, 19.

ers for North America. Brunn's mission concept was time bound, since his intent was to respond to a specific need of helping the German immigrants in North America. For him, their urgent call for help required a mission response that equaled the distressed call of the heathen. By 1886 when his society, the *Evangelisch-Lutherische Missionsanstalt*, and her school closed for lack of support, 250 students had received their preparatory theological education for the Missouri Synod in America.[89]

Not only did the Missouri Synod receive preachers from Germany, other synods such as the Iowa Synod did as well. On October 1870, Wilhelm Vilmar (1804–84), the brother of the famous Marburg theologian August Vilmar (1800–68), established in the town of Melsungen the Mission House for the Mission of Hesse (*Missionshaus für die hessische Mission*). Inspired by a presentation of the visiting professor Sigmund Fritschel of the Iowa Synod, Vilmar devoted himself to the task of raising preachers for the evangelical German immigrants in North America. Similar to Brunn's case, the instruction he provided for the young candidates was of a preparatory kind who upon arriving in North America received further education at Wartburg seminary of the Iowa Synod. In the first decade of its existence, the mission of Hesse sent out forty candidates, and in total fifty men, before the relations between Vilmar and the Iowa became strained and eventually broke.[90] Vilmar had insisted that his outgoing candidates would remain loyal subscribers to the Augsburg Confession and of his understanding of the ministry, which, however, was not the case at Wartburg. Wilhelm Vilmar had also been a leading figure in his home region in the formation of the free church, called the Lower Hesse Resistance (*niederhessische Renitenz*), which merged with other free churches in that territory to form in 1878 the Independent Evangelical-Lutheran Church in the Lands of Hesse (*Selbständige evangelisch-lutherischen Kirche in den hessischen Landen*).[91]

In the above mentioned cases, the task to help the immigrants in North America came from many support groups back in Germany who not only wished to help address the German immigrants' spiritual need but also to do so with the missionary intent to promote and preserve the pure and unadulterated Lutheran Confession.

NORTH AMERICA

Nineteenth century Lutheran missions in North America were shaped by three organizations: the General Synod (1820), the General Council (1867) and the Synodical Conference (1872). The greater evangelical ecumenical approach characterized the first two, whereas the latter pursued a stronger Lutheran confessional identity for her mission. In 1820 the General Synod formed, the first federation of Lutheran synods in North America to which

89. Stolle, *Wer seine Hand an den Pflug legt*, 62–68.
90. Stolle, *Wer seine Hand an den Pflug legt*, 69.
91. Stolle, *Wer seine Hand an den Pflug legt*, 80.

belonged the Synods of Pennsylvania, New York, North Carolina, the Joint Synod of Ohio, and the Synods of Maryland and Virginia. At the meeting of the West Pennsylvania Synod in Mechanicsburg, a central missionary society was formed at the behest of the General Synod with the intention

> to send the Gospel of the Son of God to the destitute portions of the Lutheran Church in the United States of America by means of missions; to assist for a season such congregations as are not able to support the Gospel; and, ultimately to co-operate in sending it to the heathen world.[92]

Later the name of the society was changed to The Foreign Missionary Society of the Evangelical Lutheran Church in the United States of America. Before the establishment of this central missionary society, mission had taken a congregation-based approach whereby each individually contributed to the work of foreign missions through the American Board, an inter-denominational organization. This domestic missionary work was conducted largely by the individual member synods. The General Synod sponsored foreign missions in Liberia, through the Synod of South Carolina, now a part of the United Synod in the South, which sent the African-American missionary Boston Drayton (1821–65) to Cape Palmas, the Republic of Maryland (later annexed to Liberia), Africa in 1845.[93]

Two appeals came from the foreign field to the Lutheran Church in America, one from missionary Carl Theophilus Ewald Rhenius (1790–1838), of the Church Mission Society in India, the other from Karl Gützlaff in China. It was decided to respond to the appeal of Rhenius and that John Christian Frederick Heyer (1793–1873) should go to India as the first missionary of the General Synod and of North America Lutherans. Thus, in April 1842, a hundred years after the arrival of Muhlenberg in America, missionary Heyer who was of German birth and had come to America when he was fourteen years old, left for India to become the "Apostle of Tirunelveli," a Tamil speaking region between Hyderabad and Guntur. Before that, from 1817 till 1841, he had been a home missionary laboring in difficult and widely divided fields in Pennsylvania, Maryland, Indiana, Kentucky, Illinois, and Missouri. Travelling from settlement to settlement often amid the greatest hardships, he had established churches and Sunday schools.[94] When it appeared probable that difficulties would arise on account of the connection with the inter-denominational American Board, under whose direction Heyer was to go, he resigned. In 1841 he was sent by the Ministerium of the Pennsylvania Synod, which had withdrawn from the General Synod after the first meeting.

92. Luther Benaiah Wolf, ed., *Missionary Heroes of the Lutheran Church* (Philadelphia, PA: The Lutheran Publication Society, 1911), 21.
93. *The African Repository*, Volume 43 (Washington: W. Moore Printer, 1866), 34; for a summary of the beginnings of Foreign American Lutheran Mission, see Wolf, *Missionary Heroes of the Lutheran Church*, 17–35.
94. Andrew S. Burgess, ed., *Lutheran World Mission* (Minneapolis: Augsburg, 1954), 61,

Heyer's work in the region of Guntur and Rajahmundry gave birth to the Andhra Evangelical Lutheran Church in 1927, a Telugu church, which had formed into a synod as early as 1853.[95]

The General Council of the Evangelical Lutheran Church of North America was founded in 1867 by those who desired a greater commitment to the Lutheran Confessions than what the General Synod offered. It also pursued missions in North America, mainly to the immigrants from representatives of the eleven Synods that joined it at its first convention. These developments among the Lutherans in North America left their mark on the foreign mission field. The aforementioned Lutheran church in Andhra Pradesh was divided. The southern part of the region around Guntur was taken over by the General Synod, and the churches in the northern region around Rajahmundry were given to the General Council. However, broader ecumenical cooperation continued among North American mission operations for India and other fields. From 1879, the Augustana Synod, which was established in 1860 by Swedish immigrants and a member of the United Norwegian Lutheran Church in America, that had formed in 1890, also worked in this region, supporting and connected to the work among the Santal of the Norwegian Missionary Society at Stavanger, Norway. From 1895, the Lutheran missions working in Andhra Pradesh held joint conferences biennially, and worked together with other Lutheran churches in India such as the Northern Evangelical Lutheran Church (NELC), whose roots go back to the aforementioned Norwegian Santal mission or with the South Andhra Lutheran Church (SALC). The SALC was the second Telugu-speaking Lutheran church, which traced its origin back to the year 1865 when August Mylius (1816–93) of the Hermannsburg Mission Society (HELM) in Germany began his evangelistic work in the southern part of Andhra. These efforts to unify Lutheran churches in India, which began as early as 1853, led in 1908 to the first of several All-India Lutheran conferences. In 1926, despite the language, ethnic, and regional diversity, nine Lutheran churches in India formed the Federation of Evangelical Lutheran Churches in India (FELCI) without surrendering their autonomy and identity. This Lutheran union shared a common liturgy and maintained a theological college, Gurukul in Madras. In 1998 the name was changed to United Evangelical Lutheran Church in India. Its current membership lists twelve Evangelical Lutheran Church bodies in India, of which the majority trace their roots back to either the Scandinavian (Danish, Swedish and Norwegian), North American or German missionaries.[96] The mission work of the Synodical Conference in India, particularly through its member the Lutheran Church—Missouri Synod, beginning in 1894 with her first missionary, Näther, steered her own course and from her

95. Wolf, *Missionary Heroes of the Lutheran Church*, 93–115; Martin Luther Dolbeer, Jr., *A History of Lutheranism in the Andhra Desa (The Telugu Territory of India)* (New York: Board for Foreign Missions, The United Lutheran Church in America, 1959), 41–66.

96. Dolbeer, *A History of Lutheranism in the Andhra Desa*, 179–224, 338.

work emerged the India Evangelical Lutheran Church (IELC) which established her own Lutheran college in Nagercoil.[97]

Since doctrinal interests guided Lutheranism in North America, and since certain doctrinal issues like chiliasm, pulpit and altar fellowship, and membership of secret societies were left unclarified, the Synodical Conference was founded in 1872 which became the leading voice of Confessional Lutheranism in the United States for almost one hundred years. Its mission approach was shaped and influenced by active support groups and their leaders from Germany.

The basic mission strategy at home for Lutherans in North America, whether it was the pastor, the lay person, the congregation, the district or the Synod, was that all were driven by a compassionate mission to reach out to their fellow countrymen. Scandinavian, Slovak and German Lutheran communities focused on their affiliated ethnic immigrants, but it was in particular a concerted effort of the confessional-minded Lutheran pastors of the Synodical Conference. Missionaries were stationed at important cities and ports to receive and guide immigrants in their own language to churches where they planned to settle, and itinerant preachers devoted their time and efforts to travel on horseback to gather Lutherans into worshipping communities, a strategy called *Sammelmission*. For example, Stephanus Keyl (1838–1905), the son-in-law of C. F. W. Walther and a pastor of the Missouri Synod, was called in 1869 to New York City and served until 1905 as Missouri's immigrant missionary and as caretaker of "the Pilgrim House" (*Lutherisches Pilgerhaus*) welcoming and sheltering German immigrants, as well as Swedes and Norwegians.[98] Jacob Aall Ottesen (1825–1904) was a pioneer missionary and founder of the Norwegian Lutheran Synod (1853), a tireless circuit rider to mission stations among Norwegian settlers stretching between Green Bay and Milwaukee, and around the city of Manitowoc. For the scattered German settlers in the Midwest, in particular to the hundreds of Germans in Indiana's Allen, Adams, Noble, Kendall, Whitley and Marshall Counties, the missionary Friedrich Conrad Dietrich Wyneken (1810–76) was from September 1838 onwards a circuit rider devoted to the cause of bringing them together into worshipping communities. Wyneken was affiliated with the Mission Committee of the Pennsylvania Synod. He resided in Fort Wayne, where he also pastored St. Paul's Lutheran church, while undertaking his missionary journeys in the surrounding area. Friedrich Wilhelm Hussmann (1807–81) and other missionary pastors were sent from the Bremen (missionary) Society for Protestant Germans America. There were two in 1840 and another five in 1842, of whom two came to Wyneken's assistance so that he could embark in 1841 or 1842 on his journey to

97. William J. Danker, "Into all the World," in *Moving Frontiers: Readings in the History of the Lutheran Church—Missouri Synod*, ed. Carl S. Meyer (St. Louis: CPH, 1964), 299–303.

98. Paul Rösener, *Unser erster Emigrantenmissionar, Pastor Stephanus Keyl* (St. Louis, MO: Concordia Publishing House, 1908).

Germany to seek help for the German settlers through his distress letter and through meetings with important Lutheran representatives. One important responder was Wilhelm Sihler (1801–85) from the region of Silesia, who became Wyneken's successor at St. Paul's Lutheran Church in Fort Wayne and the founder of the seminary at Fort Wayne.[99] Next to Walther and Wyneken, Sihler was a key figure in the formation of the confessional Lutheran orientation of the Missouri Synod's mission. Wyneken moved on to Baltimore and then St. Louis to serve as pastor. He succeeded C. F. W. Walther as the second president of the German Evangelical-Lutheran Synod of Missouri, Ohio and Other States (*Deutsche evangelisch-lutherische Synode von Missouri, Ohio und anderen Staaten*) established in 1847.[100]

While the promotion of Lutheran consciousness and the gathering of German settlers marked the first mission initiatives of the Missouri Synod, it soon established in 1851 a mission board, Board of Missions of the Lutheran Church—Missouri Synod, chaired by Ferdinand Sievers (1816–93), who held that position till his death in 1893. Ferdinand Sievers was born in Lüneburg, Germany. After ordination through the consistory of the Hanoverian state church and because of his connection with Wilhelm Löhe, he emigrated to North America to became the founding pastor of St Paul's Lutheran Church in Frankenlust, one of the four settlements of Franconian Lutherans in the Saginaw Valley. He conducted a number of mission trips to explore new, and to investigate current, mission sites. In 1851, he visited central Wisconsin for a possible mission site. In 1853, he visited the Bethany Mission in Michigan, and in 1856, the Minnesota Territory for mission possibilities among the Chippewa Indians and German Lutherans living there. In spite of Sievers' constant prodding and plea for missions, the year 1868 marked the official end of the Synod's mission to the Native Americans.[101]

National mission activity also extended to the Jewish community in New York in 1883 through Daniel Landsmann (1836–96) and by 1882 to the English speaking Lutherans in southern Missouri, Kansas, and Arkansas, after the Brethren of the English Conference in Missouri had petitioned the Synod to make arrangements for it. A committee was formed, which in turn obliged Pastor Andrew Baepler (1850–1927) of Mobile, Alabama to head up that important work. The Synodical Conference started mission work among the African-Americans in the city of New Orleans and the states of Arkansas and Alabama. At the Synodical Conference at Emmanuel Lutheran Church in Fort Wayne in 1877, the aforementioned Herman Amberg Preus, president of the Norwegian Lutheran Synod, submitted an important question: Had the time finally come for the Synodical Conference to direct its mission at-

99. Johann Christoph Wilhelm Lindemann, *Friedrich Konrad Dietrich Wyneken: An Evangelist Among the Lutherans of North America*, trans. Sieghart Rein (Sieghart Rein and Concordia Theological Seminary, 2010), 19.

100. Lindemann, *Friedrich Konrad Dietrich Wyneken*, 36–42.

101. Heerboth, "Missouri Synod Approach to Mission in the Early Period," 62–63; Danker, "Into all the World," 296.

tention to work among the blacks and Indians of this country? The response was affirmative. A three-member Board for the African-American Mission (Colored Mission) was formed, comprised of two pastors, Johann Friedrich Buenger (1810–82) and Karl Friedrich Wilhelm Sapper (1833–1911), and a layman from Buenger's congregation, John Umbach, all three Missouri Synod members. That same year, in 1877 at the Western District convention of the Missouri Synod meeting in Altenburg, Missouri, missionary John Frederick Doescher (1840–1916) was dispatched as the Synodical Convention's first missionary to the African-American freedmen. By 1878, he settled in New Orleans and started a Sunday School which then became Zion Lutheran Church. He opened also a second congregation, St Paul's Lutheran Church, whose facility was temporarily used for the Lutheran College that was opened in 1903 by missionary Pastor Franz Friedrich Wilhelm Jakob Lankenau (1868–1939) of the Synodical Conference. Lankenau, who authored the book, *The World is our Field: A Missionary Survey*, (1928) also opened a Lutheran college and a Lutheran parochial school. Both college and parochial school closed, in 1910 and 1925 respectively, when the Synodical Conference decided to commit her resources to work in Alabama and the college there. In 1878, Frederick Berg (1868–1939) was sent to Little Rock, Arkansas where he started St. Paul's Colored Lutheran Church and its parochial school. In the monthly English periodical, *The Lutheran Pioneer*, starting publication in 1879, the Synodical Conference kept close track of the progress of colored mission. By 1890 a total of seven mission stations existed: four in New Orleans, one in Little Rock, one in Meherrin, Virginia, and one in Springfield, Illinois. By 1894 the Synodical Conference reported that its mission among the freedmen had seven missionaries, nine teachers, thirteen congregations, 958 souls, 475 communicant members, 760 parochial and 1,042 Sunday School children. The Board members were: Karl Sapper (president), Professor Franz August Otto Pieper (1852–1931; vice president), and Professor August C. Burgdorf (1838–1930; secretary and treasurer).[102]

The mission among African Americans in North Carolina on 8 May 1889 led to the formation of the Alpha Synod of the Evangelical Lutheran Church of Freedmen in America. It consisted of four African-American pastors who were members of the North Carolina Synod with David Koonts (1844–90), the first African-American ordained in the Lutheran church, as her president. In 1891, when the North Carolina Synod failed to continue her support of the Alpha Synod, the Synodical Conference stepped in and took over the work among the African-Americans in North Carolina. The Norwegian born missionary Nils J. Bakke (1853–1921), who had served as missionary in New Orleans among the African-American population was transferred in 1891 to North Carolina, where he and compatriot missionary John C.

102. Lenker, *Lutherans in all Lands*, 798; Danker, "Into all the World," 317–321; Roosevelt Gray, "The History of LCMS Mercy Work with African Americans," 1–7; accessed 31 May 2020, https://blogs.lcms.org/2016/essay/essay-the-history-of-lcms-mercy-work-with-african-americans.

Schmidt (1870–1949) became instrumental in the formation of Immanuel College at Greensboro, at which Bakke served as president from 1903–10. Bakke should be noted for his long service in the Missouri Synod's mission among the African-Americans that had focused especially on the education of African-Americans.[103]

In the beginning years of the Missouri Synod, foreign mission amounted to support given to the German Lutheran societies of Leipzig and Hermannsburg Mission Societies until that relationship came to an end in the 1870s. Sievers' call for starting foreign mission intensified especially at that time. In 1893, the Mission Board for Foreign Missions was formed with Carl Manthey Zorn (1846–1928) and Johann Friedrich Zucker (1842–1927) as members. In 1894, at the convention at St. Charles, Missouri, the missionaries Karl Gustav Theodore Näther (1866–1904) and Franz Edward Mohn (1867–1925) were dispatched to India.[104] This mission resulted from a dispute about Scripture and the Lutheran Confessions among the Leipzig missionaries in India. A group of three Leipzig missionaries who had been sent to India in the years 1871 and 1873, namely Alfred Heinrich Grubert (1848–76), Carl Manthey Zorn, and Otto (Heinrich Theodor) Willkomm (1847–1933), who were later joined by two other missionaries, Eduard Schäffer (1842–90) and Johann Friedrich Zucker, expressed their concerns in a letter addressed to the society's leadership, the directors Julius Hardeland and Johann Heinrich Carl Codes (1813–92), over the lack of the society's commitment to confessional Lutheranism. That letter was to be treated as a letter of their resignation as missionaries of the society which they did not reverse in spite of Hardeland's visit to India in 1876 and his attempts to address the group's concerns. Stating their case in a publication, *Mannhafte Erklärung von fünf Missionaren der Leipziger Mission* (1876), they came to the defense of the Missouri Synod's doctrinal position, which all four missionaries planned to join except for Schäffer who remained behind in India.[105] On their journey from India, missionary Grubert fell ill in Germany and Willkomm was called to become the pastor of the congregation in Crimmitschau, Germany of the Evangelical Lutheran Free Church (*Ev. Lutherische Freikirche*). In the

---

103. Gray, "The History of LCMS Mercy Work with African Americans," 7–10; Christopher F. Drewes, *Half a Century of Lutheranism Among Our Colored People* (St. Louis, MO: Concordia Publishing House, 1927).

104. The Board also passed an important strategic eight-point policy statement, see Herman Koppelmann, "The First Decade of Our India Mission," *Concordia Historical Institute Quarterly* 27 (January 1955): 167.

105. "Erklärung der Missionare Grubert, Schäffer, Willkomm, Zorn, und Zucker vom November 1875," in *Quellen zur Entstehung und Entwicklung selbständiger evangelisch-lutherischer Kirchen in Deutschland*, ed. Manfred Roensch und Werner Klän (Frankfurt am Main; Bern; New York; Paris: Peter Lang, 1987), 429–41: "*Wir halten die Missourier für treue Lutheraner, für Solche, die nicht nur Lutheraner heißen, sondern es auch sind: die sich nicht herausnehmen, in allerlei Weise mit Schrift und Bekenntniß umzuspringen, sondern an beiden halten. Wir danken Gott inbrünstig dafür, daß er so tapfere Bekenner der reinen Lehre erweckt hat, und freuen uns in dem ewigen Lichte, das durch sie nun auf den Leuchter gestellt ist.*"

end, only Zorn and Zucker arrived in North America to become pastors in the Missouri Synod. Zorn became a pastor in Sheboygan, Wisconsin and then Cleveland, Ohio, while Zucker became a pastor in Brooklyn, New York, and in 1879 professor at the Concordia College in Fort Wayne, Indiana. The travel expenses were covered by C. F. W. Walther with funds from the collections at their mission festivals and that had been originally designated for the Leipzig Society.[106]

In 1892, at a meeting of Leipzig missionaries in India, Karl Gustav Theodor Näther presented a paper on verbal inspiration, in which he argued from Scripture, Matthew 20:25 in particular, for a change in the Leipzig society's leadership. He argued for a change from a hierarchical style to one that was fraternal, willing to listen to the complaints of missionaries and to accept correction. This caused tension among the missionaries and the mission leadership, with the latter issuing Näther a strong reprimand of being insubordinate. Missionary Franz Eduard Mohn supported Näther's cause. Though the society's leadership structure was *iure humano*, the Leipzig's board position remained rigid, with the result that in January 1894 both missionaries were officially dismissed from the Leipzig society. They left for Germany and joined the Evangelical Lutheran Free Church and eventually made their way to North America, where Näther and Mohn were sent out back to India in 1894 at the Missouri Synod's Convention at St. Charles, Missouri. Mohn actually arrived two years later, in 1896 after recuperating from illness in Germany. Two other missionaries from Germany joined them on the field, Otto Kellerbauer (1868–1914) and Reinhold Freche (1862–1923). Out of respect to their former Leipzig missionaries, Näther chose an area for his mission at Krishnagiri, and each of the other three missionaries established their own mission stations in close proximity along the road from Madras to Bangalore: Barugur (Kellerbauer, 1895–1914), Vanyiyambadi (Freche, 1897–1915), and Ambur (Mohn 1896–1913). Näther contracted the bubonic plague when conducting the funeral of a young boy and passed away in 1904. Näther's pregnant wife Ida returned to Germany.[107]

Lutheran mission work in India had endured a crisis. In the end, the Missouri Synod benefitted by creating its mission: the Missouri Evangelical Lutheran India Mission (MELIM). The discussions on Scripture and the Lutheran Confessions arose among the missionaries regarding doctrine and also, for Näther, pertaining to their status on the mission field in relation to the leadership back home. No questions were raised about the missionaries' status in relation to the task of raising and sharing ministry with a local, indigenous church (*bodenständige Kirche*) and her own pastors and congregations, which had already occupied the thoughts of Leipzig's first director, Karl Graul. In contrast, by the mid-nineteenth century among the English

106. Stolle, *Wer seine Hand an den Pflug legt*, 82–89.
107. Hans Kirsten, "Pioneer Missionaries of MELIM," *Concordia Historical Institute Quarterly* 56, no. 3 (Fall 1983): 116–132; Stolle, *Wer seine Hand an den Pflug legt*, 85.

speaking missionaries indigeneity was widely discussed. For example, missionary Henry Venn (1796–1873) of the Church Mission Society and chairman Rufus Anderson of the American Board of Commissioners for Foreign Missions, each proposed the strategic principles of the three self: self-supporting, self-governing, and self-propagating (self-extending).

The confessional cause in missions became one of the causes of the Synodical Conference (1872), in particular over against the Synodical Council. The Synodical Conference's members were the Illinois, Minnesota, Missouri, Norwegian, Ohio and Wisconsin synods. The Missouri Synod's own periodicals: *Der Lutheraner* and its English version the *Lutheran Witness*, *Lehre und Wehre*, an English translation of German Lutheran hymns for the English Lutheran missions, the *St. Louis Theological Monthly*, the *Missionstaube*, and *The Lutheran Pioneer*—each guided, informed and shaped the home and foreign mission of the Missouri Synod, Ohio and other states. The ecclesial confessional character of mission came to the fore also from the pulpit, for example, through a mission sermon that C. F. W. Walther preached on Isaiah 43:21 entitled "The Mission Society Established by God." Walther looked back praising the work of mission societies, yet he pushed beyond them and argued for a missionary ecclesiology:

> Nevertheless, the mission societies that had arisen and were a sign of the newly awakened Christian life were also at the same time a sign that the situation in the church as a whole was not what it ought to be. For where the situation is as it should be, it should not be necessary to form small mission societies in the church, but the whole church must itself be a great mission society. The Lord has established it to be exactly this.[108]

Walther places the missionary obligation on the church. Thus, further in the sermon he answers his own rhetorical question, "Who is it then, to whom the responsibility to preach the Gospel among all the people on earth has been committed after the death of the apostles?" as follows:

> The true mission society that has been instituted by God Himself is nothing else than *the Christian church itself*, that is the totality of all those who believe in Jesus Christ . . . This means that Christ was not content just to give faith as an invisible thing to those who belong to his church, but he also gathers them by the visible sign of Holy Baptism into outward visible congregations.[109]

By making the church the true mission society, Walther places the mission obligation on every Christian, the priestly tribe: "Let us never forget

108. C. F. W. Walther, "The Mission Society Established by God—Is. 43:21" in C. F. W. Walther, *The Word of His Grace: Occasional and Festival Sermons* (Lake Mills, IA: Graphic Publishing Company, 1978), 17–26, 19.
109. Walther, "The Mission Society Established by God," 20.

that through Holy Baptism we have all joined the mission society which God himself has established"[110] and he adds a strong ethical reprimand:

> For if the entire church is the real mission society which God Himself has established, then all those who ignore mission work and do not care to do anything for it certainly are not true and living members of the church, that is, not true Christians. They break the oath of allegiance which they have made to Christ at their baptism. They want to carry the keys of the kingdom of heaven in their hands and yet do not want to open heaven to those who are still outside. They want to be spiritual priests and yet do not do the work of a priest.[111]

We have here an ecclesiological definition of mission that became a concern for many Lutherans in the nineteenth century. Though not unanimous on ministry and church polity, they all seemed to have agreed that mission, though initially pursued by mission societies and pious believers, was ultimately an ecclesial concern. In addition, that pursuit of ecclesial mission included also an intentional oversight of the church over her missionaries' preaching and teaching, demanding from them an accountability to teach the church's faith purely and unadulterated. In his short treatise "Why Should Our Pastors, Teachers and Professors Subscribe Unconditionally to the Symbolical Writings of Our Church," Walther points out that such an unconditional subscription was required of all her preachers in the church at their ordination, namely, an oath that the Symbolical Books' doctrinal content, including their condemnations "is in full agreement with Scripture and does not militate against Scripture in any point, whether that point be of major or minor importance."[112] As a result, every missionary elect was directly responsible to the Synod's board requiring its approval to where and how to begin his work. The board for its part, as the three member board for colored mission stated at its formation in 1877, would "appoint only such pastors for missionary work who were already affiliated with a synod within the conference, and who were found worthy in doctrine and life." This procedure of selecting the candidate gave Lutheran mission both an ecclesial and confessional format, and though a child of the nineteenth century, would provide for North American mission a lasting paradigm for mission into the twenty-first century.

Klaus Detlev Schulz is a professor at Concordia Theological Seminary, Fort Wayne, Indiana.

---

110. Walther, "The Mission Society Established by God," 24.
111. Walther, "The Mission Society Established by God," 23.
112. Walther, C. F. W. "Why Should Our Pastors, Teachers and Professors Subscribe Unconditionally to the Symbolical Writings of Our Church" *Concordia Theological Monthly* 18 no. 4 (April 1947): 241–253, especially p. 241.

BIBLIOGRAPHY

Aagaard, Johannes. *Mission, Konfession, Kirche: Die Problematik ihrer Integration im 19 Jahrhundert in Deutschland.* Vols. I and II. Denmark: Gleerups, 1967.

Baierlein, Eernst R. *In the Wilderness with the Red Indians: German Missionary to the Michigan Indians, 1847–1853.* Translated by Anita Z. Boldt. Detroit, MI: Wayne State University Press, 1996.

Drewes, Christopher F. *Half a Century of Lutheranism Among Our Colored People.* St. Louis, MO: Concordia Publishing House, 1927.

Furberg, Tore. *Kyrka och mission i Sverige 1868–1901.* Uppsala: Almqvist & Wiksells Boktryckeri AB, 1962.

Graul, Karl. *Die evangelisch-lutherische Mission zu Dresden an die evangelisch-lutherische Kirche aller Lande: Vorwärts oder Rückwärts.* Leipzig, 1845.

Gray, Roosevelt. "The History of LCMS Mercy Work with African Americans." (lcms.org/blackministry).

Haccius, Georg. *Hannoverische Missionsgeschichte* II. Hermannsburg, 1910.

Harms, Hartwig. *Hamburg und die Mission des 19. Jahrhunderts: Kirchlich-missionarische Vereine 1814 bis 1836.* Hamburg: Friedrich Wittig Verlag, 1973.

Heerboth, Paul M. "Missouri Synod Approach to Mission in the Early Period." *Missio Apostolica* 1, no. 1 (May 1993): 19–26.

Imberg, Rune. "Dr. Krapf-the (Almost) Forgotten Missionary Pioneer." *Swedish Missiological Themes* 98, no. 1 (2010): 49–67.

Kirsten, Hans. "Pioneer Missionaries of MELIM." *Concordia Historical Institute Quarterly* 56:3 (Fall 1983): 116–132.

Krumwiede, Hans-Walter. *Kirchengeschichte Niedersachsens: Zeiter Band: Vom Deutschen Bund 1815 bis zur Gründung der Evangelischen Kirche.* Göttingen: Vandenhoek & Ruprecht, 1996.

Lenker, John Nicholas. *Lutherans in all Lands: The Wonderful Works of God.* Vols. 1–2. Fourth revised and enlarged edition. Milwaukee, WI: Lutherans in all lands Company, 1894.

Lindemann, Johann Christoph Wilhelm. *Friedrich Konrad Dietrich Wyneken: An Evangelist Among the Lutherans of North America.* Translated by Sieghart Rein. Fort Wayne, IN: Concordia Theological Seminary Bookstore, 2010.

Löhe, Wilhelm. *Three Books About the Church.* Philadelphia, PA: Fortress Press, 1969.

Maurer, Wilhelm. "Der lutherische Beitrag zur Weltmission der Kirche Jesu Christi." *Evangelische Missionszeitschrift* (August 1969): 170–187.

Müller, Reinhard. *Die vergessenen Söhne Hermannsburgs in Nordamerika.* Hermannsburg: Verlag der Missionshandlung Hermannsburg, 1989.

Petri, Ludwig Adolph. *Mission and the Church: A Letter to a Friend.* Translated by David Buchs. Fort Wayne, IN: Concordia Theological Seminary Bookstore, 2012.

Rösener, Paul. *Unser erster Emigrantenmissionar:Pastor Stephanus Keyl.* (St. Louis, MO: Concordia, 1908.

Scherer, James. "The Triumph of Confessionalism in Nineteenth-Century German Lutheran Missions." *Missio Apostolica* I, no. 2, (November 1993): 71–81.

Schreiner, Lothar. "Nommensen, Ingwer Ludwig." In *Biographical Dictionary of Christian Missions,* edited by Gerald H. Anderson, 499–500. New York: Macmillan Reference USA, 1998.

Stolle, Volker. *Wer seine Hand an den Pflug legt: Die missionarische Wirksamkeit der selbständigen evangelisch-lutherischen Kirchen in Deutschland im 19. Jahrhundert.* Gross-Oesingen: Lutherische Buchhandlung Harms, 1992.

Vorländer, Hermann. *Church in Motion: The History of the Evangelical Lutheran Mission in Bavaria.* Eugene, OR: Pickwick Publications, 2018.

Walther, C. F. W. "The Mission Society Established by God—Is. 43:21." In *The Word of His Grace: Occasional and Festival Sermons,* 17–26. Lake Mills, IA: Graphic Publishing Company, 1978.

Walther, C. F. W. "Why Should Our Pastors, Teachers and Professors Subscribe Unconditionally to the Symbolical Writings of Our Church." *Concordia Theological Monthly* XVIII (April 1947): 241–253.

Lutheranism in the Twentieth Century

MARK BRAUN

EARLY IN THE LAST CENTURY, Theodore Roosevelt said the Lutheran Church was "destined to become one of the two or three greatest and most important churches in the United States."[1] In 1961 Winthrop Hudson believed that Lutheranism was in position to be a "secret weapon" for Christian renewal in the modern age. The Lutheran Church, Hudson felt, was more insulated than Protestantism from "the theological erosion which so largely stripped other denominations of an awareness of their continuity with a historic Christian tradition."[2] Mark Noll wrote in 1992 that, contrasted with American Evangelicals who "waste away with panting for the supernatural quick fix," and with American liberals who "want to fix things by themselves and right away," Lutherans' sense of history "stands as a sober witness. Its wisdom lies in the realization of how great are the follies of humanity, how constant the grace of God."[3]

High praise, especially from observers outside the Lutheran tribe. Did the church body during this twentieth century live up to such lofty estimations? Lutheranism experienced an accelerated adaptation to American life, struggles in wartime Europe, numerical growth, and organizational amalgamation. Yet as the century drew to a close, Lutheranism has experienced statistical decline, uncertainty of purpose, and even a crisis of identity.

WAR ON GERMANS

In the early 1900s, while many Lutherans in the eastern United States had long since transitioned to the use of English, Synodical Conference Lutherans and other Midwest Lutheran bodies still used the languages of their

1. Theodore Roosevelt, *Presidential Addresses and State Papers* (New York: Review of Reviews Co., 1910), III, 206–207; cited by E. Clifford Nelson, *Lutheranism in North America, 1914–1970* (Minneapolis, MN: Augsburg, 1972), 136.
2. Winthrop Hudson, *American Protestantism: History of American Civilization* (Chicago: University of Chicago Press, 1961), 33, 176.
3. Mark A. Noll, "The Lutheran Difference," *First Things* 20 (February 1992): 37.

European homelands. As late as 1911, while ninety-five percent of communicants in the United Synod of the South and eighty percent of General Synod churches used English exclusively, only thirteen percent in the Ohio Synod and three percent in the Synodical Conference worshiped in English.[4]

Whatever their political leanings, many German-Americans clung fiercely to their ethnic identities. As late as 1915, the Missouri Synod's German magazine, the *Abendschule*, featured stories expressing appreciation for German political leaders and support for their cause.[5] Concordia St. Louis Professors Friedrich Bente and W. H. T. Dau played prominent roles in the American Neutrality Leagues, characterized as "rather shadowy organizations" founded to mobilize public sentiment against American involvement in the Great War.[6] But after the United States entered World War I in 1917, German Lutherans were no longer viewed as nonthreatening outsiders. Most members of foreign language synods were "only slightly incorporated into the life of their communities," and while they all anticipated acculturation would come someday," they thought that day was "far into the future, after many more generations of slow adjustment."[7]

German-American Lutheran leaders advised their members to demonstrate their allegiance to the United States. *The Lutheran Witness* advised Missouri Synod members to display the American flag, buy war bonds, and welcome speakers promoting the work of the Red Cross. But their neighbors quickly came to view German Lutherans with suspicion. The state of Minnesota established a Committee of Public Safety to investigate alleged disloyalty among state residents, especially German-Americans.[8] By early 1919 measures were introduced into the state legislatures of Ohio, Iowa, Missouri, and Nebraska, which would have made it unlawful to teach in elementary schools using any other language than English.[9] Opposition was most intense in Nebraska, where the State Council targeted three as suspicious, two of which were the state's German-American population and "conspicuous leaders" in the Lutheran Church. "Perhaps never in history," reported the Council, had it been deemed necessary for a public body "to single out by name a great church organization and appeal to the patriotism of its mem-

4. "Church News and Comment," *The Lutheran Witness* (*LuthW*) 30 (28 September 1911): 157.
5. "Aus der Zeit fuer die Zeit," *Abendschule* 61 (February 4, 1915): 417; "Der unbesieglich Wahlspruch: Mit Gott!" (18 February 1915): 449; "Deutschlands Schirm und Schutz," (29 April 1915): 609; "Der Friedens Kaiser," (29 April 1915): 618.
6. Alan Graebner, "The Acculturation of an Immigrant Church: The Lutheran Church—Missouri Synod, 1917–1929," (PhD diss., Columbia University, New York, 1965), 39–41.
7. Fred W. Meuser, "Business as Usual—Almost, 1900–1917," in E. Clifford Nelson, *The Lutherans in North America* (Minneapolis, MN: Fortress, 1975), 390–91.
8. Carol Jensen, "Loyalty as a Political Weapon: The 1918 Campaign in Minnesota," *Minnesota History* 47 (1981): 171–183; LaVern Rippley, "Conflict in the Classroom: Anti-Germanism in Minnesota Schools, 1917–1919, *Minnesota History* 43 (1972): 42–57, cited by Paul Marschke, "German Lutherans in Minnesota: Glimpses into the Americanization of a City Parish, 1890–1940," (Lutheran Historical Conference Essays, 1986), 20.
9. Niel M. Johnson, "The Missouri Synod Lutherans and the War against the German Language, 1917–1923," *Nebraska History* 56, (1975): 138–39.

bers to offset the dangerous tendencies of many of the conspicuous representatives of that organization."[10]

Wisconsin Synod Seminary Professor August Pieper, although advocating the change to English in church life, nonetheless voiced love for his mother tongue:

> It was primarily Luther who created the German language and made it the classic language of religion. Luther's whole intellect, feelings, and will were saturated with and under the control of the gospel. He made the Hebrew and Greek Bibles speak German and made them speak evangelically. It is stupid and thoughtless to say that one language is as good as another to define and transmit the gospel. Luther's German is a better vehicle of the gospel than any other modern language. Luther didn't really translate the Hebrew and Greek, he Germanized it, putting it into the language people speak at the market, or of a mother talking to her child. The church of the German Bible enjoys an unusual blessing.

Pieper considered English to be "a practical language, well-suited to the outstanding character trait of the English—materialism, the desire for what earth has to offer." He called English "a precise language" and said, "We need not fear that in the transition to English we will lose the clarity and precision of the doctrinal concepts of orthodox Lutheranism." But "the blessed warmth, the childlike quality, the bride-like beauty, the motherliness and fatherliness of the Hebrew, Greek, and German gospel can never be fully replicated in English."[11]

The language transition was easier among Lutherans who had migrated from Scandinavian countries, although often it was still painful. Some in the Augustana Synod opposed the use of English for preaching and worship on ideological grounds, but "the main reason for the reluctance to change was that most pastors simply were not very proficient in the new language and congregations generally did not demand it." As late as 1921, an estimated eighty-five percent of the sermons preached in the Augustana Synod were preached in Swedish, and few congregations used English exclusively.[12]

G. H. Gerberding of the United Lutheran Church observed in 1914, "We like to boast of the fact that the Gospel is preached in Lutheran pulpits in more languages than were heard on Pentecost in Jerusalem," but he admitted that these many languages were sometimes a "heavy cross." At the bottom of much of the

---

10. *Nebraska State Journal* (July 10, 1917); cited by Robert N. Manley, "Language, Loyalty, and Liberty: The Nebraska State Council of Defense and the Lutheran Churches, 1917–1918," *Concordia Historical Institute Quarterly* (*CHIQ*) 37, no. 1 (April 1964): 3–4.
11. August Pieper, "Unser Übergang ins Englische," *Theologische Quartalschrift* (*Qu*) 15, no. 4 (October 1918): 233–259; trans. John C. Jeske, "Our Transition into English," *Wisconsin Lutheran Quarterly* (*WLQ*) 100, no. 2 (Spring 2003): 91–92.
12. George M. Stephenson, *The Religious Aspects of Swedish Immigration* (Minneapolis, MN: University of Minnesota Press, 1932), 459, 473; cited by Maria Erling and Mark Granquist, *The Augustana Story: Shaping Lutheran Identity in North America* (Minneapolis, MN: Augsburg Fortress, 2008), 100–101.

aversion to the change to English, Gerberding charged, was "language prejudice."[13] By 1939, after the transition was mostly completed, Theodore Buenger addressed repeated the criticism, "Why did they not start English work sooner? Why did they preach the Gospel in German only?" He continued:

> It never was their policy to preach in German only. One of the silliest slanders I ever heard is that our fathers said the Word of God could not be preached in English and retain its purity. . . . Our Synod did not have enough clergymen to take care of the German Protestant immigrants, whom they were best fitted to serve. . . . We are . . . justified in claiming that we did supply the spiritual needs of the German immigrants. That has been our historic mission. It was the Lord's doing that our Synod provided, so to say, for its own household first.[14]

WAR IN GERMANY

In Germany, the Nazi party in the early 1930s increased its influence on the German parliament, and several groups developed with the intention of establishing a more distinctly German form of Christianity. One was the Confederation for a German Christianity (*Bund für deutsche Kirche*), which later called itself the German Christians or *deutsche Christen*. Another, the Faith Movement, regarded race and ethnic background to be part of God's created order; it opposed intermarriage between Jews and Christians, and refused to include Jews in the national church. Hitler supported such efforts as part of wider efforts at "coordination" (*Gleichschaltung*), bringing structures in German society into greater alignment with Nazi party goals. The Protestant Reich Church allowed only Aryan Christians to belong to the church.[15] A national synod of the German Evangelical Church issued the Barmen Declaration in 1934, which attempted to reject government claims on the churches, but the declaration was viewed differently by various church leaders. It did not address persecution of the Jews or other Nazi measures. Leaders of the Old Prussian Union Churches also met to form the Confessing Church to oppose the German Christians.[16]

In the United States, evaluations of Hitler before 1939 were surprisingly positive. American Lutherans stressed patience, driven partly by a reluctance to criticize the German government and partly by a recognition that America's house was also completely in order.[17] Especially difficult was eval-

13. G. H. Gerberding, *Problems and Possibilities: Serious Considerations for All Lutherans* (Columbia, SC: Lutheran Board of Publication, 1914), 171.
14. Theo. Buenger, "Festival Address at the Academic Service Commemorating the Centennial of the Founding of Concordia Seminary, June 3, 1939," *Concordia Theological Monthly* (*CTM*) 10, no. 8 (August 1939): 612.
15. *A Documentary History of Lutheranism: From Enlightenment to the Present* (*DHL*) 2, ed. Eric Lund and Mark Granquist (Minneapolis, MN: Fortress, 2017), 181–82.
16. Victoria J. Barnett, "Barmen Confession," in *Dictionary of Luther and the Lutheran Tradition* (Grand Rapids, MI: Baker Academic), 73–74.
17. Frederick Ira Murphy, "The American Christian Press and Pre-War Hitler's Germany, 1933–1939," (PhD diss., University of Florida, 1970), 20.

uating events in Germany before the invasion of Poland. Many Lutherans in America followed events in Europe closely because they were of German ancestry and belonged to churches which maintained fellowship of some sort with German church bodies. The evils of Hitler's rule were not initially clear to them.[18]

Christian Eduard Luthardt, in *Die Ethik in ihren Grundzügen*, had maintained as early as 1867 that it was "not the vocation of Jesus Christ or of the Gospel to change the orders of secular life and establish them anew." Christ had "nothing to do with this sphere," according to Luthardt, but allowed the secular realm to go its own way. Luthardt thus introduced a dualism in the understanding of God's governance of the world, restricting Christianity to a personal sphere but denying the church any power to comment on political issues.[19] Anders Nygren observed that although Luther drew a clear line between spiritual and temporal authority and expressly emphasized that these two realms should not be confused, Luther's teaching came to be interpreted as if he had ". . . opened the door to the secularization of society and given a completely free hand to the State."[20] Most detestable was the attack William L. Shirer made on Luther and his teaching of the two kingdoms. Shirer charged that under Luther's influence "German Protestantism became the instrument of royal and princely absolutism," while German clergy became "completely servile to the political authority of the State." Protestant pastors "quite often supported the Nationalist and even the Nazi enemies of the Republic"[21]

Such accusations ignored that Luther "provided his followers with precise definitions of the circumstances under which tyrants may be removed by force of arms."[22] From early on, churches offered resistance against the government. Dietrich Bonhoeffer refused to submit to Hitler; any notion that one kingdom was a "divine, holy, supernatural, and Christian" kingdom, the other a "worldly, profane, natural, and unchristian" one, Bonhoeffer regarded as a "vulgarization" of Luther's teaching.[23] Writing on "The Church and the Jewish Question" in 1933, Bonhoeffer acknowledged that the church was not encouraged "to get involved directly in specific political actions of the state" but recognized that the existence of the state was "grounded in God's desire for preservation in the midst of the world's chaotic godlessness." Bon-

18. John P. Hellwege, Jr., "American Lutherans and the Problem of Pre-World War II Germany," *Concordia Theological Quarterly* (*CTQ*) 80, nos. 3 and 4 (July–October 2016): 309.
19. Richard V. Pierard, "The Lutheran Two-Kingdoms Doctrine and Subservience to the State in Modern Germany," *Journal of the Evangelical Theological Society* 29 (June 1986): 195–96.
20. Anders Nygren, "Luther's Doctrine of the Two Kingdoms," *Ecumenical Reviews* 1 (Spring 1949): 301.
21. William L. Shirer, *The Rise and Fall of the Third Reich: A History of Nazi Germany* (New York: Fawcett Crest, 1962), 236.
22. Uwe Siemon-Netto, *The Fabricated Luther: The Rise and Fall of the Shirer Myth* (St. Louis, MO: Concordia, 1995), 23–24.
23. Jean Bethke Elshtain, "Bonhoeffer and the Sovereign State," *FT* 65 (August-September 1996): 27.

hoeffer nevertheless saw three possible courses of action the church could take in regard to the state: first, it may question the legitimacy of the state's actions; second, it should provide service to victims of the state's actions, even victims who are not Christians; and third, it could "not just bind up the wounds of the victim beneath the wheel" but actually "seize the wheel itself," calling out the church for its failure to create law and order.[24]

Herman Sasse wrote during the 1930s and 1940s "opposing the attempted suppression of confessional Lutheranism by false unions styled after the nineteenth century Prussian Union," by Nazi efforts to create a "united" German church, and by Karl Barth's support for a united Evangelical church to oppose Nazi encroachment against the church.[25] The land churches of Bavaria, Hanover, and Würtemberg did not fall to the Nazis. Within the confessing church movement, Brother Councils (*Brüder-Räte*) were established to oppose Nazi influence in the churches. Confessional Lutherans refused to accept the Barmen Declaration because it "confused law and gospel" and "undermined the two-governances."[26]

Lutherans in Norway "believed that Christianity and Nazism were incompatible because racism and anti-Semitism defied the Christian doctrine" of the worth of every human being. Bishop Eivind Berggrav led the Norwegian church in opposing the Nazi regime; Berggrav maintained that duty to God and conscience could also include duty to disobey a demonic or tyrannical state.[27] Norwegian bishops resigned *en masse* from the State Church in 1942.[28]

Following the war, Russian historian Moisei Mendelevich Smirin published a study of Thomas Müntzer that presented Müntzer as champion of the "people's reformation." Peasants bound to feudal landlords and deprived of even a minimum of political rights were encouraged by Müntzer to instigate revolution. According to Smirin, Müntzer envisioned "a classless society where property was held in common—a kingdom of God on earth." Müntzer judged Luther negatively, firmly believing that after the Word was given by the Lutherans, the people were forgotten. While Luther regarded salvation as a personal experience, Müntzer saw it as a "universal duty" to revolt against oppressive rule. Smirin's book "served as a catalytic element in the rise of the Müntzer legend in East Germany."[29]

---

24. *Dietrich Bonhoeffer Works*, vol. 12, ed. Larry Rasmussen (Minneapolis: Fortress, 2009), 362–66, trans. Isabel Best and David Higgins; in *DHL* 2:205–206.
25. John F. Brug, review of *The Lonely Way: Selected Essays and Letters, vol. 1 (1927–1939)*, by Hermann Sasse, trans. Matthew Harrison; in *WLQ* 100, no. 3 (Summer 2003): 237.
26. Mark Mattes, review of *Lutherans against Hitler: The Untold Story*, by Lowell C. Green; in *Logia* 17 (Epiphany 2008): 76–77.
27. Arne Hassing, *Church Resistance to Nazism in Norway, 1940–1945* (Seattle, WA: University of Washington Press, 2014), 259–63.
28. *DHL* 2:297.
29. Moisei Mendelevich Smirin, *Die Volksreformation des Thomas Münzer und der grosse Bauernkrieg*, (Berlin: Dietz, 1952); Douglas C. Stange, "A Marxist De-Lutheranization of the German Reformation," *CTM* 38, no. 9 (October 1967): 596–98.

AMERICAN REALIGNMENT

Up to World War I, American Lutherans were fragmented into as many as 150 separate bodies, divided by history, doctrine, language, distance, and loyalties to particular leaders or opposition to other leaders.[30] But change was in the air. In 1909, the General Synod invited representatives of all American Lutheran groups to a meeting to plan a joint celebration of the four-hundredth anniversary of the Reformation. Although celebration was muted by America's entry into World War I, Augustana historian G. Everett Arden concluded, "what theological debate and doctrinal discussion failed to accomplish, catastrophe achieved, namely, galvanizing Lutherans in America into common action, and creating out of their divided ranks a common front."[31]

The Norwegian Lutheran Church in America was formed in 1917, representing ninety percent of all Norwegian Lutherans in America, but it did not include the Eielsen Synod, the Church of the Lutheran Brethren, or the Lutheran Free Church.[32] The next year the General Synod, General Council, and United Synod of the South united to form the United Lutheran Church in America (ULCA), but the Swedish Augustana Synod was not included.[33]

At war's end, efforts were directed to formalizing and expanding the cooperative work that American Lutherans had begun, including a military chaplaincy, home and foreign missions, social service efforts, publicity, and publishing. The new organization, the National Lutheran Council (NLC), was formed in September 1918.[34]

In the 1920s, the Ohio, Iowa, and Buffalo Synods came close to declaring full fellowship with the Synodical Conference, but following that failed effort, these three formed the American Lutheran Church in 1930.[35] The Evangelical Lutheran Church (Norwegian), Augustana Synod, the United Evangelical Lutherans (Danish), and Suomi Lutherans (Finnish) joined the American Lutheran Church to form the American Lutheran Conference, also in 1930. The American Lutheran Church and Conference sought to maintain a middle course between the conservative Synodical Conference and more liberal East Coast Lutherans.[36]

In 1918 the Wisconsin, Minnesota, Michigan, and Nebraska Synods formed the Evangelical Lutheran Joint Synod of Wisconsin and Other States. This Joint Synod was united with the Synod of Missouri, Ohio, and Other

30. Frank S. Mead, *Handbook of Denominations in the United States*, new 8th edition (Nashville: Abingdon, 1985), 145–46.
31. G. Everett Arden, "Enroute to Unity," in Herbert T. Neve and Benjamin A. Johnson, eds., *The Maturing of American Lutheranism* (Minneapolis, MN: Augsburg, 1968), 229.
32. Mark Granquist, *A New History of Lutherans in America* (Minneapolis, MN: Fortress, 2015), 221–23.
33. Dorris A. Fleisner, "The Formation of the United Lutheran Church in America, 1918," *CHIQ* 40, no. 3 (October 1967): 143–56.
34. Nelson, *The Lutherans in North America, 1914–1970*, 18–27.
35. Nelson, *The Lutherans in North America, 1914–1970*, 28–29, 74.
36. Nelson, *The Lutherans in North America, 1914–1970*, 29–32, 78–83.

States, the "Little" Norwegian Church, and the Slovak Synod in an organic union, the Evangelical Lutheran Synodical Conference.[37]

Lutherans in the United States in 1927 totaled 2,656,158, almost a third of whom (890,671) belonged to the United Lutheran Church, followed by the Missouri Synod, (645,345), the Norwegian Lutheran Church (294,227), Augustana Synod (224,529), the Wisconsin Synod (150,395), and the Iowa Synod (149,068), with the remainder belonging to more than twenty other "churches," synods, and conferences.[38] By 1954, the total grew to more than seven million, making Lutheran churches the third largest Protestant denomination in America, trailing only Baptists and Methodists.[39]

The new American Lutheran Church (ALC) was formed in 1960, and the Lutheran Church in America (LCA) followed in 1962. The four predecessor bodies of the ALC "were all based in the Midwest, and the two largest denominations were roughly the same size." The LCA was composed of two larger bodies, the old ULCA and the Augustana synods, and two smaller bodies, the American Evangelical Lutheran Church, formerly the Danish Evangelical Lutheran Church in America, and the Suomi Synod.[40]

The Missouri Synod and other members of the Synodical Conference resisted these Lutheran union efforts. *The Christian Century* in 1948 characterized the Conference as "the negative pole of Lutheranism," and compared it to Russia in the United Nations: it ". . . organized its satellite denominations, such as the Wisconsin Synod, into an alliance behind an ecclesiastical iron curtain of non-intercourse."[41] Yet events already taking place early in the century would lead to dramatic tensions within the Missouri Synod, cause the demise of the Synodical Conference, and set in motion the realignment of American Lutheranism.

A group of Missouri Synod pastors in the Synod's English District, frustrated at the synod's heavily Germanic culture and its sluggish movement toward Americanization, formed the American Lutheran Publicity Bureau in 1914 and began publishing The *American Lutheran*, a monthly magazine in 1918.[42] Initially the Bureau sought only to urge improved methods of worship, outreach, and publicity, but by 1938 American Lutheran readers were "cheered" by efforts to bring about church union with the ALC.[43] The maga-

37. Edward C. Fredrich, *The Wisconsin Synod Lutherans: A History of the Single Synod, Federation, and Merger* (Milwaukee, WI: Northwestern, 1992), 119–42; George M. Orvick, "A Brief History of the Evangelical Lutheran Synod from 1918–1927," *Lutheran Synod Quarterly* 30, no. 2 (June 1990): 56–78; no. 3 (September 1990): 62–84; Craig A. Ferkenstad, "WELS and ELS 100 Years of Walking Together," *WELS Historical Institute Journal* (*WHIJ*) 36, no. 2 (Fall 2018): 1–17.
38. "The Latest Lutheran Statistics," *American Lutheran* (*AL*) 11, no. 4 (April 1928): 1.
39. "Lutheran Membership Passes 7 Million in U.S. and Canada," *Qu* 52, no. 4 (October 1955): 208–209.
40. Granquist, *A New History of Lutherans in America*, 282.
41. "Need Lutherans Be Skeptics?" *Christian Century* 65, no. 43 (October 27, 1948): 1134.
42. Richard O. Johnson, *Changing World, Changeless Christ: The American Lutheran Publicity Bureau, 1914–2014* (Delhi, NY: American Lutheran Publicity Books, 2018), n.p.
43. Adolf Meyer, "Convention Impressions," *AL* 21, no. 7 (July 1938): 6.

zine noted "a vast and growing 'ground swell' among the laymen of all Lutheran bodies" to receive more information on "the problem of Lutheran unity."[44] At the same time, growing opposition arose in the Wisconsin Synod and among the "Little Norwegian" Lutherans, now renamed the Evangelical Lutheran Synod (ELS), as well as among the Missouri Synod's more conservative members.[45] The ELS ultimately suspended fellowship with the Missouri Synod in 1955,[46] as did the Wisconsin Synod in 1961.[47]

Freed from Synodical Conference restraints, the Missouri Synod moved toward fellowship with the ALC. Concordia St. Louis Professor Richard Caemmerer assumed the essential unity of the Missouri Synod and the ALC; he and others understood Augsburg Confession VII, "It is sufficient for the true unity of the Christian church that the Gospel be preached in conformity with a pure understanding of it and that the sacraments be administered in accord with the divine Word" (AC VII, 2–3), in a minimalist way, not as a requirement for "uniformity in all doctrinal positions."[48] Two months before the Missouri Synod's 1969 convention at Denver, Concordia Professor Arthur Carl Piepkorn expressed extreme confidence in the Missouri Synod's upcoming vote on fellowship with the ALC. "The question [will] not be if the vote would favor authorizing" it, but "only the size of the margin in favor of it." Piepkorn further charged that delegates who might vote against the measure would be failing adequately to represent the mind of the Synod and their vote would stand "contrary to the will" of the Synod.[49]

Missouri Synod delegates approved the declaration of fellowship with the ALC that summer, but they also chose Jacob A. O. Preus to be Synod president.[50] The selection of Preus proved to be the tip of a conservative movement intent on returning the Missouri Synod to a more conservative doctrinal position. Such conservative "push-back" had been developing for some time, centered in the Confessional Lutheran Publicity Bureau, founded in 1940, and its publication, *The Confessional Lutheran*. Also in 1969, John Tietjen was chosen to be Concordia Seminary's new president, and with that the stage was set for confrontation between president and seminary.

The Missouri Synod's 1971 convention upheld the constitutionality of a Fact Finding Committee's actions and directed the seminary's Board of Control

44. "We Want the Facts," *AL* 32, no. 5 (June 1949): 4.
45. Theodore Graebner, "What Price Patience?" *AL* 33, no. 3 (March 1950): 7.
46. Paul S. Meitner, "The Mankato War (1949–1953)," *WHIJ* 29, no. 2 (Fall 2011): 2–19.
47. Edward C. Fredrich, "The Great Debate with Missouri," *WLQ* 74, no. 2 (April 1977); 157–73.
48. Richard R. Caemmerer, Sr., "Guest Editorial—A Glance at a 'Stance,'" *Currents in Theology and Mission (CurTM)* 2 (June 1975): 174–75.
49. Arthur Carl Piepkorn, "Will the Decision on Fellowship at Denver Make a Difference?" *CurTM* 40 (May 1969): 260–63.
50. Carl Lawrenz, "Some Significant Positions and Declarations at the Denver Convention of the LCMS, July 12–18, 1969" (unpublished paper, Wisconsin Lutheran Seminary essay file), 2–3.

to initiate investigations of faculty members.[51] Rather than submit to such an investigation, a majority of faculty members and most students took a self-imposed exodus from the seminary in 1974. They formed an opposition Seminary in Exile (Seminex) which lasted until 1982, then disbanded, and faculty members joined The Lutheran School of Theology, Chicago; Wartburg Seminary, Dubuque, Iowa; and Pacific Lutheran Theological Seminary, Berkeley.[52]

Preus's Fact-Finding Committee determined that numerous professors held or permitted "a confusion on the doctrine of Scripture, especially its verbal inspiration and inerrancy," presented the historical-critical method as a valid and even preferred method of biblical interpretation, cast doubt on the historical reliability of many biblical accounts, and questioned whether many of the words attributed to Jesus were ever spoken by him or were legendary inventions.[53] One professor challenged the Synod's traditional interpretation of John 10:35 and scriptural inerrancy.[54] Another charged that the term inerrancy "does not correspond to any vocable in the Sacred Scriptures" or the Lutheran Confessions, but was "a relatively young word with a limited recent history."[55] Tietjen acknowledged that since the 1950s, Concordia had been "undergoing a quiet revolution," as some faculty members in the biblical studies department had helped the seminary and the synod "come to terms with contemporary issues of biblical criticism."[56]

One of the few professors who refused to join the walkout "attributed part of Concordia's problems to the influx of too many faculty and students from the Eastern Seaboard, the periphery of the church."[57] Some held that Tietjen

---

51. *Proceedings of the Forty-Ninth Regular Convention of the Lutheran Church—Missouri Synod,* 165–66, https://files.lcms.org/wl/?id=iskV7khp2mV1mVskPB8Q1lXOCXKFRytD&path=1950-1998%2F1971%20Proceedings.pdf&mode=default&download=1&inline=1, accessed July 2020.
52. See Kurt E. Marquart, *Anatomy of an Explosion: Missouri in Lutheran Perspective* (Fort Wayne, IN: Concordia Theological Seminary Press, 1977); The Board of Control of Concordia Seminary, St. Louis, MO, *Exodus from Concordia: A Report on the Concordia Walkout* (St. Louis: Concordia College, 1977); Lawrence R. Rast, Jr., "Forty Years after Seminex: Reflections on Social and Theological Factors Leading to the Walkout," *CTQ* 80, no. 3–4 (July–October 2016): 195–215; Paul A. Zimmerman, *A Seminary in Crisis: The Inside of the Preus Fact-Finding Committee* (St. Louis, MO: Concordia, 2007). For opposing views, see Frederick W. Danker, *No Room in the Brotherhood: The Preus-Otten Purge of Missouri* (St. Louis, MO: Clayton Publishing House, Inc., 1977); Martin E. Marty, "Missouri's Exiles: Heartbreak, Ashes—and Victory," *ChrCent* 91, no. 23 (12 June 1974): 630–32; Daniel Aleshire, "Watching Hope Grow: Distant Reflections on Seminex June 2009," *CurTM* 38, no. 2 (April 2011): 84–89.
53. J. A. O. Preus, "Report of the Synodical President," (The Lutheran Church—Missouri Synod, 1 September 1972), 21–25.
54. Richard Jungkuntz, "An Approach to the Exegesis of John 10:34–36," *CTM* 35, no. 9 (October 1964), 559–60.
55. Arthur Carl Piepkorn, "What does 'Inerrancy' Mean?" *CTM* 36, no. 8 (September 1965): 577, 579, 588.
56. John H. Tietjen, *Memoirs in Exile: Confessional Hope and Institutional Conflict* (Minneapolis: Fortress, 1990), 6, 8.
57. James E. Adams quoting Professor Martin H. Scharlemann, in "Concordia 'Exiles' Commence Classes," *St. Louis Post-Dispatch* (February 20, 1974); cited by Charles K. Piehl, "Ethnicity, the Missouri Synod, and the Mission of the Church," *CurTM* 3, no. 4 (August 1976): 241.

never sufficiently understood "the thinking of ordinary Missouri pastors and people," who were "God-fearing, pious people who wanted to remain Lutheran and who believed the Bible" but were "confused and frightened by the so-called historical critical method whose apologists could never explain it and rarely knew was it was."[58] For several decades the Synod "had nearly isolated herself from events in World Lutheranism," while "theological students went to Europe and earned degrees sitting at the feet of avant-garde professors in faculties across Germany." These students then returned to the Synod "imbued in liberal higher-critical scholarship."[59]

EUROPEAN RECOVERY

After World War I, Lutherans in Europe and North America began cooperating in war relief and missions, triggering calls for a greater degree of organization to bring Lutherans together throughout the world. A first conference in Eisenach in 1923 led to the formation of the Lutheran World Convention, followed by a second meeting in Copenhagen in 1929 and a third in Paris in 1935. War in Europe caused plans to be abandoned for a time, but ties initiated between Lutheran groups in America and Europe remained strong throughout the war.

Following World War II, American Lutherans were again urged to mobilize for military chaplaincy and service to the troops, to care for "orphaned" missions, and to aid in postwar relief and the reconstruction of Europe.[60] The devastation throughout Germany, the general weakness of all European Lutheran churches, and the threat of advancing communism created huge problems for refugees and displaced persons. Lutheran mission churches in the global South often lacked support and missionary leadership.[61] Teams were sent to Europe to aid with relief efforts, refugee resettlement, and rebuilding devastated churches. Missouri Synod President John W. Behnken recalled scenes "that were to haunt us everywhere we went in Germany" of "the vast number of refugees shuffling along roads and highways, some carrying babies in arms or leading small children, others pushing and pulling little carts or carrying bundles with whatever they had been able to save from the Soviets."[62]

Lutherans also convened to resume cooperative work begun in the interwar years. The Evangelical Lutheran Free Church in Germany addressed an official letter to the Missouri Synod in 1945, and a commission of five men, including Missouri Synod President Behnken, responded, hoping "to help

58. Robert Preus, review of *Memoirs in Exile: Confessional Hope and Institutional Conflict*, in *Logia* 1, no. 1 (Reformation 1992): 70–71.
59. Paul T. McCain, "Remembering and Rejoicing: Reflections on the 150th Anniversary of Concordia," *CHIQ* 92, no. 4 (Winter 2019): 13.
60. Ernst H. Wendland, "Our Synod's First Mission Overseas," *WHIJ* 2, no. 1 (Spring 1984): 39–40.
61. *DHL* 2:258.
62. John W. Behnken, *This I Recall* (St. Louis, MO: Concordia, 1964), 94.

re-establish a Church founded on 'God's Word and Luther's Doctrine true.' God grant that [it will be] a true Lutheran church, both in doctrine and practice a Free Church."[63] In 1947, in Lund, Sweden, the Lutheran World Federation was formed, taking the place of the Lutheran World Convention.[64] At its meeting in Hanover, Germany, in 1952, the federation elected Carl E. Lundquist as executive secretary of the federation, a role he filled into the late 1950s.[65] ULCA President Franklin Clark Fry led American efforts to overhaul the remnants of the dormant Lutheran World Convention and invent the structure of the new federation.[66]

Other connections were forming in the twentieth century among the world's Lutherans. A World Conference on Life and Work was convened in Stockholm in 1925, led by Swedish Archbishop Nathan Soderblom. A second Conference on Life and Work and a separate Conference on Faith and Order met in Edinburgh in 1937.[67] American participation was limited mostly to more liberal Lutheran bodies; conservative American Lutherans were lukewarm toward ecumenism, some even remembering the unionism of the early nineteenth century Prussian Union Church.[68]

Behnken wrote that he was unable "put into words all that has been accomplished and [was] still being accomplished through these free conferences" in Germany. Papers and discussions all "centered attention on vital theological truths," and "the focus was always on the Holy Scriptures and the historic Lutheran Confessions." Behnken was pleased that Missouri "brought its influence to bear on every issue" and that its name "came to be known—and appreciated" for its "soundly confessional standards."[69] The Wisconsin Synod, though still a partner with Missouri at the time, asked:

> Was it at all the purpose of Bad Boll II to impress and to be impressed? . . . What is, we ask, the actual confessional stand of the Lutheran theologians in Germany? And what is more, we desire to know the confessional stand of the church which they represent. But which church do they represent? . . . These and other questions we ask and shall ask in view of Bad Boll I and II, questions that cannot be answered by impressions made and impressions received, however lasting and deepening these impressions may be for the participants, but only can be answered by the Scriptures and the Lutheran Confessions.[70]

63. P[aul] Peters, "The Free Church in Germany," *Qu* 42, no. 4 (October 1945): 281–82.
64. E[mund] Reim, "Lutheran World Federation," *Qu* 45, no. 1 (January 1948): 59–60.
65. Maria Erling and Mark Granquist, *The Augustana Story: Shaping Lutheran Identity in North America* (Minneapolis, MN: Augsburg Fortress, 2008), 295–96.
66. Robert H. Fisher, ed., *Franklin Clark Fry: A Palette for a Portrait*, supplementary Number of the *Lutheran Quarterly* 24 (1972): 227–28, 231–32.
67. *The Augustana Story*, 297–98.
68. *The Augustana Story*, 238–39.
69. Behnken, *This I Recall*, 117.
70. P[aul] Peters, "American Theologians' Impressions of Bad Boll," *Qu* 46, no. 4 (October 1949): 286–89.

FORMATION OF THE ELCA

It soon became apparent that the Missouri Synod's declaration of fellowship with the ALC in 1969 was ill-advised. It severed fellowship with the ALC in 1981. Jeffrey Hadden's 1967 study of Protestant ministers in the United States had revealed significant differences in belief between Missouri Synod and ALC pastors. While ninety-five percent of Missouri clergymen believed that the virgin birth of Christ was a physical miracle, only eighty-one percent of ALC pastors held the same belief; seventy-six percent of Missouri Synod pastors agreed that the Bible was "inerrant," but only twenty-three percent of ALC clergy agreed. The Glock-Stark survey of lay Protestant convictions in 1965 showed that 86 percent of Missouri Synod laymen held an unqualified belief in original sin, but only 49 percent of ALC laymen did so; similarly, 93 percent of Missouri laymen believed in the deity of Christ, but only 74 percent of ALC laymen believed it.[71]

In 1982, delegates of the ALC, LCA and AELC (Association of Evangelical Lutheran Churches), a group that formed in the Lutheran Church—Missouri Synod (LCMS) following the walkout at Concordia, met at simultaneously scheduled meetings and adopted identical resolutions to join "in forming a new Lutheran Church and to take all deliberate steps toward its earliest realization." Representatives of the three bodies established a commission for a new Lutheran church, which at its first meeting formed one task force on theology and a second on society.[72]

Richard John Neuhaus reported that a wide range of theologians, bishops, pastors, and laity offered initial support, yet Neuhaus himself was skeptical of talk about the forming of a "new church" because a new church "understood literally would be a sect."[73] He especially decried the "flaccid confessional subscription" of the proposed new church. Many Commission members reportedly favored the drafting of a "new confession for a new church" to replace historical sixteenth century confessions.[74] In 1984 came a much-publicized vote to eliminate language referring to God as "Father, Son, and Holy Spirit" in the new church's statement of faith. The very consideration of such a proposal, Neuhaus charged, said "something profoundly disturbing to many about the seriousness of our confessional commitment to the Catholic faith."[75]

Commission members acknowledged that significant doctrinal differences remained within the three synods but apparently chose to live with those differences. In 1983, the Commission affirmed, with almost no discussion, a summary paragraph on the Word of God and Scripture, which stated, "on the

71. John Warwick Montgomery, "Missouri Compromise," *Chart* 13, no 8 (17 January 1969): 50.
72. Samuel H. Nafzger, "Report on the Emerging Lutheran Church," *Concordia Journal* 10 (September 1984): 164–65.
73. "One and Nine Questions," *Forum Letter* (*FL*) 12, no. 3 (25 April 1983): 1.
74. "One and Nine Questions: Commentary no. 6, Theological Integrity," *FL* 12, no. 11 (25 November 1983): 3.
75. Edgar R. Trexler, *Anatomy of a Merger: People, Dynamics, and Decisions that Shaped the ELCA* (Minneapolis, MN: Augsburg, 1991): 60.

basis of the sacred Scriptures, the Church's creeds, and the Lutheran Confessional writings," Jesus Christ is "the Word of God, through whom God created everything" and "God incarnate, through whose person and life God fashions a new creation." The statement defined the Word of God as "God's message to us, both Law and Gospel, revealing judgment and mercy through word and deed." However, Samuel Nafzger, Executive Secretary of the Missouri Synod's Commission on Theology and Church Relations, noted that the statement refrained from ever using the terms inerrant or infallible to describe Scripture. While the Lutheran Confessions more than seventy times identify Scripture as the very Word of God, the Commission's statement "deliberately [failed] to say that Scripture is without qualification the Word of God."[76]

The Commission recognized the spiritual unity of the church but left unresolved questions on the "external unity in the church."[77] Its report, "Unity in the Context of Theological Pluralism," signaled that the new Lutheran church would continue the approach to church fellowship its predecessor churches had practiced: they sought unity not only by means of "organizational union" but more by "pulpit and altar fellowship, including common witnessing and working." Thus pulpit and altar fellowship were not expected to proceed from doctrinal unity, but would serve only as a stepping-stone toward some measure of doctrinal consensus. Practicing fellowship would continue even after attempts at reaching doctrinal unity failed.[78]

Carl Braaten agreed with Edgar Trexler, who in *Anatomy of a Merger* acknowledged that "no one ever put a church together the way the LCA, ALC, and AELC did." He expressed concern when the Commission "invented a [church] polity based on a quota system that would have far-reaching negative consequences."[79] After the merger was completed, *Lutheran Forum* warned, "our Church today is in danger of apostasy, of wholesale secularization, of trading the power of worship for the worship of power."[80] *Forum Letter* called inclusivity and multiculturalism "the twin totalitarianisms" which threatened the ELCA since its birth." It was "becoming increasingly crucial to ask why there should be a Lutheran church" at all. "If we no longer teach and believe anything in particular, and if our worship practices increasingly and so vehemently contradict what we say we believe," was there a compelling reason for the ELCA to exist?[81]

Thus the later decades of the twentieth century stood in sharp contrast to the optimism of the 1950s and 1960s, when many leaders in the ALC, LCA, and LCMS treated the question of doctrinal unity as if it already existed. By

76. Nafzger, "Report on the Emerging Lutheran Church," 165–67.
77. Samuel H. Nafzger, "The Missouri View of Lutheran Unity: Distinguishing Between Spiritual Unity and External Unity," *The Cresset* 46 (March 1983): 9–11.
78. John F. Brug, *WELS and Other Lutherans,* second ed., (Milwaukee, WI: Northwestern, 2009), 21.
79. Carl E. Braaten, "The ELCA at 20 Years: Flunking the Theological Test," *Dialog* 47 (Winter 2008): 374–75.
80. Paul R. Hinlicky, "A Time for Decision," *Lutheran Forum* (*LF*) 22, no. 1 (Lent 1988): 17–19.
81. "Captive to Myth: The ELCA in Kansas City," *FL* 22, no. 10 (7 October 1993): 1–4.

the 1990s the ELCA and the LCMS were "pulling away from each other at a significant rate." Both denominations had endured "a tremendous amount of internal strife and struggle" and had divided into "different factions and camps that greatly complicate[d] their mission and ministry."[82]

The issues of homosexuality and same-sex marriage provided the greatest cause of public strife. The 1993 statement, "The Church and Human Sexuality: A Lutheran Perspective," in the view of many upended traditional Christian teachings on sexuality. The statement's task force was charged with badly misunderstanding the nature of the gospel itself, turning it instead into a "general command to love" and disregarding "the confessional concern for distinguishing between law and gospel."[83] In 1998, *Forum Letter* expressed astonishment that the ELCA's Lutheran Youth Organization proposed a "year-long prayer emphasis for homosexual, bisexual, and transgender youth." The church's message to young people should instead have been the "classical Christian message" regarding sexuality: "Virginity is not deviancy, desires are not needs, wants are not necessities, license is not freedom, impulses can be checked, lust is not love, not all appetites should be fed."[84]

The ELCA's sexuality statement recognized same-sex unions and approved the ordination of gays and lesbians. In the year following its publication, more than three hundred congregations left the denomination in protest.[85] Nevertheless, numerous clergy and lay leaders stressed that such sexuality was consistent with their understanding of the Lutheran faith. Those who left formed two new denominations, Lutheran Congregations in Mission for Christ (LCMC, 2001) and the North American Lutheran Church (NALC, 2010), which together number more than a million members and 1,300 congregations."[86]

One extensive study of the ELCA concluded that its practices are "not based on a precise articulation of beliefs," supported by biblical proof passages, but instead on "an inclusionary interpretation of the Bible" that "invites conversations with others to learn from one another and grow together in faith." But the study found few ELCA members "familiar enough with core contents of their faith and the meanings of central Lutheran practices" to engage in such conversations. Although many within the church identify theology as one of its main strengths, outside of seminary-educated circles "the importance of theological thought is waning." Such a development is "typical for religious groups in America, most of which do not place a high value on theology as a product of history and of human thought." The re-

82. Mark Granquist, "American Lutheranism Fifty Years Ago—and Today," *LF* 43, no. 1 (Spring 2009): 27–29.
83. Bruce Foster, "You Know Neither the Scriptures nor the Power of God: An Introductory Analysis of 'The Church and Human Sexuality,'" *LF* 28, no. 1 (February 1994): 45–48.
84. "Gay Youth Events Planned," *FL* 27, no. 1 (January 1998): 1–3.
85. Jeffrey MacDonald, "Churches Leaving ELCA Estimate the Cost," *ChrCent* 127, no. 22 (November 2, 2010).
86. *DHL* 2:290–91; https://www.lcmc.net/; https://thenalc.org/.

sult will probably be that theological concerns continue to decline in importance, "replaced by religious subjectivism and a pluralization of the faith."[87]

FAITH AND LIFE

Adolf Koeberle in 1936 gave a clear presentation of the unique content of the Christian gospel:

> How does Jesus differ fundamentally from all others who have been founders of some sort of religion? He does not give directions for the purification of the soul like those which in all mystery religions are accounted the indispensable condition for any communion with divinity; He does not point man to the creative springs within his own soul that through them he might find the satisfaction of devotion; He does not make wisdom and virtue conditions of his fellowship. Just the opposite is true. Without regard to any moral attainments, spiritual fervor or intellectual wisdom, he "receives sinners and eats with them."
>
> [Christ] is not content to be one among many doors that lead to the father's house, or one way among a number of possible roads, but he calls himself "the door," "the way" that alone leads to true communion with God. He is the only bridge on which man can cross the abyss of sin that separates from God.[88]

Evidence suggests, however, that long-held distinctions between Protestant and Roman Catholic understandings of justification are fading. Protestant scholars used to be "virtually unanimous" that the word *justify* meant *to acquit* or *to declare righteous* or *to treat as righteous,* but not *to make righteous;* Roman Catholic scholars were just as insistent that *justify* meant not only *to declare righteous* but also *to make righteous.* By mid-century these "old confessional landmarks [had] become more and more out of date."[89] A presentation on justification at the Lutheran World Federation meeting in Helsinki in 1963 revealed this lack of clarity, failing to state, "God's justification of the sinner by grace, through faith, on account of the person and work of Jesus Christ, must be clearly distinguished from the life of the justified sinner to be lived by faith."[90]

Following Vatican II, a group of twenty Roman Catholic and Lutheran scholars—none of whom spoke officially for their respective church bodies—engaged in dialogue in an attempt to bridge longstanding doctrinal

87. Maren Freudenberg, *The Mainline in Modern Modernity: Tradition and Innovation in the Evangelical Lutheran Church in America* (New York: Lexington, 2018), 162, 217.
88. Adolf Koeberle, *The Quest for Holiness: A Biblical, Historical and Systematic Investigation*, trans. John C. Mattes (Minneapolis, MN: Augsburg, 1936; reprinted by St. Louis, MO: Concordia, 1982), 51–52.
89. Nigel Watson, "Justification—A New Look," *Australian Biblical Review* 18 (October 1970): 31–32.
90. Richard Klann, "Contemporary Lutheran Views on Justification," providing an analysis of Warren A. Quanbeck's "Study Document on Justification," in *CTQ* 45, no. 4 (October 1981): 290–94.

divides. Their resulting statement on justification did not settle differences, but instead allowed these differences to stand side by side "as different ways of expressing the gospel." Roman Catholic participants granted, "salvation in its totality is unconditional since it all depends on the saving will of God" but also emphasized "sanctification, reconciliation, and [the] new creation as part of justification." In their view, good works were "a part of justification and not a result" of it. Both Catholic and Lutheran participants agreed on "some general statements that salvation is by grace alone and by Christ alone," but they failed to arrive at a precise, unambiguous statement of what they meant by these terms. The closest they could come was to announce "convergences" on justification, not "agreements."[91]

In 1999 the Vatican and the Lutheran World Federation approved the *Joint Declaration on the Doctrine of Justification* by a vote of 958 to 25. Although this decision was announced with great enthusiasm, it received a lukewarm response in the press. The Vatican itself stated that the Catholic Church could "not yet speak of a consensus such as would eliminate every difference between Catholics and Lutherans in the understanding of justification." *Time* magazine reported that the Catholic Church "refuses to relinquish some cooperative agency on humanity's part through, say, penance or charity." Rome could accept the declaration "only if it is interpreted as upholding their synergistic system of salvation."[92]

In a different vein, Paul Hinlicky charged that some contemporary Lutheran leaders were abandoning the doctrine of justification by grace through faith in favor of focusing energy on "earthly happiness, be it therapeutic counseling or therapeutic politics, rather than eternal destiny; on human agency rather than human bondage; in our experience and fulfillment rather than the means of grace and discipleship."[93] Similarly, Robert Kelly noted that Lutherans "do not believe that hard work, character, positive thinking, or a winning personality will gain us anything important," but just the opposite. "With Augustine and Luther, we believe that it is just when we are at our hardworking, positive-thinking, people-influencing best that we are at our arrogant worst and farthest from God." Justification "in God's economy is a gift, given to us unconditionally in the death and resurrection of Jesus of Nazareth." Thus, holding to justification by grace alone through faith in Christ alone "contradicts the American doctrine of success.[94]

Historically, Synodical Conference Lutherans took a cautious position on the role of the church in society. The Missouri Synod "emphasized social welfare and private charities instead of collective social action." It estab-

---

91. John F. Brug, "The Lutheran-Catholic Statement on Justification," *Northwestern Lutheran* 71, no. 3 (February 1, 1984): 40–42.
92. John F. Brug, "Lutherans and Catholics Agree on a 'Differentiated Consensus,'" *WLQ* 96, no. 1 (Winter 1999): 61–64.
93. Paul R. Hinlicky, "The Future of Reformation," *LF* 25, no. 1 (February 1991): 9–10.
94. Robert A. Kelly, "Successful or Justified? The North American Doctrine of Salvation by Works," *CTQ* 65, no. 3 (July 2001): 244.

lished missions to aid indigent immigrants and assist those who suffered from fires, floods, and other catastrophes. It maintained hospitals, orphanages, hospices, and homes for the aged.[95] Theodore Graebner expressed his opposition to the social gospel in *Lehre und Wehre* and *The Lutheran Witness.*[96] In a 1927 letter to the editor of the *Chicago Daily Tribune,* Graebner maintained that political activity was ruining the spiritual mission of the church.[97] In the Wisconsin Synod, August Zich rejected church efforts to improve society as an outgrowth of Calvinism, since Calvinists have "drifted away from the real purpose of the church" but were "obsessed with an urge to benefit the human race by the application of moral precepts and laws. Having despaired of winning souls for the bliss of heaven, they attempt to bring men into a man-made heaven here on earth."[98]

In 1965, a correspondent to *The Northwestern Lutheran* asked why there had been no members of his church body at Selma, Alabama, marching for civil rights. The answer the correspondent received was in line with long-standing teaching regarding social ministry, "The answer is not that we are unconcerned," but that "it was not the business of Jesus to take over the government's functions." Where wrongs have occurred, they "should be taken care of by those to whom God has given that responsibility." Preaching the law "stands in the service of the gospel message" but "does not form a separate program of social reform." As citizens we "attend to the tasks assigned to the government. Let us not be remiss in either. But let us not hinder either function by confusing them."[99]

By contrast, the ELCA and its predecessor bodies endorsed a more activist role for the church in society. The 1964 Biennial Convention of the LCA, for example, stated that the civil rights movement had "thrust the church into a time of travail and perplexity but also of opportunity and hope." It called racial discrimination "a violation of God's created order, of the meaning of redemption in Christ, and of the nature of the church," which the church must oppose. It urged the use of all lawful means to bring about societal change, but "if and when the means of legal recourse have been exhausted or are demonstrably inadequate," Christians

> . . . may then choose to serve the cause of racial justice by disobeying a law that clearly involves the violation of their obligations as Christians, so long as they are (a) willing to accept the penalty for their actions; (b) willing to limit and direct their protest as precisely as possible against a specific grievance or injustice; and (c) willing to carry out their protest in a nonviolent, responsible

95. Jerald K. Pfabe, "The Social Gospel is No Gospel: The Critique of Theodore Graebner," *Journal of the Lutheran Historical Conference* 2 (2012): 228.
96. Theodore Graebner, "Paragraphen über den neuesten Chiliasmus," *Lehre und Wehre* 61 (August 1915): 337–50; "False Gospels," *LuthW* (7 October 1924): 363.
97. Letter, Theodore Graebner to Editor of the *Chicago Daily Tribune*, April 12, 1927; Theodore Graebner Papers, Box 36; cited by Pfabe, "The Social Gospel is No Gospel," 237.
98. Aug[ust] F. Zich, "The Social Gospel," *Qu* 31, no. 1 (January 1934): 26–29.
99. Armin W. Schuetze, "Why Weren't Our Pastors at Selma?" *NL* 52, no. 8 (18 April 1965): 120.

manner, after earnestly seeking the counsel of other Christians and the will of God in prayer.[100]

The more progressive values of the ELCA continue to be evident in statements regarding the church in society, which call on its members to "engage those of diverse perspectives, classes, genders, ages, races, and cultures in the deliberation process so that each of our limited horizons may be expanded and the witness of the body of Christ in the world enhanced."[101]

INTO ALL THE WORLD

E. Clifford Nelson noted that Lutheranism has traditionally had three geographical "centers": Germany and surrounding areas of Central Europe, Scandinavia, and North America.[102] During the twentieth century, Lutherans in Europe and America continued to take their message into all the world.

In 1924, L. H. Rullmann issued a poignant call for Lutheran schools to do mission work among African-Americans.[103] Rullmann's plea, impassioned though it was, makes for uncomfortable reading today. Consistent with attitudes of his era, Rullmann believed that "colored people," those "poor children of Ham," were "burdened with the curse of Noah" and relegated to being "servants of man." He deplored how the entire world looked down on and mistreated African-Americans, "as though God has not endowed them with a living soul." But their souls "were purchased with the blood of the Son of God. It is God's will that they shall gain eternal life just as well as whites," and so "it is also God's will that we be instrumental" in bringing them the good news. A half century later, it was reported that more than 15,000 African-American children attended LCMS elementary schools, high schools, and other educational facilities.[104]

Beginning late in the nineteenth century, the Wisconsin Synod has worked among the Apache Indians, beginning when Arizona was still a United States territory.[105] Lutherans of various bodies established missions in Alaska, decades before it became the forty-ninth state.[106] In addition, Lutherans were in Canada well before the twentieth century.[107] Lutherans have

100. "Second Biennial Convention of the Lutheran Church in America, 2–9 July 1964; in Christa Klein and Christian von Dehsen, *Politics and Policy: The Genesis and Theology of Social Statements in the Lutheran Church in America* (Minneapolis: Fortress, 1989), 267–70.
101. Freudenberg, *The Mainline in Late Modernity*, 36.
102. Nelson, *The Rise of World Lutheranism*, xii.
103. L. H. Rullmann, "How Can the Interest in Mission-Work Be Aroused and Maintained in the Pupils of Our Schools?" *Lutheran School Journal* 59 (April 1924); 125.
104. Robert H. King, ed., *African-Americans and the Local Church* (St. Louis: Concordia, 1996), 19.
105. E. Edgar Guenther, "The Lutheran Missions in Apacheland," *CHIQ* 15, no. 3 (October 1942): 71–82.
106. John E. Simon, "Some Facts about Russian and Lutheran Churches in Early Alaska," *CHIQ* 11, no. 2 (July 1938): 56–62.
107. Norman J. Threinen, *A Religious-Cultural Mosaic:* A History of Lutherans in Canada: Lutheran Historical Institute Monograph Series, Number 1 (Vulcan, Alberta: Today's Reformation Press, 2006).

initiated missionary work in Latin American countries, including Puerto Rico, beginning in 1898; Brazil in 1899; Argentina in 1905; and more recently in Haiti.[108] In Europe, Lutheran work has occurred, among other places, in Latvia,[109] Slovakia.[110] Lithuania,[111] and Russia.[112]

Three Augustana students joined a contingent of eight missionaries to India in 1912.[113] Lutherans have maintained a separate confessional stance from the Church of South India (est. 1947) and the Church of North India (est. 1970), although since 1926, some Lutherans in India have cooperated through a Federation of Evangelical Lutheran Churches of India.[114] Lutherans presently account for about two million of the 25 million Christians in India.[115]

China was a center of intensive Lutheran missionary work since before 1850, and by World War II a dozen different Lutheran groups were located around the country. Much of their work was terminated by the war and the Communist takeover. Some Chinese Lutherans moved to Hong Kong, Taiwan, Singapore, Malaysia, and beyond. There are about thirty thousand Lutherans in Japan, Lutheran numbers are increasing in Korea, and there has been a Lutheran presence in the Philippines.[116]

Lutheranism has experienced its greatest missionary expansion in Africa, where there are Lutheran churches in twenty-three countries. Most Lutheran members are in Ethiopia (6.355 million), Tanzania (5.825 million), Madagascar (3 million), Nigeria, (2.348 million), and South Africa (643 thousand).[117]

Robert Kolb has described the changing nature of world missionary work:

> As the Lutheran confession of the faith fades from the public arena of the homelands of the Wittenberg Reformation in central and northern Europe, as the Lutheran churches of the lands in east central and eastern Europe continue to recover from the Soviet persecution that followed centuries of persecution and harassment from Counter-Reformation clergy and governments, and as the immigrant churches of the Americas, Australia, and South Africa struggle with their identity in each of their specific situations, the mission churches within

108. P[aul] Peters, "Lutheranism's Efforts to Gain a Foothold in Latin America," *Qu* 50, no. 2 (April 1953): n.p.; Henrik Laur, "The Skeleton in the Closet: American Lutherans in Latin America," *LQ* 22, no. 1 (February 1970): 40–48; Henry Wittrock, "Experiences in the South American Mission,' *CHIQ* 35, no. 4 (January 1963): 131–41; Rudolph Blank, "The Lutherans in Venezuela," *Logia* 19, no. 1 (Epiphany 2010): 17–24; Mytch Pierre-Noel Dorvilier, "Lutheranism in Haiti: The Birth of a Church in Exile," *JLHC* 6 (2016): 92–100.
109. Egil Grislis, "Suffering and Hope: Two Recurrent Ideas Among Latvian Lutherans in Exile," *LQ* 22, no. 3 (August 1970): 298–318.
110. Julius Filo, "Sharing the Faith Before, During, and After Communism in Slovakia," *LQ* 16, no. 4 (Winter 2002): 433–41.
111. Darius Petkunas, "The Lithuanian Church Today," *CTQ* 73, no. 4 (October 2009): 367–72.
112. Edgars Kilpocks, "The Lutheran Church in Russia," *LQ* 3, no. 1 (February 1951): 28–30.
113. Erling and Granquist, *The Augustana Story,* 187.
114. *DHL* 2:341.
115. J. Paul Rajashekar, "India," *DLLT,* 363–66.
116. Mark A. Granquist, "North American Lutheranism and the New Ethics," in *Lutherans Today: American Lutheran Identity in the Twenty-First Century,* ed. Richard Cimino (Grand Rapids, MI: Eerdmans 2003), 171–72.
117. *DHL,* 2:339.

> the Lutheran family are growing rapidly. They are being called upon to assume more and more responsibility for ecclesiastical, social, and theological leadership among those who share the Lutheran confession of the faith.[118]

Consistent with the movement of other Christian denominations away from Western Europe and the United States and to the global south, the number of Lutherans in Indonesia is greater than the membership of the ELCA and the Evangelical Lutheran Church Canada combined, and three times as many Lutherans are in Africa as in those two North American bodies. While it is still true that more than half of all Lutherans live in Europe, all Lutheran European churches are declining. As Lutheranism moves south, its membership will shift from being among the middle class to becoming increasingly poor and marginalized. Most remarkable: "The flow of missionaries may well be reversed. As Lutheran churches in Europe and North America continue to lose membership, both Europe and North America will themselves become mission fields."[119]

FAITH AND HOPE

The Lutheran World Federation reported in 2008 that there were 69,757,570 Lutherans in the world, in 138 LWF member churches, not counting Lutherans in non-member LWF churches such as the Missouri Synod and others. But admittedly such statistics "embroil us in hazards, doubts, and ambiguities." We might like to count only those who confess unconditional subscription to the entire Book of Concord, but "such a definition is unlikely to be convincing to most of those who want to identify themselves as Lutherans."[120] This is not new; more than half a century ago, visitors to Europe reported empty pews and a culture increasingly disinterested in religion.[121]

In Germany the rise of "late modern culture" occurred between 1958 and 1973, a time sometimes referred to as the "long 1960s." Before that, mainline churches, both Roman Catholic and Protestant, enjoyed "a rather comfortable position" as "the only (morally) reliable institutions and were granted many privileges" in society. "More than 90 percent of the West German population were formal members of either Catholic or Protestant churches." But mainline churches have succumbed to the rise of this "late modern culture" that includes rejection of establishment institutions, popular alternative spiritual beliefs, and acceptance of uninhibited sexual behaviors.[122]

---

118. Robert Kolb, "The Three-Hundredth Anniversary of Lutheran Mission in India" *LQ* 21, no. 1 (Spring 2007): 100.
119. James Aageson and Arland Jacobson, "The Changing World of Lutheranism," in *The Future of Lutheranism in a Global Context* (Minneapolis: Augsburg Fortress, 2008), 1–4.
120. William Schumacher, "How Many Lutherans?" *Logia* 17, no. 1 (Epiphany 2008): 7.
121. David P. Scaer, "Reflections on a European Trip," *Springfielder* 33, no. 3 (December 1969): 15–23.
122. Jens Schlamelcher, "The Decline of the Mainline German Churches in Light of the Rise of Late Modern German Culture," *Journal of Religion and Popular Culture* 30, no. 1 (Spring 2018): 23–34.

In Scandinavia social, political, and economic shifts accelerated after the World War II. As church attendance and participation continued to decline, Christians attempted to maintain their position in society through the development of Christian Democratic parties. A majority of Scandinavians still maintain membership in the state church and support it through their taxes.[123] Long-term trends, however, remain unclear.[124]

Between the year of its founding, 1988, and 2013, ELCA membership dropped from 5.2 million to 3.9 million, a 20 percent loss.[125] The number of ELCA congregations also declined from 11,069 in 1990 to 9,533 in 2012.[126] Some project that the ELCA will disappear by simple attrition about the year 2046, with the LCMS following a year or so behind.[127] The year 1969 marked the high water mark in the Missouri Synod, when it had 2,778,238 members. Between 1969 and 2011, the Synod shed 546,380 members, a 19.67 percent loss. Over that same time, the non-Hispanic white population of the United States, the population that most closely mirrors the ethnic makeup of Missouri, increased 8.9 percent. Since 2011, the LCMS has been losing members at a more rapid pace. The decline is captured in the number of infant baptisms by decade: 1969—65,569; 1979—55,540; 1989—52,479; 1999—45,901; 2009—28,627.[128] The Wisconsin Synod gained 21,000 to 25,000 baptized members in each of the two decades between 1969 and 1978, but has lost 22,400 members in the years 2014–18. Conservative projections are that the WELS will lose 188,000 members by 2059; a more drastic projection has the WELS losing 261,000 members, reducing it to a church body of 93,000 baptized, less than two-thirds the size it was in 1927.[129]

What faith and hope do Lutherans have, after we have now come one-fifth of the way into the twenty-first century, with no change of trends apparent? Assessments are easy to come by.[130] Here are three voices:

---

123. Harald Hegstad, "The Lutheran and Ecumenical Identity of Church of Norway," in Anne-Louise, et. al., eds., *Exploring a Heritage: Evangelical Lutheran Churches in the North* (Eugene, OR.: Pickwick Publications, 2010), 301–319.
124. Gary G. Yerkey, "The Church of Sweden's Nonbelievers," 24 January, 2013, *DHL*, 2:298.
125. Mark Granquist, "Ways to be Lutheran: New churches experiment with polity," *ChrCent* 131, no. 8 (4 April 2014): 12–13.
126. "Congregation Totals for ELCA," *Potpourri Reports* (2012); cited by Freudenberg, *The Mainline in Late Modernity*, 13.
127. Frederick Niedner, "'Come over to M.I.T.—and Concordia—and help us': Some thoughts on *promissio* and *mission* in academe, and a twenty-first century promise-truster's guide to avoiding a host of false dilemmas that lie between Athens and Jerusalem," (presented to the Third International Crossings Conference, St. Louis, 25–27 January 2010), 1.
128. Heath R. Curtis, "LCMS and Demographic Decline," *Gottesdienst* 21 no. 2 (Trinity 2013): 13–14.
129. Jonathan Hein, "Connecting to a Changing Culture," presentation to the Biennial Convention of the Wisconsin Ev. Lutheran Synod, 2019, https://synodadmin.welsrc.net/download-synodadmin/convention-resources-2019-synod-convention/?wpdmdl=3530&ind=1564776467350, accessed July 2020; compare "The Latest Lutheran Statistics," *AL* 11, no. 4 (April 1928): 1.
130. Kathryn A. Kleinhans, "Why Now? The Relevance of Luther in a Post-Modern Age," *CurTM* 24, no. 6 (December 1997): 488–95.

Many among us see our American culture as the enemy. They tell us that what is "American" is per se inimical to Christianity. This, they say, is what's wrong with American Evangelicalism: it is too American. They picture the church as a "little flock" standing against the world, against the incursion of American individualism, or democratism, or commercialism, or Deism . . . .Of course, there is much in American culture that is contrary to Christian faith. Often, however, these assertions are made by people who are not always as alert to their own cultural biases as they claim to be. If it is negative to be too "American," how is it better to be too "German," or "British," or "Scandinavian'?"[131]

What will Lutheranism look like in the twenty-first century? Under God's grace we will confess the prophetic and apostolic narrative of Christ with fresh clarity and precision . . . .

The way that we think about ourselves, about our children, about our parents, about our spouse, about our work, about our play—all will be grounded and nurtured by the narrative of God's love and gracious presence in Christ. We will confess Him not in the enthusiasms of our private, choice-driven religiosity, but in the catholic creeds and confessions which expound the One whom the prophets and apostles herald. When that Christology is confessed, then our every moment is defined as significant for it is lived . . . before the blessed and Holy Trinity, who defines beginning and end, and who offers freely and fully in the crucified Messiah the life that is whole and real and forever.[132]

Real renewal and growth of Lutheranism in America calls for confessional integrity and a firm commitment to the biblical teachings confessed in the Book of Concord, a burning interest in sharing the message of sin and grace with every part of the population of our land, and a gospel-motivated eagerness to share the message of salvation on the part of our lay people . . . .A secondary factor in such a renewal is a balance between preserving the best of our traditional customs and forms of worship and openness to the best of new forms of worship which arise in our own time and which are appropriate to our own culture. Such a movement would not, of course, be a guarantee of numerical success because it may be argued that as many people leave the visible church because of preaching which is too biblical as leave because of preaching which is not biblical enough. But a Lutheranism which devoted itself to such goals would be a cause which would be worth fighting for and one which its followers would not have to be ashamed of when they have to give an account of their stewardship.[133]

Mark Braun is Professor of Theology at Wisconsin Lutheran College, Milwaukee, Wisconsin.

---

131. J. A. O. Preus III, "What Did It Mean to be Lutheran Today? Addressing Contemporary Issues with the Historic Christian Faith," in *What Does It Mean to Be Lutheran: The Pieper Lectures* (2000: Concordia Historical Institute and the Luther Academy: 2000), 85–86.
132. Dean O. Wenthe, "What Did It Mean to be Lutheran in the Twenty-First Century?" in *What Does It Mean to Be Lutheran*, 98.
133. John F. Brug, "The Future of Lutheranism," *WLQ* 84, no. 3 (Summer 1987): 233–34.

BIBLIOGRAPHY

MEMOIRS

Behnken, John W. *This I Recall.* St. Louis, MO: Concordia, 1964.

Braaten, Carl E. *My Ecumenical Journey: Ecumenical Experiences and Perspectives of an Evangelical Catholic Theologian.* Delhi, NY: ALPB Books, 2018.

Scaer, David P. *Surviving the Storms.* St. Louis, MO: Luther Academy, 2018.

Tietjen, John H. *Memoirs in Exile: Confessional Hope and Institutional Conflict.* Minneapolis, MN: Fortress, 1990.

HISTORIES

Aaberg, Theodore A. *A City on a Hill: A History of the Evangelical Lutheran Synod.* Mankato, MN: Evangelical Lutheran Synod, 1968.

Aageson, James and Arland Jacobson. *The Future of Lutheranism in a Global Context.* Minneapolis, MN: Augsburg Fortress, 2008.

Baepler, Walter A. *A Century of Grace: The Missouri Synod, 1847–1947.* St. Louis, MO: Concordia, 1947.

Braun, Mark E. *A Tale of Two Synods: Events that Led to the Split between Wisconsin and Missouri.* Milwaukee, WI: Northwestern, 2003.

Cimino, Richard, ed. *Lutherans Today: American Lutheran Identity in the Twenty-First Century.* Grand Rapids, MI: Eerdmans 2003.

Erling, Maria and Mark Granquist. *The Augustana Story: Shaping Lutheran Identity in North America.* Minneapolis, MN: Augsburg Fortress, 2008.

Fredrich, Edward C. *The Wisconsin Synod Lutherans: A History of the Single Synod, Federation, and Merger.* Milwaukee, WI: Northwestern, 1992.

Granquist, Mark. *A New History of Lutherans in America.* Minneapolis, MN: Fortress, 2015.

Grundmeier, Timothy D. "'The Language Question': Theological Conflict over the Transition from German to English among Synodical Conference Clergy, 1887–1953." Master's thesis, Mankato State University, 2011.

Gurgel, Stephen Scott. "The War to End All Germans: Wisconsin Synod Lutherans and the First World War." Master's thesis, University of Wisconsin-Milwaukee, 2012.

Johnson, Jeff G. *Black Christians: The Untold Lutheran Story.* St. Louis, MO: Concordia, 1991.

Johnson, Richard O. *Changing Word, Changeless Christ: The American Lutheran Publicity Bureau, 1914–2014.* Delhi, NY: ALPB Books, 2018.

Lueking, F. Dean. *Mission in the Making: The Missionary Enterprise among Missouri Synod Lutherans, 1846–1963.* St. Louis, MO: Concordia, 1964.

Nelson, E. Clifford. *Lutheranism in North America, 1914–1970.* Minneapolis, MN: Augsburg, 1972.

Nelson, E. Clifford, ed. *The Lutherans in North America.* Philadelphia, PA: Fortress, 1975.

Nelson, E. Clifford. *The Rise of World Lutheranism: An American Perspective.* Philadelphia, PA: Fortress, 1982.

Schuetze, Armin W. *The Synodical Conference: Ecumenical Endeavor.* Milwaukee, WI: Northwestern, 2000.

Stanford, Craig S. *The Death of the Lutheran Reformation: A Practical Look at Modern Theology and Its Effects on the Church and the Lives of Its People.* Fort Wayne, IN: Stanford Publishing, 1988.

Trexler, Edgar R. *Anatomy of a Merger: People, Dynamics, and Decisions That Shaped the ELCA.* Minneapolis, MN: Augsburg, 1991.

Index

C ◆

D ◆

E ◆

F ◆

G ◆

N ◆

O ◆

P ◆

Q ◆

R ◆

S ◆

T ◆

U ◆

V ◆

W ◆

Y •

Z •

Made in the USA
Las Vegas, NV
06 May 2021

22575016R00099